Freud and the Problem of Sexuality

SUNY series, Insinuations: Philosophy, Psychoanalysis, Literature

Charles Shepherdson, editor

Freud and the Problem of Sexuality

BRADLEY RAMOS

SUNY PRESS

Cover art: Bob Thompson, *The Good Samaritan*, 1965. Oil on pressed board. Collection of DePaul Art Museum, gift of Samuel and Blanche Koffler 2012.120. © Michael Rosenfeld Gallery LLC, New York, NY

Published by State University of New York Press, Albany

© 2024 State University of New York

All rights reserved

Printed in the United States of America

No part of this book may be used or reproduced in any manner whatsoever without written permission. No part of this book may be stored in a retrieval system or transmitted in any form or by any means including electronic, electrostatic, magnetic tape, mechanical, photocopying, recording, or otherwise without the prior permission in writing of the publisher.

For information, contact State University of New York Press, Albany, NY
www.sunypress.edu

Library of Congress Cataloging-in-Publication Data

Name: Ramos, Bradley, 1989– author.
Title: Freud and the problem of sexuality / Bradley Ramos.
Description: Albany : State University of New York Press, [2024] | Series: SUNY series, Insinuations : philosophy, psychoanalysis, literature | Includes bibliographical references and index.
Identifiers: LCCN 2023029209 | ISBN 9781438496764 (hardcover : alk. paper) | ISBN 9781438496788 (ebook) | ISBN 9781438496771 (pbk. : alk. paper)
Subjects: LCSH: Freud, Sigmund, 1856–1939. | Sex (Psychology) | Sex—Philosophy | Psychoanalysis.
Classification: LCC BF173.F85 R36 2024 | DDC 150.19/52—dc23/eng/20231218
LC record available at https://lccn.loc.gov/2023029209

10 9 8 7 6 5 4 3 2 1

Contents

Acknowledgments	vii
Citation Conventions and Abbreviations	ix
Preface: Sexuality without Teleology	xiii
Introduction: The Problem of Sexuality	1

Part 1. Sexual Problems: Complicating *Trieb* and Instinct

Chapter 1	The Problem with Popular Opinion	15
Chapter 2	The Problem with the Instinct: Strachey's Revenge	37
Chapter 3	The "Impossible Difference" between *Trieb* and Instinct	59

Part 2. Three Essays on Freud's Theory of Infantile Sexuality

Chapter 4	The Role of the Other in the Genesis of Sexuality	73
Chapter 5	Auto-Hetero-Erotism: Making Space and Time for the Object in Freud's Infantile Sexuality	85
Chapter 6	Perversion and Pervertibility of the Instinct	109

Conclusion: No Exceptions	131
Notes	141
Bibliography	167
Index	185

Acknowledgments

First and foremost, I must thank the following people and acknowledge the profound impact their friendships have had on my life: Adrian Johnston, who introduced me to the love of learning and wisdom; Elizabeth Rottenberg, who taught me the joys of reading and writing; and David Maruzzella, who showed me the necessity of philosophical conversation. Without their generous support and invaluable insights this book would not have been possible. Furthermore, I must thank Michael Naas, Peg Birmingham, and Sean Kirkland, who also took the time to read this book at various stages in its development and provide me with thoughtful comments. It was a privilege to have had so many skilled and careful readers help me along the way.

Additionally, and so as not to leave anyone out, I owe an immeasurable debt of gratitude to all my friends and family for everything they have done for me. I cannot thank them enough. Specifically, I must thank Claire Patterson for her love, support, and kindness throughout this process. I would also like to thank Christopher Rigling. Without our psychoanalytic work together, many of these insights would have never come to light. I should also like to thank DePaul University for providing me with the opportunity to pursue much of this research.

Finally, I would like to thank Rebecca Colesworthy, Susan Geraghty, and Laura Glenn at SUNY Press for their hard work, patience, and feedback throughout the editing and production process of this book. Any faults herein remain my own.

Citation Conventions and Abbreviations

The following citation conventions and abbreviations are used for texts frequently cited. The published English edition is cited where applicable, and I have silently modified or provided my own English translations throughout when necessary. For texts that are frequently cited, unless otherwise noted, the citations are formatted with the English translation first and the original edition second. For other foreign language texts that are crucial to the argument or concern matters of translation, both the original and its English translation are cited according to *The Chicago Manual of Style*.

Works by Sigmund Freud

I have adopted the following convention throughout for in-text citations of Freud's work. Unless otherwise noted, all translations are taken from James Strachey's *Standard Edition of the Complete Psychological Works of Sigmund Freud*. Each citation from the *Standard Edition* is formatted as SE, followed by the volume number and page number, which is followed by its corresponding location in the *Gesammelte Werke*: (SE #: #/GW #: #). On a few occasions, for the sake of the argument, I will refer directly to the revised translation of the 1905 edition of the *Three Essays*. In those cases, since the 1905 edition is out of print in German, I do not cite the German original.

GW: *Gesammelte Werke*. 18 vols. Frankfurt am Main: Fischer, 1940–1968.
N: *Gesammelte Werke, Nachtragsband, Texte aus den Jahren 1885 bis 1938*. Ed. Angela Richards in collaboration with Ilse Grubrich-Simitis. Frankfurt am Main: Fischer, 1987.

SE: *The Standard Edition of the Complete Psychological Works of Sigmund Freud.* 24 vols. Trans. James Strachey in collaboration with Anna Freud, assisted by Alix Strachey and Alan Tyson. London: Hogarth, 1953–1974.

RTE: *Three Essays on the Theory of Sexuality: The 1905 Edition.* Trans. Ulrike Kistner. Ed. Phillipe Van Haute and Herman Westerink. London: Verso, 2016.

Works by Jean Laplanche

LD: *Life and Death in Psychoanalysis.* Trans. Jefferey Mehlman. Baltimore: Johns Hopkins University Press, 2013. *Vie et mort en psychanalyse.* Paris: Flammarion, 1970.

Cop.: "The Unfinished Copernican Revolution," in *Essays on Otherness.* New York: Routledge, 1999, 53–85. "La révolution copernicienne inachevée," in *La révolution copernicienne inachevée: 1967–1992.* Paris: Presses Universitaires de France, 1992, iii–xxxv.

FB: *The Temptation of Biology: Freud's Theories of Sexuality; followed by, Biologism and Biology.* New York: Unconscious in Translation, 2015. *Le fourvoiement biologisant de la sexualité chez Freud,* in *Problématiques VII.* Paris: Presses Universitaires de France, 1993, 9–126.

Pul.: "Drive and instinct: distinctions, oppositions, supports, and intertwinings," in *Freud and the Sexual.* New York: Unconscious in Translation, 2011, 5–26. "Pulsion et instinct," in *La sexualité élargie au sens freudien.* Paris: Presses Universitaires de France, 2008, 7–25.

Trois.: "The *Three Essays* and the Theory of Seduction," in *Freud and the Sexual.* New York: Unconscious in Translation, 2011, 249–66. "Les *Trois Essais* et la théorie de la séduction," in *La sexualité élargie au sens freudien.* Paris: Presses Universitaires de France, 2008, 241–56.

Works by Louis Althusser

Dec.: "The Discovery of Dr. Freud," in *Writings on Psychoanalysis: Freud and Lacan.* New York: Columbia University Press, 1996, 85–105. "La découverte du docteur Freud," in *Écrits sur la psychanalyse.* Eds. Olivier Corpet and François Matheron. Paris: Éditions Stock/IMEC, 1993, 195–219.

Sur.: "On Marx and Freud," in *Writings on Psychoanalysis: Freud and Lacan.* New York: Columbia University Press, 1996, 85–105. "Sur Marx et Freud," in *Écrits sur la psychanalyse.* Eds. Olivier Corpet and François Matheron. Paris: Éditions Stock/IMEC, 1993, 222–45.

Works by Jacques Derrida

G: *Of Grammatology.* Trans. G. C. Spivak. Baltimore: Johns Hopkins University Press, 1997. *De la grammatologie.* Paris: Éditions de Minuit, 1967.

OT: *On Touching: Jean-Luc Nancy.* Trans. Christine Irizarry. Stanford: Stanford University Press, 2005. *Le toucher, Jean-Luc Nancy.* Paris: Galilée, 2000.

Works by Jacques Lacan

Mirr.: "The Mirror Stage as Formative of the *I* Function as Revealed in the Psychoanalytic Experience," in *Écrits: The First Complete English Edition.* Trans. Bruce Fink in Collaboration with Héloïse Fink and Russell Grigg. New York and London: W. W. Norton & Company, 1999, 75–81. "Le stade du miroir comme fondateur de la fonction du Je," in *Écrits.* Paris: Éditions du Seuil, 1966, 93–100.

Sign.: "The Signification of the Phallus," in *Écrits: The First Complete English Edition.* Trans. Bruce Fink in Collaboration with Héloïse Fink and Russell Grigg. New York and London: W. W. Norton & Company, 1999, 575–84. "La signification du phallus," in *Écrits.* Paris: Éditions du Seuil, 1966, 685–97.

Subv.: "The Subversion of the Subject and the Dialectic of Desire in the Freudian Unconscious," in *Écrits: The First Complete English Edition.* Trans. Bruce Fink in Collaboration with Héloïse Fink and Russell Grigg. New York and London: W. W. Norton & Company, 1999, 671–702. "Subversion du sujet et dialectique dans l'inconscient freudien," in *Écrits.* Paris: Éditions du Seuil, 1966, 793–828.

Preface

Sexuality without Teleology

Over the last few decades a thousand discourses about sexuality have bloomed. As such, renewed attention has been paid to the psychoanalytic theory of sexuality in contemporary philosophy, gender studies, and queer theory. However, much of the literature in these fields often tends to engage with psychoanalysis as it has been filtered through the works of Jacques Lacan, Michel Foucault, or personal experience.[1] This study instead aims to put forward a rigorous reading of Freud's own writings, especially his often overlooked *Three Essays on the Theory of Sexuality*.[2] However, the purpose of this study is not to force Freud to be agreeable to these contemporary discourses by opposing the supposedly unproblematic aspects of his writings to those that are deemed to be problematic.[3] Rather, this study seeks to let Freud speak for himself and then along the way to address some of the contemporary—if sometimes anachronistic—charges leveled against him. The argument is that by returning to Freud's writings there is still something unexpected and revolutionary to be found in his theory of sexuality.

For throughout his entire career Freud dared to put forward a theory of sexuality that was without any teleology.[4] At the (beginning and) end of the day, Freud always sought to situate psychoanalysis within the tradition of modern natural science[5]—insofar as the latter seeks to rid our understanding of nature of any inherent teleology.[6] In addition, as a thinker following on the heels of Darwin, Freud argued that this nonteleological account of nature applied to even the most seemingly stubborn of human phenomena such as sexuality. In so doing, Freud was led to treat sexuality itself as a *problem*, since throwing the traditional teleological explanations of sexuality into question now demands that we attend to the complexities at work in every manifestation of sexuality. This is such a radical gesture that, once taken seriously, it will force us to reevaluate how we understand even some of the more supposedly "problematic" aspects of Freud's writings (such as the Oedipus complex). This, in turn, will allow us to see how such aspects of his writings might furnish us with the means to challenge the very heteronormative and biologistic ideology that Freud is often charged with shoring up.

As will become evident in what follows, if sexuality is stripped of any inherent teleology, if sexuality becomes a problem, then any given manifestation of sexuality is in this sense no more or less unique. Thus, as a clinician, observing how sexuality consciously and unconsciously unfurled in the free associations of his patients, Freud aimed to provide a robust account of it that was equal to the diversity manifesting in his sessions. What Freud discovered—far from shoring up any sort of heteronormative or biologistic ideology—was that the diversity of sexualities turned out to be the rule rather than the exception. What this means is that—if such terms make sense anymore—what was before considered to be normal and natural turns out to be much more perverse; and what was considered to be perverse and unnatural itself becomes natural. By thinking through this *problematic* logic of the natural-unnatural, we will begin to see part of what is so disturbing about Freud; namely, he urges us to renounce our fantasy of sexual exceptionality and along with it any privileged access that such a sexuality would supposedly—by virtue of its very exceptionality—grant to, for example, epistemology, temporality, ethics, politics, or even some sort of pure enjoyment or hidden pleasure.

When it comes to contemporary ethical-political concerns about Freud's psychoanalytic theory of sexuality, what this study seeks to demonstrate is that any attempt to articulate and administer a sexual morality based on a norm, based on an exception, is inevitably doomed to undermine itself because it is fundamentally at odds with the very nature of sexuality. Aware of this fact, what Freud left us with is a theory of sexuality that not only forces us to grapple with the ways that we all consciously and unconsciously reproduce the (hetero)normative society of which we are a part; but a theory of sexuality that also furnishes us with the tools necessary for understanding these processes of normalization. Such tools will allow us to rigorously combat both the overwhelmingly heteronormative popular opinion of Freud's own time and its contemporary variations that seek to condemn him with just as much vehemence. Thus, the wager I would like to put forward is that the only way of forging any fruitful or effective theory and practice concerning sexuality is through a robust conception of it. This begins first and foremost by understanding what sexuality is.

Introduction

The Problem of Sexuality

Philosophy's Problem with Sexuality

This study seeks to pursue a rigorously philosophical line of questioning, namely, what is (the nature of) sexuality? And it seeks to do so through the lens of Freud's psychoanalytic theory of sexuality. Yet it is admittedly difficult to find two more ambivalent bedfellows than the founder of psychoanalysis and those who have taken on the tradition of Western philosophy that extends back to ancient Greece. On the one hand, Freud's own ambivalent relationship with philosophy is well known and well documented.[1] He famously liked to claim that he tried to stay as far away from it as possible, so as not to taint his psychoanalytic thought with it.[2] On the other hand, philosophers themselves have spilled quite a lot of ink on Freud's various ideas, while being careful to keep him at an arm's length, making sure not to count him as one of their own.[3] However, just because Freud is not a philosopher, by his or the philosopher's standards, does not necessarily mean that he does not have something interesting to say to philosophy. In fact, I would argue that it is, on the contrary, precisely *because* Freud is not a philosopher, that is, precisely *because* of his status on the margins of philosophy, that he is able to offer a unique challenge to philosophy. And his challenge, I argue, is this: keep on philosophizing!

This is because sexuality, which Freud put front and center in his psychoanalytic theory, has traditionally been a problem for philosophy. With few exceptions,[4] sexuality has proved to be a stumbling block that has continued to trip up philosophers for millennia. For some reason, whenever philosophers are forced to dirty their hands with it, sexuality often becomes a point at which they seem to suddenly stop philosophizing: losing their deepest insights, failing to consequently apply their own philosophical program, or flat-out contradicting themselves. Perhaps this goes without saying, but losing insights, failing to be consequent, and contradicting oneself have always represented major concerns for philosophers.

Traditionally, in order to deal with the problem of sexuality, philosophers have often tended to repeat a gesture that can be traced all the way back to Plato's final text, the *Laws*. In Book I of the *Laws*, right in the middle of a heated debate about drinking alcohol, temperance, and the "art of pleasure," the apparent protagonist of the dialogue, the Athenian Stranger, suddenly mentions sexuality for the first time: "whether one makes the observation in earnest or in jest, one certainly should not fail to observe that when male unites with female for procreation the pleasure experienced is held to be due to nature [*kata physin*], but contrary to nature [*para physin*] when male unites with male or female with female, and that those first guilty of such enormities [*tolmēma*] were impelled by their slavery to pleasure (Plato 2001, 635C)."

For the Athenian Stanger, there are two forms of sexual pleasures: those that are in accordance with nature and those that are contrary to nature. According to this scheme, heterosexual intercourse for procreation (and only heterosexual intercourse for procreation) is the sort of sexuality that produces pleasure in accordance with nature, *kata physin*. Every other sexual pleasure is contrary to nature, *para physin*. As such, those who engage in heterosexual intercourse for procreation abide by the (natural) law, and those who do not are no more than unlawful slaves to their nonnatural pleasure. In succumbing to such nonnatural pleasures, the latter are committing a *tolmēma*,[5] an enormity or a crime, against the very law of nature itself.

But then suddenly the dialogue moves on without dwelling on the subject any longer, and the interlocutors continue trading jabs over alcohol abuse in their respective city-states. Plato himself does not have much else to say about sexuality, until it irrupts into the dialogue again much later in Book VIII.[6] Suddenly the Athenian Stranger can sense that sexuality is beginning to threaten his discourse about how to create and govern a stable social order. According to the Athenian Stranger, all those nonnatural sexual pleasures contrary to nature should be considered excessive and, as a result, a threat to any stable social order. To remedy this problem, the Athenian Stranger argues that institutional laws should be erected in order to reflect, protect, and enforce the natural law of heterosexual intercourse for procreation (Plato 2004, 838A–839B). In other words, these excessive nonnatural sexualities must be suppressed by institutional laws that will force them to conform with the natural law.

Such an idea seems to present us with an interesting philosophical problem, namely, that when it comes to sexuality the Athenian Stranger must call on artificial means (that is, institutional laws) in order to force the natural into existence. Yet, Plato himself seems to ignore this problem entirely. Once these laws are articulated and put into place sexuality is supposedly dealt with once and for all, and the dialogue again moves on from and never returns to the topic of sexuality.

At least chronologically speaking, this would appear to be Plato's final word on sexuality. At first glance it would seem to be in tension with some of his earlier works concerning love and sexuality. Unlike, say, the *Symposium*, in which sexuality and Eros arguably play an integral role in almost every aspect of human life, in his final dialogue it is only briefly addressed when it almost inconveniently surges into the text, only to be suppressed back into the margins. It is certainly worth noting that this suppressive gesture operates on both the theoretical and the textual registers. Theoretically speaking, Plato divides sexuality into natural sexuality (which conforms to the law of nature) and nonnatural sexuality (which must be suppressed and forced to conform to the natural law). Textually speaking, this normalizing and naturalistic schema allows the interlocutors of the dialogue to avoid talking about sexuality any further, relegating it to the margins of the text.

And it is this very gesture that becomes the dominant one in the history of philosophy. Throughout the history of philosophy, we see philosophers repeatedly attempt to pronounce the final word on sexuality by dividing it into the categories of natural and nonnatural, relegating it into the margins of philosophical thought and reflection.

Even in Plato's earlier works such as the *Phaedrus* and the *Symposium*, in which sexuality plays a much more prominent and positive role, it is still arguably something to be transcended and left behind on the way to a higher appreciation of true love and beauty. Or take Aristotle. As Emanuela Bianchi argues in *The Feminine Symptom*, Aristotle seeks to couch an entire "patriarchal metaphysics" in the division between the biological difference between men and women and the supposed natural attraction between them. This conception of sexuality and sexual difference certainly plays itself out in his understanding of nature, which spans several of Aristotle's texts (Bianchi 2014, 2). For example, in section II of Book I of the *Politics*, when musing about the structure and role of the family in political life, Aristotle declares that procreation is a natural desire that human beings share in common with plants and animals (Aristotle 2013, Book I). Furthermore, in probably his longest and most sustained musings on sexuality, in the *Generation of Animals*, Aristotle's analysis of sexual difference and reproduction leads him to the conclusion that sexuality itself is governed by a natural teleology toward heterosexual reproduction (Bianchi 2014, 1–2). Of course, anything that deviates from this teleology and begins to complicate his conception of nature and sexuality is almost conveniently glossed over in Aristotle's analyses (Bianchi 2014, 74). Or take Epicurus, who conceived of the sexual intercourse between a man and a woman as natural and sought to banish sexuality to the margins of human existence because it is excessive and should be avoided (Brennan 1996, 348). The Stoics, too, seemed to share similar views on sexuality. Cicero, for example, who otherwise often vociferously disagreed with the Epicureans, agreed with Epicurus's marginalization of sexuality, condemning the passions aroused by it. He appears to have had even more severe remarks about homosexuality (Cicero 2002, 64–67); and, at any rate, he considers a man's love for a woman to be much more "permissible" by nature (Cicero 2002, 65). Or take Augustine. In the *Confessions*, Augustine describes sexuality in terms of a dangerous impulse that must be squelched at all costs. Although the theme of sexuality continuously irrupts into Augustine's confessions, he tirelessly struggles to suppress it by repeating this familiar gesture. For example, in Book II of the *Confessions*, he tries to fend off the dangerous sexual impulses of his childhood (Augustine 1982). Furthermore, in *On Marriage and Concupiscence*, Augustine goes so far as to claim that marriage and procreative sex are the natural domain of sexuality, while every other carnal pleasure is considered to be evil, sinful, and unnatural. Later Scholastics also display a similar struggle against sexuality in their writings. For example, in his *Summa Theologica*, Aquinas sought to discover what is natural about sexuality by understanding what human sexuality shares with that of the animals. He, then, strategically attempts to remove sexuality from sight by confining it to the conjugal bed and, at the same time, going so far as to condemn every other sexual pleasure as a sin against nature (Aquinas 2000, IIa–IIae). Or take Rousseau, who famously carries on Augustine's confessional tradition and, in his own *Confessions*, continuously struggles against any and every nonnatural sexual impulse that threatens to corrupt his natural purity. Or take Descartes. In the *Passions of the Soul*, his last philosophical treatise, which is dedicated to a sweeping account of the human passions, Descartes only briefly mentions sexuality a single time. In Article 90, he claims that nature itself has established sexual difference as a means of attracting two people of the opposite sex together for sexual union (Descartes 1989, Art. 90). Or take Kant. Throughout his career, Kant continuously found himself mobilizing his philosophical arsenal against sexuality. Whenever sexuality comes up in Kant's discourse, he attempts to suppress it by organizing it into the moralizing categories of natural procreative sex and unnatural and dangerous perversions (Soble 2003). Or take Hegel, who in his treatment of marriage in the *Elements of the Philosophy of Right*, interestingly notes that human sexuality (with all of its complex rituals of courting and marriage) seems to exceed and defy the natural impulse to simply procreate (Hegel 2012, 201–6). However, immediately after pointing this out, Hegel attempts to wrangle sexuality back into the conjugal bed, relegating it to its supposedly natural purpose of procreation (Hegel 2012, 206–8). Slavoj Žižek suggests that Hegel has to go so far as to come into direct contradiction with his own philosophical insights about nature and sexuality in order to accomplish this suppression of sexuality (Žižek 2012). Or take a more contemporary example like Thomas Nagel, who seeks to couch the division between natural sexuality and nonnatural perversions in psychological—rather than physiological or biological, but nevertheless naturalistic—terms (Nagel 1969).

As we can see, sexuality has always been on the minds of philosophers, and there is nary a philosopher who has not sought to pronounce the final word on it. Time and again sexuality *is mentioned*, it does come up, and more often than not it is treated only as a problem that must be quickly sorted into the categories of the natural and the nonnatural, then dismissed, suppressed, and done away with. Thus, we might ask ourselves: Why this dismissive and suppressive treatment of sexuality? Why the categories of natural and unnatural sexuality? And what, for that matter, is so threatening about sexuality to philosophy such that it must be suppressed and marginalized in this way?

Taking the Problem of Sexuality Seriously

Of course, these are precisely the sorts of questions that Freud forces us ask. This is because, according to Freud, sexuality is something whose very nature, and by its very nature, confronts us as a problem. However, contrary to much of the tradition of Western philosophy, for Freud sexuality is a problem that must be confronted head on. In other words, rather than being a problem that must be dealt and done away with, sexuality is a problem that must be taken seriously *as a problem*. In fact, in an often overlooked and absolutely crucial footnote contained in Freud's groundbreaking *Three Essays on the Theory of Sexuality*, Freud declares that for psychoanalysis every manifestation of what we call "sexuality"—even the most obvious and straightforward examples of it, that is, even what we would all unquestioningly consider to be sexual (e.g., intercourse between a man and a woman)—is itself *a problem, ein Problem*, that "needs elucidating" because it is not a "self-evident fact": "from the point of view of psychoanalysis the exclusive sexual interest felt by men for women is also a problem [*ein Problem*] that needs elucidating and is not a self-evident fact" (SE 7: 146n/GW 5: 44n). As a problem, then, which comes to us from the ancient Greek verb *pro-ballein*, literally meaning "to throw before," sexuality is something thrown before us, something that confronts us, something that challenges us. It does so not as something pregiven, predefined, or predetermined, but rather as something demanding an investigation—one that does not anticipate in advance where it should lead.

It is precisely as a problem, then, that we will treat sexuality in what follows by turning to Freud's theory of sexuality as it is spelled out primarily in his *Three Essays*. Such a reading demands that we read Freud not with the hope that he will provide us with a more palatable solution to the problem of sexuality. Instead, we will read Freud as problematizing sexuality, in other words, as reactivating or rehabilitating the problem of sexuality. That is, we will read Freud as raising sexuality back to the dignity of a problem, as treating sexuality as the problem it already was and always is.

Despite his urgent plea to treat sexuality as a problem, Freud himself has often been faulted for surreptitiously *normalizing* and *naturalizing* sexuality, thereby himself obfuscating the problem. Although he promises to do otherwise, so the story goes, Freud himself nonetheless pronounces his own final word on sexuality, which looks disappointingly like that of the philosopher. According to such accusers, the symptoms of Freud's naturalistic and normalizing tendencies are exhibited in many aspects of his work. Look no further than, for example, the following evidence: his treatment of sexuality as an instinct; his emphasis on the stages of libidinal development; his focus on genitality; his preoccupation with sexual difference; and his essentializing conception of femininity and masculinity. What all these indictments share in common is the effort to fault Freud for falling prey to the following mistakes in his work: (1) he hastily turns sexuality into something innate, functional, and teleological; and/or (2) he speciously grounds a binary between the normal and the abnormal in eternal, ahistorical, and often phylogenetic structures. In both cases, the problem is that no matter how hard he tries, Freud nevertheless treats what is supposed to be contingent, fluid, acquired, and sociohistorically constructed as necessary, fixed, innate, and predetermined by nature.

However, what such detractors fail to take seriously is precisely the ways in which Freud's treatment of sexuality *as a problem* informs his analysis of it. In what follows, I will argue that by treating sexuality as a problem Freud comes to challenge the very *naturalistic* gesture for which he is often faulted. And far from pronouncing the final word on sexuality, Freud instead succeeds at opening up a series of questions that challenge us to rethink the nature of sexuality. As such, the question for us in what follows is not whether Freud himself is a naturalist, but rather, what does the nature of sexuality look like when we take Freud's problem of sexuality seriously?

Beginning to Read Freud's Theory of Sexuality Philosophically

But how should such an investigation begin? Our investigation will begin as Freud himself began; and it is my contention that (despite his ambivalence toward philosophy) Freud begins his investigation rather *philosophically*. For if sexuality is a problem and not a "self-evident fact"—that is, not something that is pregiven, predefined, or predetermined in advance—then we are necessarily forced to ask ourselves the question: what *is* sexuality?[7] After all, what is it about all the (for lack of a better word) "stuff" that we call "sexual," which makes it sexual in the first place?

Of course, such a question will, without a doubt, remind us of the (in)famous Socratic *ti esti* question, the "what is . . . ?" question. And at this point it is worth remembering that in Plato's earlier, so-called definitional dialogues,[8] the ones in which Socrates poses the "what is . . . ?" question to his interlocutors, he does so in order to demonstrate that their subject matter (whether it be piety, courage, temperance, justice, friendship, etc.) is something along the lines of what we are here calling a *"problem,"* in the Freudian sense. In fact, Plato can be seen as portraying a Socrates who is at pains in these dialogues to get his interlocutors just to the point of seeing that their subject matter is not a self-evident fact and, therefore, needs elucidating. In this way, Socrates challenges his interlocutors to treat their subject matter not as it immediately appears to them, or perhaps better said: not *only* as it appears to them, and not *only* in terms of their preconceived notions of it. Instead, he challenges those initial appearances and preconceived notions in order to show that the matter at hand is something worthy of deeper investigation. However, the specifically philosophical difficulty of this approach is that by virtue of throwing these initial appearances and preconceived notions into question, the investigation can no longer be mapped out in advance by prevailing opinions, definitions, norms, or practices. As such, Socrates and his interlocutors must forge their way through the subject matter without any assurances of where it will lead.

Likewise, Freud challenges us to do the very same thing when he problematizes sexuality in the *Three Essays*. By reading Freud's theory of sexuality in the *Three Essays* as the reactivation or the reproblematization of a problem, this forces us to read his work just as he approaches the problem of sexuality itself—namely, without trying to force or determine in advance where our investigation shall lead and without imposing our preconceived notions of Freud's work on it (or at least being open to the possibility that our preconceived notions about it could be wrong). Instead, we must follow it in all of its various vicissitudes wherever it should lead with the idea that there is still something surprising and novel to be found in it. What this has in store for us, as philosophers, is the ability to keep on philosophizing, allowing us to do so precisely at a point where philosophers have traditionally tended to become rather unphilosophical.

Freud's Confrontation with Popular Opinion

Now the analogy between Socrates and Freud's respective methods of investigation begins to diverge at crucial moments.[9] However, they do share another similarity in how they begin: much like the Socrates of Plato's definitional dialogues, Freud will begin his investigation into the question about the nature of sexuality by first turning to the self-professed experts in sexual matters. This includes anyone who believes that they have a definitive definition of what sexuality is, which Freud groups under the heading "popular opinion," *die populäre Meinung*. It is important for us to understand that when referring to "popular opinion" Freud does not only have in mind his scientific and medical contemporaries, but also each and every one of us. Throughout his work Freud repeatedly emphasizes the fact that we all take ourselves to be experts when it comes to matters concerning sexuality. Of course, this is no accident because we have all wrestled with—and continue to wrestle with—the problem of sexuality ourselves. This is a struggle that we can trace all the way back to our childhoods, during which time we were consumed with burning questions about the nature of sexuality.

Now, our present investigation will not be concerned so much with the origins of these questions, nor with the reasons as to why they are so pressing for us (which itself would demand and deserve a rich investigation of its own[10]). Instead, we will focus our attention, as Freud does in the *Three Essays*, on the ways in which popular opinion attempts to deal with these demanding questions. Curiously enough, the way that popular opinion attempts to deal with this problem looks a lot like the way that the tradition of philosophy has attempted to deal with this problem. It is no coincidence, then, that at the outset of the *Three Essays*, Freud claims that the "poetic fable" in Plato's *Symposium* (that is, Aristophanes's famous speech) is a beautiful reflection of popular opinion.[11] In what follows, we will see that, like the philosopher, popular opinion attempts to avoid the problem of sexuality altogether by establishing a normalizing and naturalistic definition of sexuality. Repeating a familiar gesture, popular opinion seeks to divide sexuality into a *natural instinct for heterosexual intercourse and reproduction* and the *unnatural perversions of that instinct*. By attempting to organize sexuality into these categories, popular opinion repeats a millennia-long tradition dating at least as far back as Plato's *Laws*, hoping this time to have finally pronounced the last word on sexuality and buried the problem once and for all.

However, immediately at the outset of the *Three Essays*, Freud seeks to contest this eulogy, this (normalizing and naturalistic) final word on sexuality. In so doing, Freud does not intend merely to "critique" popular opinion, that is, in other words, to show that popular opinion is simply wrong to define sexuality in this way and that he, Freud, has a much better definition of it. No, the point for Freud is to resuscitate the problem of sexuality and confront popular opinion with it. In so doing, Freud hopes to provoke the expert in all of us to challenge ourselves to go beyond our preconceived notions of what we think sexuality is. By challenging our common opinions about sexuality, Freud is able to show that popular opinion, despite itself and on its own terms, actually knows (without knowing that it knows) something more about the nature of sexuality than its normalizing and naturalistic definition immediately implies or explicitly seeks to accomplish. In other words, Freud's insights about the nature of sexuality are already (unknowingly) contained within popular opinion; Freud is just going to point out these insights and develop them—the consequences of which we will attempt to systematize in what follows.

Chapter Outline

In part 1, we will trace some of the consequences that this problem of sexuality has created in the reception of Freud's work.

In chapter 1, we will turn to and reevaluate Freud's confrontation with popular opinion in the *Three Essays*. This confrontation is an important and often overlooked aspect in the development of Freud's theory of sexuality. Specifically, for our purposes, it will help us begin to articulate the problem at work in popular opinion's normalizing and naturalistic definition of sexuality. Through Freud's engagement with popular opinion, we will be in a much better position to specify what exactly is meant when we say that sexuality is a problem.

In chapter 2, we will see how this problem of sexuality has continued to play itself out in the reception and, more specifically, the translation of Freud's work. Special attention will be paid to the debates surrounding James Strachey's infamous translation of the term "*Trieb*" as "instinct." By turning to the eminent philosopher, psychoanalyst, and translator, Jean Laplanche, we will begin problematizing the traditional choice between either "drive" or "instinct" as the translation of Freud's "*Trieb*." We will show that the problems that arise in the translation of Freud's *Trieb* shed light on a much more difficult problem at the heart of his theory of sexuality.

In chapter 3, we will continue to complicate the classic *Trieb* and instinct distinction by asking whether the complications that arise from this distinction are a problem for Freud (that is, whether Freud himself just had difficulty maintaining a clear distinction between the two terms in his work) or if there is something deeper at work. That is, we will wonder whether this is a problem in the thing itself, that is, sexuality. Relying on the work of Louis Althusser, we will attempt to chart a course through Freud's work that will illuminate a new way of understanding Freud's *Trieb* as border- or limit-concept and, as such, the "impossible" relation it forms with the natural instinct.

In part 2, we will begin a three-part investigation into Freud's theory of infantile sexuality. In chapter 4, we will begin with Laplanche's magnificent study of Freud's *Three Essays* in his 1970 text, *Life and Death in Psychoanalysis*, in order to begin giving a robust account of the complex relation between infantile sexuality and the instinct. Along with Laplanche and Freud, we will begin to trace sexuality back to its origins in order to give a genetic account of it. By investigating the characteristics of what Freud famously and provocatively called "infantile sexuality," we will find that the origins of sexuality are structured in a complex relation with the other qua caregiver.

In chapter 5, our question into the role of the other in infantile sexuality will lead us to the work of Jacques Derrida. We will stage a debate between Derrida and a contemporary revisionist reading of psychoanalytic autoerotism, which seeks to purge the other altogether from infantile sexuality in the name of rescuing Freud's theory of sexuality from heteronormativity. Through a detailed discussion of auto-affection we will demonstrate the necessity and inescapabilty of the other in infantile sexuality, even in autoerotism. This will provide us with an opportunity to revisit the problem of sexuality in light of more contemporary concerns about Freud's work and provide a heterodox and spirited defense of the much-maligned Oedipus complex. We will argue that even the supposedly most normative aspects of Freud's work can furnish us with the tools necessary for challenging the very normativity with which he is often charged once we take the problem of sexuality seriously.

In chapter 6, we will return to Laplanche's *Life and Death in Psychoanalysis* in order to continue fleshing out our understanding of infantile sexuality. What we will see is that there is a problem at the origin of infantile sexuality. Through Laplanche's innovative reading of Freud's *Three Essays*, we will be led to the claim that infantile sexuality as such is a perversion because it comes about as a deviation from the instinct. Working with and against Laplanche's idea of infantile sexuality as the perversion of a weak and premature natural instinct, we will come to challenge some of Laplanche's own tendencies to reduce the instinct-*Trieb* relation to a mere opposition. In so doing, we hope to shed even more light on the origins and nature of sexuality in the unfolding of the self-differentiating *Trieb*-instinct relation.

In the conclusion, we will seek to show how Freud's understanding of sexuality as a perversion of the natural instinct challenges many contemporary attempts to treat sexuality as an exception in various ways. In so doing, we will seek to show how Freud's problem of sexuality, in turn, challenges us to abandon the gesture of problematization itself. In this way, we hope that Freud's theory of sexuality will continue to provoke questions, discussions, and debates about the nature of sexuality.

Part 1

Sexual Problems: Complicating *Trieb* and Instinct

Chapter 1

The Problem with Popular Opinion

The editorial history of Freud's *Three Essays on the Theory of Sexuality* alone reveals how important this text was for his psychoanalytic theory as such. It was one of the few texts—alongside monumental and foundational psychoanalytic works such as the *Interpretation of Dreams* and the *Psychopathology of Everyday Life*—that Freud felt the need to update again and again in light of fresh discoveries in his work. After its initial publication in 1905, four subsequent editions of the *Three Essays* were published in 1910, 1915, 1920, and 1924. Each time Freud took great pains to revise, ameliorate, and add to the original work, and ultimately the 1924 edition of the text was almost twice the length of the original. In chapter 2 of our present study, we will consider some of these alterations to the text in more detail, and in chapter 5 we will address some of the controversies surrounding them. At any rate, suffice it to say that the sheer volume of alterations to the original text serves to underscore not only how central the ideas presented in this text were to Freud's psychoanalytic theory, but also the fact that they were always open to alteration as psychoanalysis itself continued to develop as a discipline—a point that we will attempt to drive home in chapter 3.

Despite the numerous alterations to the text, however, its general structure, trajectory, goal, and provocation remained the same. In this text, Freud set out, at a very general level, to investigate the nature of sexuality and challenge our prevailing theories about it. As the title indicates, the work is composed of three essays, each of which takes up an investigation into a separate aspect of Freud's theory of sexuality.

1. In the first essay, "The Sexual Aberrations," Freud begins with a polemic against the theory of sexuality espoused by

what he calls "popular opinion." According to Freud, popular opinion, for reasons that we will investigate, seeks to establish a normative and naturalistic definition of sexuality, according to which whatever tends toward heterosexuality is normal and natural, while everything else is abnormal and perverse. Freud, on the contrary, will turn to these so-called sexual aberrations in order to show how they challenge popular opinion and, more importantly, see what they might reveal to us about the nature of sexuality itself. The present chapter of this study will be concerned with unpacking the significance and the stakes of the confrontation between Freud and popular opinion in "The Sexual Aberrations" and beyond.

2. The second essay, "Infantile Sexuality," gives us an elaborate account and mounts a sophisticated defense of Freud's most controversial and provocative claim in the text—namely, that sexuality extends all the way back to our childhood, and even as far back as our infancy. However, what Freud calls "infantile sexuality" looks nothing like popular opinion's so-called sexual instinct for heterosexual intercourse, but rather is defined by being what Freud calls "polymorphously perverse." The entire second part of our study will be dedicated to a detailed examination of the most important aspects of Freud's theory of infantile sexuality: for example, infantile helplessness; polymorphous perversity; the relation of sexuality to the vital instincts; the significance of the infant's relation to its caregiver; and autoerotism.

3. The last of Freud's *Three Essays*, "The Transformations of Puberty," provides us with an account of the changes undergone by the human organism during puberty and the effect that this reproductive maturation has on our conception of sexuality. This, of course, becomes a major problem for Freud in light of the previous two essays. Since the human organism is in many ways born premature, especially in terms of its reproductive maturity, which does not take place until much later in life, the ability to reproduce only appears after infantile sexuality has established itself as the dominant force in libidinal life. In this way, the polymorphous perversion of infantile sexuality somehow seems to precede what popular

opinion comes to call the "normal" and "natural" instinct for reproduction. This idea that perversion precedes instinct will only further complicate our understanding of sexuality, which we will address in chapter 6.

Although each of these three essays tackles a separate aspect of Freud's theory of sexuality, there is nevertheless an underlying logic that unfolds over the course of the text—a logic that has continued to produce problems in the translation and reception of Freud's work. The entire first part of our present study will attempt to shed light on this logic (chapter 1), trace out some of the problems that it produces (chapter 2), and unpack some of the consequences that it has for our understanding of Freud's theory of sexuality (chapter 3).

Popular Opinion Revisited: A Serious Consideration

Freud himself begins the *Three Essays* with an open declaration of war against the popular opinion, *die populäre Meinung*, of sexuality. Yet, few have taken Freud's complicated and fecund relation with popular opinion as seriously as Freud himself did. In fact, if it is even remarked upon at all, the term *popular opinion* is often construed as little more than a mere rhetorical device against which Freud will develop his own theory of sexuality.[1] In this way, it is often treated as little more than an unsophisticated straw man—in which Freud either overeagerly reduces all of his scientific and medical contemporaries to a mere footnote,[2] or makes a hasty generalization about all the various lay discourses concerning sexuality[3]—which he can then easily critique, reject, and oppose. However, popular opinion is much more than a mere rhetorical device for Freud; it is something that he felt demanded to be taken seriously, as we see Freud confront popular opinion time and again throughout his career. This was because popular opinion always lurked in the numerous criticisms, objections, oppositions, and resistances to his psychoanalytic theory (even within the psychoanalytic movement itself[4]). It also reared its head time and again in his psychoanalytic practice.[5] Although the terminology that Freud uses to designate popular opinion does not always remain constant throughout his oeuvre,[6] it nonetheless shapes many of his most important works and breakthroughs.[7] In this way, Freud's confrontation with popular opinion in the *Three Essays* amounts to much more than an isolated incident in which he caricatures a few of his contemporaries. It was a major battle in his war of attrition against popular opinion. As such, Freud's treatment of popular opinion in the *Three Essays* demands a serious consideration.

As it stands, some lingering confusion still exists in the secondary literature concerning who exactly Freud has in his crosshairs with the term *popular opinion*.[8] However, it is clear that what is at stake for Freud is that—whether it finds its guise in a doctor, a scientist, a psychoanalyst, a mother, a father, a patient, a child, a religious figure or institution, or a philosopher—popular opinion always has "quite definite ideas about the nature [*ganz bestimmte Vorstellungen von der Natur*]" of sexuality (SE 7:135/ GW 5: 33). Freud claims that these "definite ideas," defining ideas, *ganz bestimmte Vorstellungen*, or perhaps even definitive ideas, always take the form of a definition that, in one way or another, presupposes a naturalistic and normalizing framework. This definition almost invariably makes a biological assumption that defines sexuality as "analogous" to something like hunger and, as such, something that human beings share in common with animals: "The fact of the existence of sexual needs in human beings and animals is expressed in biology by the assumption of a 'sexual instinct [*Geschlechtstrieb*],' on the analogy of the instinct of nutrition, that is of hunger" (SE 7: 135/GW 5: 33). By modeling sexuality on the analogy of hunger, popular opinion seeks to define it strictly in terms of what we would today be tempted to call a *natural instinct*. Just as, for example, the natural instinct of hunger can be understood as a force that impels an organism toward objects of nutrition (which are then ingested and digested with the aim of nourishing the organism and lowering the tension built up in it by hunger), sexuality is supposedly nothing other than the force that attracts the organism toward a sexual object (through which the organism aims to lower its sexual tension).

During Freud's own time, this sexual instinct was widely understood in terms of what his contemporaries called the "*Geschlechtstrieb*." As Arnold Davidson points out, Freud's contemporaries used this term quite ubiquitously and systematically to talk about an innate instinct for reproduction (Davidson 1987, 265). In other words, the *Geschlechtstrieb* was conceived as an instinct that serves a *particular vital function* (i.e., the reproduction of the species) and has a preestablished *aim* and *object* (i.e., genital union with a member of the opposite sex)—all of which, of course, is determined in advance by nature.

According to Freud, though, if we were to take a step back and scrutinize popular opinion's definition of sexuality, we will find that it is full of "errors, inaccuracies, and hasty conclusions" (SE 7: 135/GW 5: 33). For there are all kinds of manifestations of sexuality that ultimately do not fit this rigid and narrow definition. Off the top of our heads, we can all certainly think of many examples that we would consider to be "sexual," which nonetheless do not conform to popular opinion's *Geschlechtstrieb*. Of course, popular opinion itself could just bury its head in the sand and dismiss these examples as simply not being sexual at all. However, the problem here for popular opinion is that it still considers these various manifestations of sexuality to be sexual as well. After all, it is popular opinion, and not Freud (as Freud himself points out), that labels anything that does not conform to or deviates from the *Geschlechtstrieb* as a "*sexual* aberration."

How can it be the case, then, that popular opinion points to this one thing, the *Geschlechtstrieb*, as being definitive of the nature of what sexuality is, yet at the same time acknowledges that the domain of sexuality stretches well beyond these confines? This is not a rhetorical question simply meant to dismiss popular opinion, but rather one that needs to be taken seriously. How could anyone who takes seriously the study of sexuality attempt to define it strictly in terms of the *Geschlechtstrieb*, while nonetheless acknowledging the sexual aberrations as being sexual as well?

In seeking to define sexuality in this way, popular opinion clearly seeks to establish an opposition between the *Geschlechtstrieb* and the so-called sexual aberrations that deviate from it. This, among other things, is meant to create a certain structural, if not ontological, hierarchy that prioritizes the supposedly normal and natural over the abnormal and unnatural. This prioritization of the natural instinct (which comes first) over the sexual aberrations (which only come about secondarily as a deviation from the supposed sexual instinct) is made explicit in the normalizing, and even moralizing, framework within which popular opinion often inscribes these terms: on the one hand, there is the good, sometimes divine, sexual instinct for heterosexual intercourse, and, on the other hand, there are the bad, abnormal, degenerate, deviant, perverse, and unnatural sexual aberrations. Of course, like the philosophers who we discussed in the Introduction, popular opinion privileges the *Geschlechtstrieb* as the paradigm of sexuality in an attempt to suppress and marginalize the so-called sexual aberrations. However, as we will see in what follows, these supposedly suppressed sexual aberrations will repeatedly return to cause problems for popular opinion's naturalistic and normative framework.

What Freud wants to demonstrate in the first of his *Three Essays* is that even under the slightest bit of interrogation the line dividing the normal/

natural from the abnormal/unnatural begins to blur and dissolve—so much so that it seems like what popular calls normal and natural turns out to be rather perverse, and what it considers to be abnormal and unnatural turns out to be the rule rather than the exception. The harder popular opinion tries to keep the normal and natural pure and free from the perversity of the sexual aberrations, the more popular opinion finds itself mired in a problem: twisting itself inside out, tying itself up in contradictions, and struggling to maintain the opposition between them. And it is this very problem to which Freud draws our attention because it is this problem that should be taken seriously—not simply dismissed as being contradictory or problematic—since it reveals something fundamental about the nature of sexuality as such, which will demand that we completely and radically rethink what we commonly understand sexuality to be.

Popular Opinion as *Doxa* in the Rigorous Sense of the Term

Before moving on to a detailed discussion of Freud's interrogation of popular opinion, it is worth dwelling on a concern that Jonathan Lear raises about Freud's confrontation with popular opinion. This will help us understand not only the stakes of Freud's confrontation with popular opinion, but also the method with which he will do so. For just by virtue of challenging popular opinion, Freud demands something very difficult of the reader. He demands that we challenge our own understanding of sexuality and put it into question. This, of course, is no easy feat when it comes to our common opinions and beliefs, especially those concerning sexuality. However, according to Lear, this radical gesture—a quintessentially psychoanalytic gesture, to be sure—in and of itself raises some serious concerns about Freud's theory of sexuality. In his philosophical introduction to Freud, Lear worries that, ultimately, Freud might not provide us with any meaningful discussion or definition of sexuality. In fact, this is precisely because whatever Freud comes to call "sexuality" differs so greatly from that of popular opinion: "If Freud's conception of sexuality differs that much from the popular conception, why should we think of it as sexuality? Why not think of it—whatever it is—as something else? This is an important question and one that has not yet been answered accurately" (Lear 2005, 55). According to Lear, if Freud seeks to challenge the "popular conception" of sexuality in such a radical manner that it completely undermines our spontaneous conception of it, then we have to ask ourselves why Freud should insist on calling whatever he is investigating "sexuality" at all. For Lear, there has not been a sufficient and satisfying response to this concern and, as such, this presents a major problem for Freud's theory of sexuality (if it could still be called that).

However, Lear's analysis risks overlooking a crucial move that Freud makes in his treatment of popular opinion in "The Sexual Aberrations." This is a point worth stressing because it will become very important in our investigation of Freud's *Three Essays*. It is not that he, Freud, simply disagrees with popular opinion and, consequently, endeavors to put forward his own definition of sexuality, which is completely different from that of popular opinion, and which he thinks is more accurate and more comprehensive. After all, why would Freud even waste his time engaging with popular opinion at all, if it were so far off the mark? What Freud wants to show in the first essay is that popular opinion itself is already working with a much more sophisticated, complex, and complicated (albeit latent) understanding of what sexuality is. Under a little scrutiny and reflection, this understanding will come to light and lead us to a deeper conception of the nature of sexuality, which Freud will try to spell out in the remainder of the *Three Essays*. In this way, popular opinion serves Freud as a sort of *doxa*—not in the traditionally understood sense of a "mere" opinion (. . . that he can easily critique and dismiss for some other opinion)—but rather in the sense that is produced when taking into account the "double valence" of the ancient Greek verb *dokein* from which *doxa* comes. As the ancient Greek philosophy scholar, Sean Kirkland, claims, "*dokein*" means both "to have an opinion about something" and "to appear to be something" (Kirkland 2013, 24). Kirkland further points out that the word *dokein* is etymologically related to the deponent verb *dechesthai*, which means something like: to take, to accept, to receive, or to welcome (Kirkland 2013, 25). Taken as such, *dokein* can be understood as a "receiving"—a receiving of an understanding that always somehow seems to point beyond what is immediately received (Kirkland 2013, 25).

For our purposes, we can see that in the first essay Freud receives popular opinion's definition of sexuality, this *doxa*, and takes seriously the ways in which it already points beyond itself to a deeper understanding of sexuality. As such, far from merely talking about something completely different than what popular opinion calls "sexuality," Freud takes seriously the ways in which popular opinion considers sexuality to be much more complex and complicated than its definition appears to be. Thus, it is not simply a matter of convention: it is not that popular opinion calls sexuality one thing, while Freud calls it another. What Freud wants to show us is that popular opinion itself already considers sexuality to be that very "something else" that Lear sees as constituting a problem for Freud's theory of sexuality. In this way, Freud takes popular opinion seriously not just as something that needs to be reckoned with, which should be overturned and done away with, but as something that, almost despite itself, reveals something to us about the fundamental nature of sexuality.

Freud will, then, as psychoanalysts are demanded to do, listen with great care to what popular opinion has to say about sexuality, taking it at its word, even when its word seems to fall apart, because this falling apart itself tells us something about the nature of sexuality as such. In this way, we can say that for Freud popular opinion knows (without knowing that it knows) something more about the nature of sexuality than its definition appears to put forward. And what it knows is this: that when it comes to the nature of sexuality there is a necessary possibility of deviation built in it. Or, to paraphrase Freud from the end of "The Sexual Aberrations": what is innate in sexuality is perversion (SE 7: 171/GW 5: 71). In other words, *the nature of sexuality itself is perversion*. And it is this apparently confusing formulation that Freud arrives at through his interrogation of popular opinion, to which we will now turn our attention.

Freud's Cross-Examination of Popular Opinion in "The Sexual Aberrations"

With this in mind, we can now turn to the details of Freud's interrogation of popular opinion in the *Three Essays*. Freud begins his cross-examination of popular opinion by bringing our attention to the way that popular opinion tends to organize the "sexual aberrations" into two major categories, which make up the first two sections of "The Sexual Aberrations": (1) deviations in respect of the sexual object; and (2) deviations in respect of the sexual aim. Having divided the sexual aberrations into these two categories, Freud can begin systematically interrogating popular opinion's attempt to define the nature of sexuality in terms of the *Geschlechtstrieb* against the so-called sexual aberrations.

Perversion, or Why Sexuality Cannot Be Simply Defined in Terms of the Sexual Aim

We will begin with the second section, deviations with respect to the sexual aim, because it makes Freud's strategy for interrogating popular opinion abundantly clear. Freud—borrowing from popular opinion's definition of sexuality—defines the *sexual aim* as "the act towards which the instinct [*Trieb*] tends." The sexual aim, then, is the act or activity that one *aims* at in order to release their sexual tension. With this in mind, Freud will turn to popular opinion in order to see how it would define this sexual aim based on its attempt to explain sexuality in terms of the *Geschlechtstrieb*. As such, for popular opinion the sexual aim would be nothing other than "the union of genitals in the act known as copulation, which leads to a release of the sexual tension and a temporary extinction of the sexual instinct—a satisfaction analogous to the sating of hunger" (SE VII 149/ GW 5: 48–49).

Again, modeling sexuality on the analogy of hunger (as popular opinion is wont to do), it declares that the sexual aim is genital union, which leads to a sating of sexual tension. Evidently, what makes this activity sexual is that it involves the union of the *sex* organs and the release of *sexual* tension. However, it seems difficult to discern what exactly popular opinion claims the ultimate aim of sexuality is: is it the release of sexual tension, that is, an orgasm, which happens as a result of genital union? Or, is it genital union, of which the orgasm is merely a side effect or by-product? Either way, Freud is happy to let popular opinion have its cake and eat it too with this definition, since he will show that neither genital union nor the orgasm can be defining of sexuality as such.

Freud immediately points to several examples, which popular opinion calls "perversions," that is, examples of sexuality that deviate from its definition of sexuality in terms of the *Geschlectstrieb*—examples, it is worth emphasizing again, that popular opinion itself still, curiously enough, considers to be sexual. For example: voyeurism and exhibitionism, sadism and masochism, and even certain forms of touching and kissing. Since these acts do not conform to the sexual aim of the *Geschlechtstrieb*, popular opinion considers them to be *perversions* that *deviate*, in one way or another, from the sexual aim of genital union, intercourse, and orgasm.

We can see that in all of these perversions genital union need not be the aim. In fact, the genitals, and certainly genital union, may not even come into play at all. The actions of a Peeping Tom, for example, are certainly called sexual, even if all that transpires is looking. We can certainly imagine a Peeping Tom who does not even look at the genitals of another, touch their own genitals, have an orgasm, or even intend to have an orgasm while looking. Yet, there is something nonetheless sexual about the looking of a Peeping Tom. What that is popular opinion cannot say, so it dismisses the Peeping Tom simply as being a pervert.

Now to push things a little further than Freud did in his own day: one might also think of certain practices known as "edging" or "orgasm denial," which popular opinion would no doubt consider to be sexual. In such cases the aim is to come as close as possible to an orgasm only, in the end, to prevent it altogether. In other words, the sexual aim is precisely to prevent what popular opinion considers to be defining of the sexual aim in order to do the exact opposite—not lowering tension, but instead heightening it without release.

Such perverse counterexamples begin to leave popular opinion with a problem: it must either disavow the sexual aspect of these perversions, or it must acknowledge them as sexual and fall into direct contradiction with its own definition of the sexual aim. Its only solution so far is to call them *sexual*, but try to dismiss, suppress, and even repress them as sexual *aberrations*. In other words, they are sexual, but perhaps not *really* sexual in the true sense of the word because they are merely inadequate expressions of the true sexual function.

Freud, on the contrary, instead of dismissing these perverse counterexamples, takes them seriously as revealing something about the nature of sexuality as such—namely, that sexuality can be present in various acts (not just the union of the genitals or the orgasm) such that even the most innocuous and everyday acts like looking can have, as Freud puts it, a "sexual tinge," *sexuell betonten* (SE 7: 157/GW 5: 56). Somehow, whatever we call sexuality can come to contaminate and tinge any activity whatsoever in such a way that even looking, eating, speaking, walking, and so on can be considered sexual. The consequences of this are far-reaching for Freud's theory of sexuality. For what this implies is not just that the sexual aim is more diverse or, perhaps, is a "spectrum" of different aims. Rather, what this means is that *sexuality cannot be defined in terms of the sexual aim*, because any activity whatsoever can become tinged with sexuality in this way. As such, popular opinion's attempt to divide sexuality into a normal/natural sexual aim and an abnormal/unnatural sexual aim begins to fall apart. There is no natural sexual aim that can considered normal, because the nature of sexuality as such is to tinge any activity whatsoever with sexuality. In this way, *what was considered to be a perversion turns out to be part of the very nature of sexuality itself.*

Homosexuality, or Why Sexuality Cannot Be Defined Strictly in Terms of the Sexual Object

In the first section of "The Sexual Aberrations," deviations in respect of the sexual object, Freud puts popular opinion's attempt to define sexuality in terms of the sexual object into question in a very similar manner. According to popular opinion, another component of what makes something sexual is an attraction toward a sexual object. In this way, it is the object that is sexual; and sexuality *is* just the attraction to that (sexual) object. But what, we might ask, makes an object sexual in the first place? According to popular opinion, the sexual object can, of course, be defined as a member of the opposite sex. In this way, the "sexualness" of the object is defined in terms of the genitals of the opposite sex. In other words, what sexuality *is*, then, is just the very attraction one has toward a member of the opposite *sex*. However, Freud immediately challenges popular opinion's attempt to define sexuality in this way, and not without a hint of sarcasm: "It comes as a great surprise therefore to learn that there are men whose sexual object is a man and not a woman, and women whose sexual object is a woman and not a man" (SE 7: 136/GW 5: 34). If sexuality is defined as that which attracts someone to the opposite sex, it should surprise us that there are people who are *sexually* attracted to members of the same sex. In fact, it is on popular opinion's own terms that these deviations from the (hetero)sexual object are considered to be sexual at all. Again, Freud is just pointing out this inconsistency in popular opinion's account of sexuality. After all, it is popular opinion itself that labels people attracted to members of the same sex as homo*sexuals* and, thereby, ordering homosexuality in the world of sexuality. Thus, Freud's "great surprise" here—and there is a great surprise here—is not so much that we find people who do not conform to this narrow heteronormative definition of sexuality. That is not really much of a surprise. Rather, the great surprise here is that popular opinion still considers these homosexual attractions *to be sexual at all* given that it seeks to define sexuality in terms of the attraction to a member of the opposite sex.

This apparent contradiction leaves popular opinion with a huge problem concerning its definition of the nature of sexuality—namely, how can it be the case that sexuality is defined as the attraction toward a member of the opposite sex, if the attraction toward a member of the same sex is also considered to be sexual? It seems that whatever sexuality *is* it is more than just the attraction to a member of the opposite sex.

Popular Opinion's Problem with Homosexuality

It is clear that popular opinion has a problem with homosexuality—namely, that it acknowledges it as sexual, yet it attempts to exclude it from its definition of sexuality. In Freud's 1920 case study, "The Psychogenesis of a Case of Homosexuality in a Woman," which itself constitutes one of his most direct confrontations with popular opinion in his psychoanalytic practice, Freud documents, among other things, the ways in which popular opinion gets itself into and tries to wriggle itself out of this very problem.

In this text, Freud reports undertaking the treatment of a young woman who is about eighteen years of age. Her parents have taken her to see Freud after she was left severely injured from jumping off a building in an attempted suicide. The young woman leapt from a building, Freud tells us, immediately after her father had caught her in public with her love interest—a woman almost ten years her senior, whom she had been expressly forbidden from seeing. Freud explains that the parents desperately sought his help in order to bring their daughter back to a "normal state of mind." They hoped, of course, to relieve their daughter of her depression and suicidal tendencies, but also to cure her of her homosexuality as well, which they viewed as a sign of "degeneracy" and the source of her problems. (Little did they suspect that Freud had no intentions of "curing" any of his patients of their homosexuality.[9]) Furthermore, if Freud's psychoanalytic work was not enough to cure her of her homosexuality, then the father had yet another trick up his sleeve to rid her of it. Freud reports: "If [psychoanalysis] failed, he still had in reserve his strongest countermeasure: a speedy marriage was to awaken the natural instincts [*natürlichen Instinkte*] of the girl and stifle her unnatural tendencies [*unnatürliche Neigungen*]" (SE 18: 149/GW 12: 274). Should psychoanalysis fail, the father's next step to cure his daughter's homosexuality was going to be to use artificial means (a forced marriage) in order to combat her "unnatural tendencies," *unnatürliche Neigungen*, and restore her natural (sexual) instincts, *natürlichen Instinkte*. In this way, the father views the young woman's homosexuality as a degeneracy of her natural instinct—that is, as an unnatural tendency that deviates from her innate, natural attraction toward a member of the opposite sex. The parents hoped that Freud would be able to awaken their daughter's supposed natural instinct for a member of the opposite sex, which supposedly lay dormant within her, and stifle her so-called unnatural homosexual tendencies. And if he failed, then a marriage should do the trick. (It is worth remarking here that, just like the Athenian Stranger in the *Laws*, the father attempts to use artificial means to force the supposedly natural into existence.)

By framing their appeal in this way, the parents come to perfectly embody popular opinion: they consider their daughter's homosexuality to be sexual and yet try to disavow it as not really being sexual insofar as it is merely a deviation from her natural sexual instincts. On the one hand, the young woman's sexuality becomes *a problem* for her parents only and precisely insofar as they admit that it is sexual in one way or another. It is only in its being sexual that her homosexuality can be seen to come into conflict with her supposed natural sexual instinct. On the other hand, as a mere tendency or degeneracy, that is, not a part of her true and innate sexual nature, her homosexuality can supposedly be cured and brought back to the natural state from which it deviates.

Now, much like the young woman's parents in "A Case of Homosexuality in a Woman," popular opinion in the *Three Essays* attempts to wriggle out of this self-inflicted problem in a similar way. Popular opinion declares homosexuality to be a degeneracy, but a degeneracy with a twist, since it considers it to be an "*innate* indication of nervous *degeneracy* [*angeboren Zeichen nervöser Degeneration*]" (SE 7: 138/GW 5: 36). In this way, homosexuality is curiously considered to be both something innate and something degenerate. How could this be? How could homosexuality be both innate and a deviation from what is considered to be innate?

Unfortunately, popular opinion itself does not recognize the genius of this almost paradoxical formulation, which would force us to think of homosexuality, and perhaps sexuality as such, as something that is both innate (i.e., as originary, as original, or as natural) *and* as a degeneracy (i.e., as a deviation from the origin, as acquired, or as unnatural). (Freud himself will pick up on this paradoxical formulation and develop it further later in the text, and we will return to it ourselves in what follows). For now, suffice it to say that Freud is happy to continue pushing popular opinion's confused attempt to deal with homosexuality to its breaking point: "We are therefore forced to a suspicion that the choice between 'innate' and 'acquired' is not an exclusive one or that it does not cover all the issues involved in [homosexuality]" (SE 7: 140/GW 5: 39). What is at stake for Freud, then, at this point in his interrogation of popular opinion is that by attempting to account for homosexuality as either something innate or something acquired does nothing, in the end, to tell us what about homosexuality makes it *sexual*. Freud continues,

> The nature of inversion is explained neither by the hypothesis that it is innate nor by the alternative hypothesis that it is acquired. In the former case we must ask in what respect it is innate, unless we are to accept the crude explanation that everyone is born with his sexual instinct [*Sexualtrieb*] attached to a particular

sexual object. In the latter case it may be questioned whether the various accidental influences would be sufficient to explain the acquisition of inversion without the co-operation of something in the subject himself. (SE 7: 140/GW 5: 39)

According to Freud, as we can see, neither the innate nor the acquired alone exhausts the complexities at stake in the nature of homosexuality. As such, popular opinion cannot define homosexuality as being derivative of heterosexuality, that is, as being a deviation from or a degeneracy of some supposed heterosexual instinct, nor can popular opinion claim that it is something innate or natural, because this would come into direct contradiction with its definition of sexuality in terms of an innate heterosexual instinct for reproduction.

If we have been harping on what appears to be an obvious and straightforward point, it is because there is a subtle—yet significant and major—shift at this point in the text. For Freud, the question here is no longer about whether or not popular opinion is able to account for the sex of the person to whom one could become attracted in its definition of sexuality. In other words, he is no longer concerned with whether or not popular opinion's definition is comprehensive enough to include homosexuality within it. Rather, it is popular opinion's own waffling on this subject that leads Freud to a different set of concerns, namely, whether the attraction toward a sexual object is sufficient enough to define what sexuality *is* in the first place. This is because popular opinion has gained no ground in its own attempts to define sexuality in terms of the person to whom one is attracted. Not only does this definition in no way exhaust popular opinion's own understanding of what it considers to be sexual. It is also clear that even on its own terms neither the attraction toward the heterosexual or homosexual object tells us anything about why heterosexuality or homosexuality are considered to be sexual at all.

More Objects, More Problems: Fetishism, or Why Sexuality Cannot Be Defined in Terms of the Sexual Object

Under the duress of Freud's line of questioning concerning the sexual object, popular opinion will attempt to offer up yet another defense. We can almost hear popular opinion retort in the *Three Essays*, "sexuality is just the attraction towards a person in general, whether that be a person of the same sex or the opposite sex." However, Freud already has a response of his own in waiting, pointing to the fetishists, or those people for whom the sexual object is not even a person at all: "Well," we can almost hear Freud say, "if that is your new definition of sexuality, then it comes as an *even greater surprise* that there are people whose sexual object is not a person of the opposite sex, but not even a person at all!"

In fact, a quick survey of the field of the fetishists shows that many people are sexually attracted to many different objects, such that it appears as though anyone could de jure become attracted to any object whatsoever. What the fetishists show us is that the object to which one becomes attracted is so highly variable that it is in no way decided in advance. The fact that someone could become attracted to, say, an animal, an inanimate object, an idea, a sound, a smell, a taste, and so on shows that there is no single object that defines sexuality as such. One could just as easily become attracted to a person of the opposite sex as a person of the same sex, or even some animate or inanimate object. Thus, there is nothing about these various objects themselves that tell us why the attraction toward them is sexual.

This variability of the object shows us that sexuality, the *Trieb*—what is left once we take the *Geschlecht*—(that is, the sex/gender of the object toward which one is attracted) out of the *Geschlechtstrieb*—is initially independent of the object and, therefore, cannot be defining of it. In this way, the object itself does not tell us why the attraction toward that object is sexual in the first place, nor does it explain why a given object is sexual. In fact, we can now see that popular opinion's definition of sexuality in terms of the sexual object is shown to be circular: according to popular opinion, sexuality is the attraction toward the sexual object, and what makes that object sexual is just the sexual attraction toward that sexual object.

Popular Opinion's Kettle Logic

By seeking to define sexuality in terms of the sexual object of the *Geschlechtstrieb*—that is, as the natural, instinctual attraction toward a member of the opposite sex—popular opinion soon finds itself plagued with a sort of kettle logic. Freud's first recorded mention of what has become known as "kettle logic" comes in his *Interpretation of Dreams*. At the end of his famous discussion of the dream about Irma's injection, Freud famously states, "the defense put forward by the man who was charged by one of his neighbors with having given back a borrowed kettle in a damaged condition" (SE 4: 119–20/GW 2: 125). The man's three-pronged defense, as is well-known, is that:

1. he had given the kettle back undamaged;
2. the kettle already had a hole in it when he borrowed it; and
3. he had never borrowed the kettle in the first place.

Freud will later, in his *Jokes and their Relation to the Unconscious*, call this kettle logic a "piece of sophistry" (SE 8: 61–62/GW 6:65–66). Of course, the "sophistry" at work here is that each of these individual propositions taken alone would represent an acceptable defense; however, taken together they come to violate the principle of noncontradiction: for example, the kettle could not have been given back undamaged if it already had a hole in it; it could not have been given back (damaged or not) if it was not borrowed in the first place; and so on. In other words, by trying to mount an absolutely irrefutable defense the man ends up defeating his own argument.

Now we can see the same kettle logic is implicitly at work in popular opinion's attempt to define sexuality in terms of the sexual object. As Freud shows in his interrogation of popular opinion, the latter holds three incompatible positions. According to popular opinion, sexuality is:

1. *just* the attraction to a member of the opposite sex;
2. *not just* the attraction toward a member of the opposite sex, but to any object; and
3. not the attraction toward the object at all.

Freud shows that popular opinion implicitly maintains all three of these positions in its confused attempt to define sexuality, and all three statements taken together would ultimately come into contradiction with each other.

It is important to remember, though, that Freud brings up this "piece of sophistry" in the *Interpretation of Dreams* not to dismiss his dream about Irma's injection as being nonsensical, but instead to take this "illogical" kettle logic of the dream seriously as disclosing something to us about nature and construction of dreams (SE 4: 119–20/GW 2: 125). Freud will come to claim that the nature of dreams follows a certain logic (albeit a logic that seems to defy our everyday ways of thinking, which are arguably structured by the principle of noncontradiction). I would argue that the same idea is at work implicitly in Freud's treatment of popular opinion in the *Three Essays*. Freud wants us to take popular opinion's kettle logic seriously as disclosing something to us about the nature of sexuality itself—not just that popular opinion is simply wrong about sexuality.

Now, the problem with popular opinion is that it does not take its kettle logic seriously. Thus, on the one hand (and we will return to this later), Freud demands that we take seriously the fact that popular opinion considers sexuality to be naturally heterosexual despite the overwhelming evidence to the contrary, which it itself points out to us. We might, then, ask ourselves: why does popular opinion remain so obstinately attached to the idea (or fantasy) of this normative and naturalistic definition of sexuality? On the other hand, and this concerns us presently, Freud does not simply dismiss the contradictory twists and turns of popular opinion's account of sexuality. Rather, he takes it seriously as revealing something about the nature of sexuality itself. Just as it is the case in the *Interpretation of Dreams* and in *Jokes and their Relation to the Unconscious*, the point Freud is trying to make is not that we should simply dismiss what is going on here as a piece of sophistry or as a confused and contradictory account of sexuality. It is not that this kettle logic turns out to violate the principle of non-contradiction and should, therefore, be discarded as absurd or nonsensical. Rather, this logic should be taken seriously, and taken seriously as proper to the workings and movement of the thing itself: the dream-work, the joke-work or, in this case, sexuality. What sets Freud apart from popular opinion, then, is that he takes this kettle logic seriously and, in so doing, forces us to think through it in order to understand what sexuality is.

The Soldering of the Object and Weak Directionality

What Freud discovers in the twists and turns of popular opinion's attempt to define sexuality in terms of the *Geschlechtstrieb* is that what is "essential and constant [*Wesentliche und Konstante*]" in sexuality must be something other than the attraction to the sexual object (SE 7: 149/GW 5: 48). In other words, since the object is variable, the object itself and the attraction toward that object cannot be defining of what sexuality *is*. One can think, for example, of a mundane object like food. Food is often considered to be the object of the instinct of hunger, yet we can think of many instances in which we would say that food is considered to be a sexual object. Why do we consider food to be sexual in certain instances and not others? What makes certain interactions with food sexual? We do not seek to answer these complicated questions here, but from them we can see that there must be something other than the object itself that constitutes it as a *sexual* object.

Yet, we need to be careful. Despite the fact that the object is not what is defining of sexuality, this does not mean that the object itself plays no role in sexuality whatsoever, and we will return to this crucial argument again in chapter 5. For now, it is important to note that just because the object is not defining of sexuality as such, the object itself is absolutely integral for understanding what sexuality *is*. In other words, it may not be a sufficient condition of sexuality, but it sure is necessary. This is because sexuality only becomes manifest to us in the attraction to an object. It is impossible to think of sexuality that is not directed toward an object of some sort (a point we will flesh out in some detail in chapter 5). In this way, popular opinion is correct to lay a certain amount of emphasis on the sexual object, but it is its insistence on the object being defining of sexuality *as such* that is misplaced.

All of this still leaves Freud with a pressing question: if one could de jure become attracted to any object whatsoever, such that it is not decided in advance, then how does one become attracted to an object in the first place? In dismantling popular opinion's attempt to define sexuality in terms of the object and *Geschlectstrieb*, Freud is admittedly left with very few resources to explain the origins and the nature of this attraction toward the sexual object (SE 7: 146/GW 5: 46). However, Freud does not despair over this lack of material or the fact that the question cannot be immediately answered. In fact, it is precisely the lack of material and the absence of a solution that leads him to another (more important) observation: "Nevertheless, our investigation has put us in possession of a piece of knowledge which may turn out to be of greater importance to us than the solution of that problem" (SE 7: 146–47/GW 5: 46). Here, we see that Freud fights to keep this question concerning the nature of sexuality open, rather than shutting the question down by immediately providing an answer to it. It is the question itself, and not the answer, that will provide Freud with further insights.

Freud continues, then, specifying what this important piece of information is.

> It has been brought to our notice that we have been in the habit of regarding the connection between the sexual instinct [*Sexualtrieb*] and the sexual object as more intimate [*innige*] than it in fact is. Experience of the cases that are considered to be abnormal

has shown us that in them the sexual instinct [*Sexualtrieb*] and the sexual object are merely soldered together—a fact which we have been in danger of overlooking in consequence of the uniformity of the normal picture, where the object appears to form part and parcel of the instinct [*Trieb*]. It seems probable that the sexual instinct [*Geschlechtstrieb*] is in the first instance independent of its object; nor is its origin likely to be due to the object's attractions. (SE 7: 147–48/GW 5: 46–47)

For now, let us set aside the three variations on the German term *Trieb* at work in this passage until chapter 6 and continue to consider the relation between sexuality and the sexual object. Given the frequency of the so-called normal picture—given, that is, that a statistical majority of people seem on the surface to conform to the *Geschlechtstrieb*—popular opinion falls into the trap of assuming that the sexual object is "part and parcel" of sexuality. It assumes that the *Trieb mitzubringt*, brings with it, the sexual object. In other words, because so many people engage in heterosexual intercourse, popular opinion assumes that sexuality must, then, have a predetermined, natural attraction toward a member of the opposite sex determined in advance. For popular opinion, the *Trieb*—that force through which sexuality is manifest—and the heterosexual object are considered to be so intimately connected that the attraction is innate, instinctual, and natural. Accordingly, it must just be the nature of sexuality to be attracted to a member of the opposite sex, and everything else must be some deviation from this. However, Freud has shown that the connection between sexuality, the *Trieb*, and the sexual object is not as "intimate," *innige*—that is, not as innate, instinctual, and natural—as popular opinion assumes.

As Freud has shown, anyone could in principle have become attracted to any object whatsoever, such that it is de jure highly variable, and such that there is no innate, natural connection to the object decided in advance. This leads Freud to conclude that the *Trieb* as such and the sexual object must be initially independent of each other or, at least, that sexuality is not reducible to the attraction to/from the object. Since there is no innate or natural bond that is decided in advance between the *Trieb* and the sexual object, Freud declares that the two must be attached together, or "soldered," *verlötet*, in some secondary way.

This soldering, as Elizabeth Rottenberg points out, is a "trope" that suggests that the connection between *Trieb* and the object cannot be reduced to a pregiven binary alternative (in this case, innate/acquired, normal/abnormal, natural/unnatural). Instead, she suggests that the connection itself is unnatural or nonnatural, since it is "an artificial joining that is in no way assured by nature," though she adds: "it may have a naturalizing effect" (Rottenberg 2019, 91). In other words, although this soldering is un- or nonnatural insofar as it is not decided in advance by the nature of the *Trieb*, this does not preclude it having a naturalizing effect, or becoming part of the nature of the *Trieb*. In other words, because one can in principle become attracted to any object whatsoever, the possibility of becoming attracted to, or soldered to, any object whatsoever must already be contained within the *nature* of sexuality itself. What is essential and constant to the nature of sexuality, then, is neither the heterosexual object nor the sexual object in general, but rather the *very possibility* of becoming soldered to an object.

It is not the object or the attraction to an object that makes it sexual, then, but this secondary soldering to the object. In other words, an object becomes sexual in its being soldered to the *Trieb*, the process of which for an individual can only be revealed in and through the psychoanalytic situation. We can now see the sort of contradiction at work in popular opinion that Freud forces us to think through—namely, that the *nature* of sexuality is this *secondary* soldering to the object, which itself is part of the nature of sexuality. We can no longer conceive, then, along with popular opinion, of some natural sexuality that is magically attracted to a heterosexual object. Instead, and this is a product of popular opinion's own understanding of sexuality, the nature of sexuality is in this soldering of the *Trieb* to any object whatsoever.

The problem for Freud concerning the nature of sexuality—and this seems to be what separates him from not only the popular opinion of his day, but contemporary discourses about sexuality as well—is one of understanding how the *Trieb* becomes soldered to an object that is not determined in advance. In other words, how is it the case that the *Trieb*, despite its inherently nonteleological nature, nonetheless comes to take on what we might call a "weak directionality"? After all, as we have shown, although it is not *inherently* attracted to certain objects, the *Trieb* does nonetheless become soldered to them. Thus, the *Trieb* is "directional" in the sense that it does tend toward certain objects. Of course, part of the strategical use of the term *directional* here is meant to avoid connotations of teleology, in which case the purpose, aim, and object of sexuality would be decided in advance as a final cause. Furthermore, this "weak directionality" is considered "weak" in the sense that it is not inherent, innate, or decided in advance; it comes into being secondarily, so to speak, and the routes it takes toward its objects are circuitous, plastic, malleable, exchangeable, contingent, and open to alteration and sublimation. However, as we will show in more detail in chapter 5, it is important to keep in mind that sexuality does serve a certain purpose for the organism, even if this purpose is not a reproductive one that is determined in advance.

The Nature of Sexuality: Innate Perversion

Ultimately, for Freud, what all of these examples of the sexual aberrations show us is that what is essential and constant in sexuality—what sexuality *is*—is neither definable in terms of the sexual object (because the sexual object is de jure highly variable), nor the sexual aim (because any act whatsoever can become tinged with sexuality). In other words, sexuality cannot be defined in terms of its aim or object, because neither the aim nor the object does anything to tell us about what sexuality *is* or what makes any specific aim or object sexual in the first place. There must be something beyond any given aim or object that makes this aim or object sexual, which popular opinion itself hints at when it calls the sexual aberrations "*sexual.*" Thus, even on its own terms, sexuality begins to spill out of the narrow confines of popular opinion's attempt at a rigid definition, extending so far beyond it as to come into direct contradiction with it.

Freud demands that we take these contradictions seriously as revealing something about the nature of sexuality, because what popular opinion shows (without knowing that it shows this) is that sexuality itself is structured by a certain blurring of the binary opposition between the so-called natural and unnatural, which popular opinion tries to cover up with a fig leaf of a normalizing and naturalistic definition. However, as we have seen, this normalizing and naturalistic definition begins to fall apart such that we can conclude that the nature of sexuality is, in fact, the secondary soldering to an object, which can then come to tinge any activity and object with sexuality.

If sexuality can deviate from the supposed normal and natural sexual object, becoming soldered to any object whatsoever, then this means that the possibility for this deviation is always already built into sexuality. Freud himself seems to say as much when he declares at the end of "The Sexual Aberrations" that the possibility for perversion is something that lies innate in everyone: "The conclusion now presents itself to us that there is indeed something innate lying behind the perversions but that it is something innate in everyone, though as a disposition it may vary in its intensity and may be increased by the influences of actual life. What is in question are the innate constitutional roots of the sexual instinct [Sexualtrieb]" (SE 7: 171/GW 5: 71). For Freud, when we ask about the innate "constitutional roots" of sexuality, when we ask about the origins or the nature of the *Trieb*, we are led to the fact that the possibility for perversion is something lying innate in within it. When it comes to sexuality, perversion is not, in this way, a deviation from what is innate, but rather what is innate is this possibility for deviation. In other words, the nature of the *Trieb* itself is perversion, which, in turn, will begin to complicate the ways that we understand the relation between the *Trieb* and the instinct.

Chapter 2

The Problem with the Instinct

Strachey's Revenge

For Jean Laplanche, Freud's confrontation with popular opinion in the *Three Essays* constitutes a moment of upheaval, an event, *un événement*, not only in Freud's own thought, but also in our collective understanding of sexuality as such (Trois. 249/241). This is because, according to Laplanche, Freud puts forward a revolutionary theory of sexuality that challenges popular opinion and, as a result, the instinctual model of sexuality as such. If popular opinion, as Freud shows, seeks to define and confine sexuality strictly in terms of the *Geschlechtstrieb*, that is, strictly in terms of a sexual instinct for heterosexual intercourse and reproduction, Freud opens up a way of thinking the *Trieb* that breaks with any and every biologistic and instinctual model of sexuality that presupposes it is an innate instinct with a predetermined teleology. As we have shown in chapter 1, Freud's *Trieb* has no predefined aims or objects determined in advance toward which it tends. Unlike an instinct, then, with its predetermined teleology, according to Laplanche, the *Trieb* proper is an "almost blind," *quasi aveugle* force—a force, that is, which seeks "satisfaction rather than some preestablished end" (FB 14/21). Freud's revolution, then, the event of the *Three Essays*, was to have shown how the *Trieb* itself breaks from the instinct and, in this way, to have himself theoretically and conceptually broken with popular opinion's biologistic-instinctual model of sexuality.

However, like any revolutionary discovery, its incompleteness and undecidability leave it open to three counterrevolutionary forces:

1. It can be met with hostile criticism, resistance, and opposition—and is, thereby, subject to ruthless suppression;

2. Its true insights can be misrecognized, distorted, disregarded, or even ignored—and, thereby, its revolutionary force completely undermined; or

3. It risks becoming codified, institutionalized and, in this way, normalized—and, thereby, its polemical force neutralized.

Thus, throughout his career, Laplanche continued to find himself in a familiar position: attempting to galvanize and unleash the revolutionary and polemical potential of Freud's theory of sexuality against these three reactionary tendencies. For Laplanche, these threats come from all sides. Just to name a few: Kleinian psychoanalysts (FB 110–11/123–24), a certain brand of Lacanianism (Pul. 8–9/10), hermeneutic interpreters (Laplanche 1992a; 1999a; 2020a), Herbert Marcuse (Laplanche 1992d; 2020b), and philosophers of all stripes[1] (Laplanche 1999c, 162–63; 2015a). There is always a suspicion that friends as well as foes are guilty of betraying Freud's momentous discovery and slipping back in the very biologistic-instinctual interpretations of his work with which Freud had broken. In the face of what he sees as pernicious and dangerous threats to Freud's theory of sexuality, Laplanche continuously found himself struggling to reaffirm, revivify, and redeploy the revolutionary and polemical moments of Freud's theory of sexuality. For Laplanche, to affirm to the Freudian revolution, then, is to constantly return to it and reaffirm it. Its provocation and polemic must always be reactivated and redeployed. Laplanche's strategy for doing so is to constantly return to Freud's work and redevelop underemphasized aspects of it in order to continuously draw lines of demarcation between the revolutionary and reactionary moments.

Like Freud before him, then, who constantly confronted popular opinion in the development of his theory of sexuality, Laplanche takes it as his mission to continuously combat popular opinion in the form of the biologistic-instinctual interpretations of Freud's theory of sexuality, even in Freud's own work. In this way, Laplanche was led to wage an unrelenting war against the dominant interpretations of Freud's theory of sexuality on two separate fronts. On the one hand, Laplanche took aim at those who, however unwittingly, were guilty of *biologizing* and *instinctualizing* Freud's theory of sexuality—that is, reducing the *Trieb* to nothing more than an instinct, which loses the innate perversity of sexuality in the process. On the other hand, Laplanche sought to confront the *anti-instinctual interpretations* of Freud's work, which he saw as attempting to erase the instinct altogether from Freud's theory of sexuality, thereby losing the specificity of Freud's discovery. In this way, Laplanche sought to protect the perversity and safeguard the specificity of Freud's theory of sexuality.

Laplanche against the Biologizing-Instinctualizing Interpretation of Freud's Theory of Sexuality

Given the enormous magnitude that Laplanche ascribes to the relation between *Trieb* and instinct in Freud's work, it is curious and worth remarking (along with Laplanche himself, to be sure) that Freud never, at any point in his work, directly compares, contrasts, associates, distinguishes, equates, differentiates, opposes, or otherwise explicitly relates *Trieb* with instinct. While there are perhaps a few places where Freud might be seen to do so implicitly,[2] the German term *Instinkt* itself—which would be the direct cognate of the English word *instinct*—only appears a handful of times in any form throughout Freud's entire body of work. Even fewer times, does it appear in any significant proximity to the term *Trieb*. How can it be the case, then, that such a crucial conceptual relation develops between these two terms, if Freud himself never puts them into direct relation, and especially when he uses one of them only sparingly?

According to Laplanche, despite the fact that Freud himself never *explicitly* thematizes the relation between these two terms, the latter does do so *implicitly* throughout his work. In fact, as we will see, for Laplanche, the *Trieb*-instinct relation comes to define the very development of Freud's theory of sexuality as such. For Laplanche, the clearest, albeit implicit, thematization of the relation between these two terms can be found in the opening paragraphs of Freud's *Three Essays*: "The clearest thematization is the famous passage from the beginning of the *Three Essays*. . . . The word instinct is never pronounced, but it is well and truly there under the title of what Freud calls the 'popular opinion of sexuality'" (Pul. 9/10). For Laplanche, it is precisely the popular opinion of sexuality and, consequently, its biologistic and instinctual understanding of sexuality as the *Geschlechtstrieb* against which Freud will oppose his own theory of sexuality in the *Three Essays*. Thus, under the heading of—what I am calling here—the *biologizing-instinctualizing interpretations of sexuality*, Laplanche is primarily concerned with those who, in accordance with popular opinion, attempt to reduce sexuality to a biological, or biologistic, instinct.

Laplanche's polemics against such reductive interpretations of sexuality extend at least as far back as his magisterial 1970 text, *Life and Death in Psychoanalysis*. There, Laplanche defines the instinct in the following manner: "[The instinct] is a preformed behavior whose framework is hereditarily fixed, and which is repeated [*se répète*] according to modalities that are relatively adapted to a certain type of object" (LD 10/21). An instinct, for Laplanche, is something that is "preformed," decided in advance, and fixed by heredity, passed down from one generation to the next through phylogeny. In this way, it has its ends—in this case the object toward which it tends—and the pathways for securing that object decided in advance. As he puts it some three decades later in "Pulsion et instinct":[3] "there is the hereditary, fixed, adaptive character with a somatic tension from the beginning, a "specific action," a satisfying object, leading to a lasting lowering of tension" (Pul. 12/13). In this way, the instinct is defined by some somatic tension that remains completely endogenous. There is both a "specific action" and a "satisfying object," which are both pregiven and fixed by heredity, and through which the given somatic tension is to be relieved. As we can see, what is crucial for Laplanche is that everything happens within the organism: some somatic tension arises within it, which can be relieved in and through some preformed and adaptive biological framework with which the organism is born. For example, in hunger, some endogenous tension arises in the organism, which can be quelled through the "specific action" of ingesting and digesting the "satisfying object," or food, all of which is said to be a part of the organism's biological nature passed down by heredity.

When it comes to sexuality in particular, these biologizing-instinctualizing interpretations usually (but not always) come in the form of a reproductive model of sexuality, in which case sexuality is defined as an innate instinct that serves the function of heterosexual intercourse leading to the reproduction of the species—what today might be characterized as heteronormative, essentialist, or functional models of sexuality. In this way, there is a predetermined teleology that is defined both by the "specific action" (i.e., heterosexual intercourse) and the "satisfying object" (i.e., a member of the opposite sex), which serves a functional, self-preservative purpose (i.e., reproduction of the life of the species), and follows an already premapped out developmental plan (i.e., the maturation of the reproductive system during puberty). All of this determines the sexuality of the organism in advance because it is something that the organism carries with it from birth, passed down to it through phylogeny and fixed by heredity.

All the emphasis here should be laid on the *innate* or the *pre*. For Laplanche, these biologizing-instinctualizing interpretations include *anything* that smacks of the innate when it comes to sexuality: the endogenous, the hereditary, the phylogenetic, and so forth. In other words, *anything* that *pre*supposes that there is anything *pre*given about sexuality (no matter how much emphasis is laid on reproduction or no matter how psychoanalytic it may appear) is to be considered a biologizing-instinctualizing interpretation. For example, Laplanche points to Karl Abraham's infamous stages of libidinal development as an example of such a biologizing-instinctualizing interpretation of sexuality (FB 28, 72–73/36, 83–84)—in which the evolution of the libido follows an inherent plan that is determined in advance, unfolding in a rigid teleology toward genital primacy. This would also apply to any theory of sexuality that describes, for instance, homosexuality as being something innate, that is, something part of human nature or something one is simply born with, as is the case in Aristophanes's poetic fable in Plato's *Symposium*. In both cases, some aspect of sexuality is treated as innate or pregiven in advance and, in this way, all of sexuality is, therefore, according to Laplanche, treated as an instinct. For Laplanche, these pre-, un-, or even anti-Freudian biologizing-instinctualizing interpretations completely miss the spirit of Freud's own long and protracted war of attrition against the popular opinion of sexuality (LD 14/27–28; Pul. 9/10).

The problem with the biologizing-instinctualizing interpretation is that by one-sidedly reducing any aspect of sexuality to the instinct, such interpretations serve, in the end, to suppress, or even repress, Freud's singular and momentous discovery of sexuality. By turning sexuality into an instinct, these interpretations—no matter how Freudian or psychoanalytic they claim to be—inevitably neutralize the perverse aspects of the *Trieb* and, thereby, reinscribe it within a functional and teleological framework.

Laplanche against the Anti-Instinctual Interpretation of Freud's Theory of Sexuality

To combat these biologizing-instinctualizing interpretations, Laplanche continuously sought to defend the specificity of Freud's theory of sexuality and to preserve the perverse characteristic of Freud's *Trieb* against the instinct. However, Laplanche was, of course, not the first to highlight the perversity at stake in Freud's theory of sexuality. In fact, Laplanche was neither the first nor the only one to take up arms against the overwhelming profusion of biologizing-instinctualizing interpretations of Freud's work. Many had already sought to combat these same biologizing-instinctualizing interpretations by radicalizing Freud's *Trieb*, claiming that it has nothing whatsoever to do with the instinct. According to these *anti-instinctual interpretations*, the only way to defend Freud's theory of sexuality is to eradicate the instinct from it. This is what, for example, according to Laplanche, led Jacques Lacan at one point in his career to declare provocatively and polemically (but also, it must be said, wrongly[4]) that Freud never wrote the word *instinct*—and accordingly, that he only wrote the word *Trieb*, which has nothing to do (etymologically or conceptually) with the instinct (Lacan 1983, 6; 1966c, 834).[5] Such was the zeal to eradicate the instinct from Freud's work altogether. While these overzealous gestures doubtlessly carry on the polemical spirit of Freud's confrontation with popular opinion, Laplanche argues that they only do so at a cost. In so doing, they one-sidedly and regrettably give rise to another set of problems, because they underestimate the importance of the implicit opposition between *Trieb* and instinct, through which Freud articulates his theory of sexuality. As such, they risk losing the specificity of the *Trieb* altogether.

For Laplanche, the only way to preserve the perversity and safeguard the specificity of Freud's theory of sexuality, that is, to protect the *Trieb* from collapsing entirely back into the instinct, is to oppose them. In other words, the sexual domain must be opposed to the nonsexual domain. At times, as we will see in chapters 4 and 6, this opposition is one that Laplanche himself will seek to complicate.[6] However, Laplanche seems to invariably highlight the foundational nature of this distinction and its importance for understanding Freud's theory of sexuality. For example, in *Life and Death in Psychoanalysis*, Laplanche writes: "[Freud's] entire theory [of sexuality] is founded on conflict, and conflict implies duality [*dualité*]; it is necessary that there is something opposed [*s'oppose*] to sexuality" (LD 26/46). Or, as Laplanche writes elsewhere in *Le fourvoiement biologisant chez Freud*:[7] "I will thus end with this affirmation: the specificity of the sexual is affirmed only when the existence of the non-sexual domain is reaffirmed, in a certain fashion, at least potentially" (FB 26/35). According to Laplanche, the specificity, the very existence even, of sexuality can only be maintained against the domain of the nonsexual, which of course for Laplanche is synonymous here with the instinctual. Without the domain of the instinctual, the specificity of the *Trieb* will be forever lost.

Furthermore, without some kind of distinction between *Trieb* and instinct, any theory of sexuality risks, according to Laplanche, regressing into the most vulgar and abstract "pansexualism," in which everything is considered to be sexual.[8] This vulgar and abstract pansexualism would, in turn, only lead to a desexualization of sexuality: "the danger is . . . that of desexualization. In a word, if everything is sexual, then nothing is sexual. 'Sexual' becomes a word without consequence" (FB 101/113). If everything is sexual, then nothing is sexual. Without the nonsexual instinct against which sexuality is opposed, there is nothing specific to the latter. Laplanche, in "Pulsion et instinct," will come to chastise Lacan for precisely this: "Here, I cite Lacan: 'Freud never wrote the word instinct.' Henceforth, the drive occupies the entire field. Furthermore, interpreted as 'drift [*dérive*],' by a play on words with the English word 'drive,' we are henceforth 'all-adrift [*tout-dérive*],' in the realm of the 'all drive [*tout pulsion*].' But drifts from what? For, if the drive does not drift from the instinct, how can we say that it drifts?" (Pul. 8–9/10). If the instinct is erased altogether, if the instinct is reduced to nothing, then the *Trieb* becomes everything and everywhere and, at the same time, nothing and nowhere. Without the instinct, according to Laplanche, the true perversity, the drifting of the *Trieb*, which we will discuss at length in chapter 6, loses all its meaning because there is nothing from which it drifts. We are, thus, left all adrift. As such, the polemical force of Freud's theory of sexuality and its specificity are dissolved into nothingness, and its most crucial and valuable insights, and especially their polemical force, are completely lost.

Ultimately, the problem with the anti-instinctual interpretations is that by one-sidedly erasing the instinct, they surreptitiously erase the *Trieb* with it. And in a certain sense, attempting to immunize Freud's work altogether from the instinct, curiously enough, does not do enough to protect it from the instinct—quite the contrary. In fact, according to Laplanche, there is nothing to prevent these anti-instinctual interpretations themselves from unwittingly falling prey to a biologizing-instinctualizing interpretation.[9] In this way, the biologizing-instinctualizing and anti-instinctual interpretations become two sides of the same coin.

For Laplanche, the solution to this problem is to hold the instinct at a proper distance, theoretically and conceptually speaking, in order to prevent contaminating the *Trieb* with the instinct. As such, the instinct always retains a crucial structural role in Laplanche's account of Freud's theory of sexuality. Just because sexuality is that which puts into question and breaks with the instinct, does not mean that the instinct completely disappears.[10] For Laplanche, then, the only way to preserve the specificity of Freud's theory of sexuality is to thematize this very relation between *Trieb* and instinct, which as we will see in chapters 4 and 6 is much more complicated and complex than a mere opposition.

Laplanche against the Instinct in Translation, *un rabattement*

Historically speaking, the anti-instinctual interpretation of Freud's work grew primarily out of a reaction to the way Freud's work—and in particular the term *Trieb*—was being translated. When Freud's work began to be translated out of German into other languages, there was a dominant trend to translate the *Trieb* as "instinct" and its various cognates in other languages. According to Laplanche, this "folding back," this *rabattement*, of the *Trieb* into the instinct in translation has created a "problem of translation," *problème de traduction*, that has plagued psychoanalysis for about a century now (Pul. 8/9). For Laplanche (and many others), this biologizing-instinctualizing translation has not only given rise to profuse and pervasive confusion regarding Freud's texts themselves, but it has also led to a proliferation of biologizing-instinctualizing interpretations of Freud's work. As such, the need for a solution to this problem of translation is urgently felt.

Trieb (Translated) as Instinct 1: "Traduttore—traditore!"

The difficulties in translating "*Trieb*" from German—not just in Freud's work, but in general—are well known and well documented.[11] In order to deal with this difficulty, James Strachey aimed to translate Freud's "*Trieb*" into English as "*instinct*," consistently and systematically throughout his monumental twenty-four volume *Standard Edition of the Complete Psychological Works of Sigmund Freud*.[12] Everywhere that one reads the word "instinct" in the *Standard Edition*, one can be sure (or rather, as we will discuss, almost sure) that the German term being translated is "*Trieb*." Strachey was, of course, not the only, or even the first, to translate "*Trieb*" as "instinct" (or its various cognates in other languages). However, even if Strachey was not the first, his translation was certainly the most influential. With the publication of Strachey's seminal translation of Freud's mammoth body of work, "instinct" became the standardized, institutional translation of Freud's *Trieb* across multiple languages. In this way, Strachey's translation came to corroborate and vindicate earlier translations of

"*Trieb*" as "instinct" (e.g., Marie Bonaparte's translations of Freud's work into French or Abraham Brill and Ernest Jones's earlier translations into English) and to influence subsequent translations of Freud's complete works into Spanish and Italian.

Despite becoming the standard translation, Strachey's rendering of "*Trieb*" as "instinct" has been met with considerably less than univocal support. The term *instinct* is, after all, at least a curious translation choice etymologically speaking. For the German language already avails itself of a cognate for the English word *instinct*: *Instinkt*. Thus, if Freud meant something along the lines of what we in English call an instinct, it seems like he could have very well used the German term *Instinkt*. Yet, Freud chose to deploy the term "*Trieb*" when elaborating his theory of sexuality in particular and his psychoanalytic theory in general, and not—as Strachey's translation may suggest—the word *Instinkt*. However, everything is further complicated by the fact that Freud *does*—although sparingly—have recourse to the German word *Instinkt* throughout his work, which is a word that Strachey also, curiously, decides to translate as "instinct."[13] It is even more regrettable, then, that Strachey chose to collapse these two different German terms (*Trieb* and *Instinkt*) into the same English word *instinct* in his translation. In so doing, Strachey's translation is seen to give rise to four major complications

1. Despite his best editorial efforts to distinguish between Freud's different usages of both German terms in his editorial footnotes (by indicating the "handful of instances" where Freud writes "*Instinkt*" instead of *Trieb*—a curious gesture that in itself already seems to betray the importance of their distinction), Strachey's translation risks introducing unnecessary ambiguity into the text. By homogenizing these two German terms into the same English word, one can never be sure whether the term being translated is *Trieb* or *Instinkt* (unless, of course, one has recourse to the German original). This becomes a serious problem at decisive moments in Freud's work. For example, in the 1920 case study, "The Psychogenesis of a Case of Homosexuality in a Woman," which we discussed in chapter 1, Strachey translates the German word "*Instinkt*" as "instinct," without following his own editorial protocol and noting that Freud uses "*Instinkt*" and not *Trieb*.

2. Although these two German terms have, no doubt, as Laplanche points out, "parallel etymologies" (LD 9/21), Strachey's decision to collapse them in his translation runs roughshod over the difference between them, however etymologically minimal it may be. The very fact that Freud employed these two similar, but different, terms is not something that should be so hastily swept under the rug of translation.

3. This is a more serious charge: Strachey's translation risks equivocating *Trieb* with *Instinkt*. These are two terms that seem to take on opposed (or, at least, different) conceptual meanings in Freud's technical vocabulary. Such an equivocation proves to be extremely troublesome when, for instance, Strachey translates a term like "*Sexualtrieb*" (an absolutely central term, to be sure) into English as "sexual instinct." Such an equivocation risks something much worse than merely introducing unnecessary ambiguity into the text because, as Laplanche points out, "the term *Instinkt* is used to designate something entirely different from what is described elsewhere as sexuality" (LD 10/21). Indeed, the term *sexual instinct*, as will be shown, becomes almost a contradiction in terms.

4. As commentator after commentator has pointed out, the semantic resonances of the word "instinct" in English (and its cognates in other languages) runs completely contrary to what Freud began to articulate with his concept of *Trieb*.[14] The *Trieb*, as we have seen according to certain interpretations, is simply not an instinct. More recently, Mark Solms, for example, who has taken on the task of revising Strachey's *Standard Edition*, while acknowledging that there are difficulties in translating the term "*Trieb*," has said that Strachey's translation is not only a problem but an "erroneous translation" (Solms 2013, 206–7). Some have even gone so far as to claim that all the confusion surrounding the interpretation of Freud's theory of sexuality can be traced back to this mistaken translation.[15]

For Laplanche, these complications constitute the "pernicious character" (Pul. 9/10) of Strachey and company's translation of "*Trieb*" as "instinct" (and its cognates). The problem with Strachey's translation is that he collapses the crucial and indispensable distinction that Freud maintained between these two terms, even if it was only implicitly developed in the text. Thus, the word *instinct*, like the very concept itself, is seen to be too specific and too determined—too determining—which, according to Laplanche, ultimately comes to obfuscate what is truly at stake in Freud's theory of sexuality (Pul. 8–10, 25/9–11, 32).

As a result, Strachey's translation has cemented his legacy in the lineage of biologizing-instinctualizing interpretations of Freud's work, ultimately betraying Freud's most revolutionary insights by folding them back into an instinctual framework, forever burying *Trieb* under the instinct in his translation. He is, thus, guilty of going astray from Freud's *Trieb* and sending anglophone readers and other translators astray in the process. For betraying Freud's *Trieb*, Strachey has been villainized as a traitor to the Freudian cause, and his critics' rallying cry has been, to quote a play on words that Freud references in his *Jokes and their Relation to the Unconscious*: "*Traduttore—traditore*!" Strachey: translator, traitor!

Trieb (Translated) as "Instinct" 2: Strachey's Self-Defense

To avoid the complications outlined above, it has become commonplace to insist on a more etymologically faithful translation of Freud's German. As such, many have lobbied for "*Trieb*" to be translated into English as "drive"[16] (and "*pulsion*,"[17] or even "*dérive*,"[18] in French). In French, such efforts are already complete. With the publication of *Les œuvres complètes de Freud*, under the scientific direction of Jean Laplanche, "*Trieb*" has been systematically rendered as "*pulsion*." With the publication of Mark Solms's *Revised Standard Edition*, the same will soon be true in English, in which "*Trieb*" will be systematically translated as "drive." (Although such efforts were already under way in, for example, Ulrike Kistner's recently updated translation of Freud's 1905 version of the *Three Essays on the Theory of Sexuality*.) Such translations seek not only to maintain the distinction between *Trieb* and *Instinkt*, but also to protect Freud's *Trieb* from becoming too instinctual and undoing, what they see as the damage done by Strachey's biologizing-instinctualizing translation—a supposedly simple etymological solution for (what turns out to be) a complex conceptual problem.

However, in response to the mounting criticism of his choice to translate "*Trieb*" as "instinct," which was already taking shape during his own time, Strachey adamantly defended his position. In fact, Strachey dedicated an entire section of his "General Preface" to the *Standard Edition* chronicling the trials and tribulations of translating a term like Freud's "*Trieb*." There, in a section titled "Notes on Some Technical Terms whose Translation Calls for Comment," Strachey indicates that he was already aware of suggestions to translate "*Trieb*" as "drive," and—lamenting first and foremost the limits of the English language[19]—he dismisses this supposedly simple etymological solution as, in fact, being too complicated and too neologizing. Although the term *drive* as noun, qua sexual drive, has become commonplace for us today, it was not to be found in *The Oxford English Dictionary* at the time. Furthermore, however technically it may be used in Freud's text, the term *Trieb* is nonetheless an everyday German term. Thus, to translate it as "drive" would have been to invent a new meaning for the word *drive* and substitute it for an everyday term. Strachey asks us why we would introduce English neologisms for colloquial German terms, especially if it threatens to change the nature of the text. Moreover, and more importantly, Strachey offers a few words of warning to his critics, pointing them to a set of much more difficult issues concerning the translation of this term.

Strachey points out the magnificently indefinite nature of Freud's *Trieb* and the manifold, complex, and polyvalent ways in which Freud uses the term throughout his work. Faced with the challenges of translating such a conceptually rich and rigorous, yet also magnificently indefinite, term such as Freud's "*Trieb*," Strachey claims to have done the only "rational thing," which in this case was "to choose an obviously vague and indeterminate word and stick to it" (Strachey 1953, xxv). By choosing a term that Strachey saw as "vague" and "indeterminate" and using it consistently and systematically, Strachey hoped to have allowed space for all the complex, polyvalent, and manifold meanings of *Trieb* to take shape of their own accord in the text: an indeterminate word for an indeterminate concept. After all, what could possibly go wrong so long as "the same English word is invariably used for the German original" (Strachey 1953, xxv)? According to Strachey, all one has to do is read the text, and read it carefully, in order to see how Freud develops this term throughout his psychoanalytic writings.

In fact, given the manifold meanings of "*Trieb*" that Strachey picks up on in Freud's work, the former intends to flip his detractors' accusations on themselves, challenging those who seek such neat and clean etymological solutions to the complex set of problems opened up by the *Trieb* and its translation. In his "Notes on Some Technical Terms whose Translation Calls for Comment," he cautions his detractors: "It requires, I think, a very brave man seriously to argue that rendering Freud's Trieb by 'drive' clears up the situation. It is not the business of a translator to attempt to classify and distinguish between Freud's different uses of the word. This job can be safely left to the reader, provided that the same English word is used invariably for the German original" (Strachey 1953, xxv). For Strachey, then, the issues surrounding the translation of Freud's *Trieb* go much deeper than purely etymological concerns. They point to something else at stake in the concept of *Trieb* itself, which ultimately goes beyond concerns over the "correct" etymological transposition of words from one language into another.

As Arnold Davidson points out in his article, "How to Do the History of Psychoanalysis: A Reading of Freud's *Three Essays on the Theory of Sexuality*," many of Freud contemporaries employed the term *Trieb* (and not *Instinkt*) to describe something like the very instinct for heterosexual copulation, for which many of Strachey's detractors will come to criticize him: "Since many of Freud's contemporaries, among them, Krafft-Ebing, used *Trieb*, Freud's terminology did not constitute a break with previously established terminology. It is not the introduction of a new word that signals Freud's originality" (Davidson 1987, 265). In other words, Freud did not just choose a different word from his contemporaries to talk about sexuality. In fact, Freud's innovation had nothing to do with simply introducing a new term, a neologism, into the German language—so why should Strachey do so in English? Rather, his innovation consisted in putting an everyday term like *Trieb*—with all its conceptual baggage and the preconceived ideas about it—into question, complicating it, and then giving it new meanings and richer determinations within his psychoanalytic framework. This is, of course, the same strategy Freud employed in his confrontation with popular opinion, but now at the level of the term *Trieb* itself. The point is that Freud takes an everyday German word and bends it toward his usages, and the same should be possible in English. As such, simply choosing a term that seems etymologically closer to Freud's German alone will not suffice to settle the complex set of issues plaguing the *Trieb* and its translation. Strachey, for his part, leaves this task to the reader.

Trieb (Translated) as Instinct 3: Strachey's Revenge

Translation itself always held a crucial, albeit somewhat ambivalent,[20] status in Laplanche's analytic and interpretative (in his particular sense of the terms[21]) approach to Freud's work. In *Life and Death in Psychoanalysis*, for example, translation provides Laplanche with a pivotal point of departure for his first systematic and sustained treatment of Freud's theory of sexuality. There, in the first chapter, Laplanche focuses his brief, yet decisive, discussion of translation on the "transposition" of terminology from one language into another, focusing specifically on the translation of the term "*Trieb*" in Freud's work. What Laplanche shows is that translation—even taken in this narrow sense—performs a certain amount of work on the material being translated, which ultimately has the power to both "guide" and "misguide" us: "The guiding thread of our discussion will be the notion of drive [*pulsion*], *Trieb*, and the couple that it forms with another term, instinct. If it is true that terminology and, above all, its transposition from one language into another can guide but also misguide us, the problems of translation have introduced in the present case a confusion that is far from being extinguished" (LD 9/21). As Laplanche highlights here, the work of translation always risks misguiding us, leading us astray, because something can always be lost in translation. The translation of Freud's work is no exception. In fact, such is the case with the translation of *Trieb*, which has, more than any other term, as Laplanche points out, given rise to profuse and pervasive confusion that is far from having been resolved. Yet, Laplanche expresses some qualified sympathy for Strachey's translation here. He goes on to stress (almost echoing Strachey's own self-defense) that the confusion here is not entirely reducible to the "meticulousness," *méticulosité*, of the translator alone (LD 9/21). In fact, Strachey's self-defense has, curiously enough, proven to be somewhat prophetic, since concerted efforts to clear up the situation by demanding etymological fidelity to Freud's German have not succeeded in clearing up the confusion altogether. After all, despite numerous struggles to purge Freud's texts of the instinct, we are all nonetheless still talking about it. Thus, the confusion surrounding Freud's *Trieb*, which is marked by Strachey's translation and its discontents, is symptomatic. The trace of the instinct on the *Trieb* has not been and will not be fully erased. No amount of etymological hand-wringing seems to make the stain of the instinct disappear. As such, the confusion here points to something in Freud's "*Trieb*" itself that allows it to be put into relation with the instinct in the first place.

Even Lacan, the great defender of Freud's "*Trieb*," who fought so adamantly and tirelessly against any contamination of the *Trieb* by the instinct, writes the following in the later stages of his career:

> Notice the ambiguity of the word "*Trieb*" has taken on in psychoanalytic stupidity, instead of people striving to grasp how this category is to be unpacked. The category is not without ancestry, I mean the word is not without usage already, one that goes back a long way, as far back as Kant, but what it is useful

for in analytic discourse would merit our not rushing in and translating it as "instinct." But after all, these slippages do not occur for no reason. And although for a long time I have been emphasizing the aberrant character of this translation, we are nevertheless within our rights to benefit from it. (Lacan 1991, 15–16; 2007b, 14)

Just as the sexual aberrations reveal something more fundamental about sexuality in the *Three Essays*, the supposedly "aberrant" translation of "*Trieb*" as "instinct" reveals something about the *Trieb* itself. In this case, the "slippages" in the work of translation are precisely that, slippages, in the sense of parapraxes. They do not happen for no reason, as there is a certain logic at work in the slippage itself. In other words, the aberrance of the translation is a part of the concept or text itself. As such, Freud's *Trieb* must be tinged in some way with the instinct if these slippages are to occur in the first place. Thus, as a rejoinder to Lacan, we might also say that we should not rush in to translate "*Trieb*" as "drive" either.

For Laplanche, however, the source of these slippages is Freud himself. It is Freud, despite the revolutionary force of his own discovery, who often falls prey to the "temptation," *la tentation*, of these same sorts of biologizing-instinctualizing tendencies (FB 19, 76/25, 86). After all, such interpretations, if they are interpretations at all, do not come out of nowhere; there must, of course, be something within Freud's texts that is open to such interpretations if they are to occur in the first place. According to Laplanche, then, the *rabattement* of the *Trieb* on the instinct in translation reflects a certain *rabattement* in the text itself, since "Freud will not cease to fold-back [*rabattre*] the [*Trieb*] onto an instinctual model" (Pul. 10/11).

For Laplanche, it is crucial for us to understand that Freud himself is partially responsible for opening the door to these reactionary, instinctual tendencies because he ultimately left his revolution incomplete, *inachevée* (Cop. 81/xxxii). According to Laplanche, it is Freud himself who will sometimes collapse back into an instinctual understanding of the *Trieb* and sexuality. As such, these reactionary tendencies in the reception of his work are themselves only a symptom—a symptom that highlights a certain tension in Freud's work itself, namely, his oscillation to and from the instinct.

Whatever the case may be, it is to Strachey's merit that he reveals this very tension in Freud's texts through his supposedly erroneous translation. As Laplanche himself points out in *Le fourvoiement biologisant chez Freud*: "When a thought passes through the trial of translation [*l'épreuve de la traduction*], some constants or gravitations are found, which are not explicit for the author nor even for their German speaking reader" (FB 29/38). The work of translation reveals certain hidden or implicit "gravitations" in the text, which might go unnoticed for German speakers reading the text in their native language. Through the trial, "*l'épreuve*," of translation, in passing through what is foreign, the gravitation of the *Trieb* toward the instinct becomes explicit in Freud's work.[22] As such, the confusion here between *Trieb*, drive, and instinct is not purely accidental, stemming solely from the idiosyncrasies and errors of the translator. In a certain sense, Strachey is correct and justified to translate "*Trieb*" into English as "instinct," according to Laplanche, *because Freud himself will often succumb to conceptualizing the* Trieb *as an instinct.*

For Laplanche, then, it is Freud who goes astray from his own revolutionary discovery, and nowhere is this going-astray, this *fourvoiement*, more apparent than in the history of the publication of Freud's *Three Essays*. However, as we will seek to demonstrate in chapter 3, this tendency toward the instinct is not a mere idiosyncratic quirk or misstep on Freud's part either. It is something necessary in the concept of the *Trieb* itself—a topic on which Laplanche, as we may already begin to see, will seem to wavier. For now, however, we will return editorial history of the *Three Essays* in order to understand what Laplanche claims is Freud's going-astray.

Laplanche against the Instinct in Freud, *un fourvoiement*

A Brief Editorial History of the Three Essays

The *Three Essays* always stood as a cornerstone of Freud's thought. As we know, it was a text so important that it demanded him to return to it again and again throughout his career, and it received significant revisions in light of the major discoveries and developments in the twists and turns throughout Freud's intellectual itinerary. As such, the *Three Essays* underwent notable and substantial alterations when it was republished in 1910, 1915, 1920, and 1924, sedimenting layer upon layer of modifications, most of which came in the form of additions and footnotes to the original text. The 1924 edition became the final, official version published in the first collections of Freud's work and is still the same edition used in the German *Gesammelte Werke*, as well as in Strachey's *Standard Edition* and Laplanche's own *Les Œuvres complètes de Freud*. Despite valiant editorial efforts by Strachey and

Laplanche to indicate Freud's alterations to the text (which are not existent in the *Gesammelte Werke*) through their meticulous footnotes, the original 1905 version remains buried under the subsequent editions. Before turning to Laplanche's account of the significance of Freud's changes to the text, we will briefly recount the material pertinent to our discussion that he added to the *Three Essays* in each of the editions in order to help us understand what is at stake here.

In 1910, Freud returned to the *Three Essays* in order to add a short preface, five footnotes, and roughly five other minor alterations to the original text. In his brief preface to the 1910 edition, Freud concedes that there are many "deficiencies" and "obscurities" in the original text, but he importantly claims to have resisted the "temptation," *Versuchung*, of introducing new research into the text, which would "have destroyed its unity and documentary character" (SE 7: 130[23]). In other words, Freud did not wish in 1910 to alter the substance of the text, despite having years of subsequent psychoanalytic research to add to his theory of sexuality. Freud's additions and alterations to the text in 1910 are, true to his word, indeed for the most part only clarificatory and expository in nature.[24]

However, already in 1910 Freud feels that the ideas put forward in the original 1905 edition need to be open to alteration. In the preface to the 1910 edition, Freud expresses his wish that the book will "age rapidly" and that "what was once new in it may become generally accepted, and that what is imperfect in it may be replaced by something better" (SE 7: 130). It is telling that Freud would later, as Strachey points out, drop the 1910 preface altogether from the subsequent editions. (As such, this preface has subsequently disappeared entirely from the *Gesammelte Werke*, but was rescued in Strachey's *Standard Edition*.) All of this, of course, leaves open the possibility that Freud will no longer think of the text strictly in terms of its documentary character and will succumb to the "temptation" to supplement it with new research.

In 1915, he does precisely that. 1915 represents, in terms of volume, Freud's most significant revisions to the text. In 1915, Freud adds another preface, drops the 1910 preface altogether, adds twenty-one footnotes, and makes roughly twenty-six other revisions to the text, adding anywhere from a word or a sentence to entire paragraphs and sections. Among other things, Freud found it imperative to defend his psychoanalytic claims about sexuality, as tensions with Jung and Adler began to boil over. Freud began to oversee the rise of revisionist and reactionary tendencies (or as Freud later calls them in a footnote to the Wolf Man case study—which he claims is a supplement to his polemics against Jung and Adler—"*Umdeutungen*," or "twisted re-interpretations" as Freud apparently suggested it be translated into English[25]) within psychoanalytic circles. As such, Freud felt forced to shore up and reconsolidate the major claims of the psychoanalytic theory of sexuality in order to defend them from these internal threats.

Additionally, during the intervening years the *Trieb* itself is subject to substantial reconsideration, especially in the essays that came to be known as the "Metapsychological Papers." All of this material begins to seep its way into his 1915 revision of the *Three Essays* in significant ways.[26] Freud also adds entire sections in the second essay on infantile sexuality, including: the "Sexual Researches of Childhood" (SE 7: 194–97/GW 5: 95–97) and "The Phases of Development of the Sexual Organization" (SE 7: 197–200/GW 5: 98–101). In the latter section, "The Phases of Development of the Sexual Organization," Freud explicitly takes on board Karl Abraham's infamous stages of libidinal development: that is, the evolution of the libido from the oral stage to the anal stage to the genital stage.

In 1920, Freud adds yet another preface, fifteen footnotes, and roughly fifteen other alterations to the previous text. At this time World War I has ended, which prompts Freud to return to the *Three Essays* and champion its lasting relevance—perhaps a swipe at those who thought the war neuroses had finally disproved the dominance played by sexuality in the development of neuroses.[27] In the preface, Freud takes yet another swipe at those who oppose his theory of sexuality, by appealing to an unlikely ally: philosophy. Here, Freud calls upon great philosophers to assuage the fears of his doubters and detractors. Freud's emphasis on the dominant role played by sexuality in the life of human beings is no different, he claims, than what is found in Schopenhauer's philosophy (SE 7: 134/GW 5: 32). Furthermore, Freud goes on to liken the discoveries of psychoanalysis to Plato, warning his detractors that "anyone who looks down with contempt upon psychoanalysis from a superior vantage-point should remember how closely the enlarged sexuality of psychoanalysis coincides with the Eros of the divine Plato" (SE 7: 134/GW 5: 32).[28] The Oedipus complex is also mentioned for the first time in the *Three Essays* in a footnote added in 1920 (SE 7: 162n/GW 5: 62n).

Four years later, in 1924, Freud returns to the *Three Essays* for the last time. This time he does not add another preface, keeping his additions to eleven footnotes and roughly seven other alterations to the previous text. In addition to clarifying points made in earlier editions of the text, Freud also points readers to his 1923 article "The Infantile Genital Organization," in which he posits the existence of the infamous "phallic stage" prior to the genital stage proper in Abraham's theory of libidinal development (SE 7: 199n/GW 5: 100n).[29]

The 1905 *Three Essays*, un événement

While Freud eventually found it imperative and necessary to break from the documentary character of the *Three Essays* and update it in light of subsequent psychoanalytic discoveries, Laplanche provocatively claims that the subsequent editions only obscure and mystify the initial discovery of the perversity of the *Trieb* in the 1905 *Three Essays*. For Laplanche, Freud's subsequent additions to the original text are neither a deepening of the revolution that took place in 1905, nor a clarification of the issues at stake in the text. They only serve to complicate things further. In fact, overall, the subsequent additions to the text represent, according to Laplanche, a going-astray, *un fourvoiement*, from the original insights of the 1905 text, as Freud moves further and further away from his discovery of the perversity of the *Trieb* and gradually slips back into an instinctual model of sexuality.

In a talk given in 2005, titled "The *Three Essays* and the Theory of Seduction," Laplanche claims that if one wants to experience the true revolutionary and polemical force, the "traumatizing" effect even, of Freud's *Three Essays*, one must begin by pruning away the layers of the subsequent editions in order to return to the original 1905 text.

> To really feel this "enigmatic" or "traumatizing" aspect, we should refer to the event [*l'événement*] of 1905, that is, to the first edition of the *Three Essays*. In the French edition, of which I was the scientific director, we decided to highlight in the margins, in a consistent way, all the passages dating to the subsequent editions: 1910, 1915, 1920, 1924. I advise you to practice the same thing in your own volume of the *GW* or the *S[E]*, then read only the 1905 edition. The effect is gripping, upending. (Trois. 241)

Laplanche urges his readers, whether they work in German, French, or English, to prune away the subsequent alterations to the text and read the 1905 edition in its supposedly pure state. In so doing, one is in the position to view "the event," *l'événement*, that is Freud's 1905 *Three Essays*— the effect of which is "gripping" and "upending." (Upon reading this suggestion, I, myself, bought a copy of the *Three Essays* in order to cross out everything added after 1905—a tedious process, to be sure, whose effect was less gripping or upending and more like reading a redacted document from a government cover-up.) For Laplanche, however, the "gripping" and "upending" effect comes from what is no longer in the text and, thus, what is able to return to the fore.

> Everything that seemed well known, the "stages" of libidinal development, narcissism, the progressive evolution towards genital primacy, all that has disappeared. What remains is, then, a strange, almost baroque text nonetheless supported by strong lines of force. It is, above all, the incessant affirmation of infantile sexuality with its specificities: partial drives, erotogenic zones, leaning-on, etc. It is also the affirmation of the originary "polymorphous perversity," and its eventual integration in genital pleasure under the form of foreplay. (Trois. 249–50/241–42)

By peeling away the subsequent editions of the *Three Essays*, one is left with a "strange" and "almost baroque" text. More importantly, though, by removing the alterations after 1905, everything that later comes to obfuscate the event of 1905 is stripped away with it. Everything that reeks of the instinct, the innate, the teleological, and the functional is conveniently erased from the text, and one can safely wash their hands of all the supposedly problematic aspects of Freud's later thought. No more heteronormative and pathologizing Oedipus complex. No more developmental schema predetermined in advance, following a steady teleological development from the oral stage to the anal stage to the phallic stage to the genital stage. No more sexist phallic stage at all. No more primacy of the genitals and the implicit functional purpose of reproduction. No more narcissism and the one-sided focus on the ego of the infant, risking an endogenous account of the genesis of sexuality (FB 76–77/87–88). No references to Eros and the supposedly impoverished account of sexuality that comes with it, which Laplanche declares is completely contrary to what psychoanalysis first discovered as sexuality (LD 123–24/185). No opposition between life and death drives, which Laplanche sees as the final result of Freud's *fourvoiement*, his most egregious going-astray, the most damning evidence of his reduction of sexuality to the instinct (FB 109/123; LD 122–23/186).

Later, in chapters 4, 5, and 6, we will question whether returning to the 1905 edition of the text truly represents, even on Laplanche's own terms, an advance in Freud's thinking about sexuality. However, for now we can see that for a certain Laplanche by removing what is commonly thought of as quintessential to Freud's theory of sexuality, we are supposedly left with the true insights of Freud's theory of sexuality discovered in the *Three Essays*. For Laplanche, what is left is the perversity and the specificity of the *Trieb*, and everything that comes along with it: infantile sexuality, polymorphous perversity, and so on. By returning to the 1905 edition of the *Three Essays*, one is able—to borrow a turn of phrase from Marx apropos of Hegel—to prune the instinctual shell in order to get to the polymorphously perverse kernel at the heart of Freud's theory of sexuality. Without the subsequent editions of the text, the reader is supposedly left with a *Trieb* in all its polymorphously perverse glory—that is, a *Trieb* properly opposed to and free from even the possibility of being contaminated by the instinct.

Chapter 3

The "Impossible Difference" between *Trieb* and Instinct

In the previous chapter, we demonstrated how the problem of sexuality is exemplified in the translation of Freud's *Trieb* and, as a result, in the reception of his work. Through the work of translation, a tension seems inevitably and necessarily to arise between the *Trieb* and the instinct. On the one hand, we saw that the *Trieb is never completely reducible to the instinct*, as was the case in Strachey's infamous translation of "*Trieb*" as "*instinct.*" In this case, the *Trieb* always comes to complicate and undermine this very reduction. On the other hand, *the trace of the instinct can never be entirely erased from the* Trieb *altogether*, as Laplanche demonstrated was the case in his repudiation of the anti-instinctual interpretations of Freud's work, because the *Trieb* is always dependent in some way on the instinct. Thus, no matter how translators seek to situate the *Trieb* with respect to the instinct, we nonetheless find ourselves entangled in a web of sexual problems, as every supposed solution to the problem of sexuality via translation finds itself surreptitiously saddled with yet another set of problems.

The concern motivating this chapter is understanding whether this problem of sexuality is, as Laplanche claims in "The *Three Essays* and the Theory of Seduction," due to a temptation on Freud's part for the biological and instinctual, from which he was lamentably unable to escape. In other words, we will wonder whether this problem of sexuality is owed to a mere idiosyncratic quirk on Freud's part to sometimes, however wittingly, favor the biologistic over his own psychoanalytic insights into sexuality, or whether this has to do with the nature of sexuality itself. That is, whether this relation and tension with the instinct is necessary and endemic to the *Trieb*.

Althusser on the Impossibility of Defining Freud's *Trieb*

In one of his few explicit and direct engagements with Freud, in a little-discussed text he initially wrote in 1976, "The Discovery of Doctor Freud," Louis Althusser puts his finger on precisely this problem in Freud's work. In this text, Althusser finds himself reevaluating and questioning certain of his own tendencies to privilege Jacques Lacan's work as the pinnacle of psychoanalysis.[1] To do so, he seeks to play up Freud against what he sees as certain nonscientific tendencies in Lacan's work. What Althusser seeks to do is draw out, if at all possible, the specificity of Freud's scientific discovery of the unconscious. This is, of course, as we will see, a central concern that preoccupies Althusser whenever he approaches Freud, Lacan, or psychoanalysis in general: the task is always to delineate and articulate that which makes psychoanalysis scientifically revolutionary and groundbreaking (Althusser 1996c; Althusser et al. 2014, 7n, 362n; Althusser 1993a, 26–29; 2015, 85; 2014, 287–303; 1996a, 14–15; 1996d).[2] In "The Discovery of Doctor Freud," in particular, Althusser attempts to do so by highlighting the difficulty Freud has in defining one of the core concepts of his psychoanalytic work—the infamous *Trieb*: "First, the concept of *pulsion* [*Trieb*]. It is an extremely interesting concept because Freud never arrived at a satisfying definition of it, which did not prevent the concept from 'functioning' very suitably in metapsychological 'theory' and in practice. Why this impossibility to define it? Not because of its imprecision, but because of the impossibility of thinking its precision theoretically" (Dec. 102/217). As we will see, Freud spent much of his career constantly working and reworking his conception of the *Trieb*, never arriving at a definitive, or "satisfying," definition of it. Yet, the curious thing here, according to Althusser, is that this did not prevent the concept from "functioning" within Freud's metapsychological theory. In other words, the "impossibility" that Freud runs up against in defining the *Trieb* did not prove to be an insurmountable obstacle to his metapsychological theory—quite the contrary. The question for us then becomes: how is it the case that the "impossibility" of defining the *Trieb* did not become, in turn, an impossibility for Freud's metapsychological theory as such? And why, for that matter, is the *Trieb* impossible to define in the first place?

Althusser is indeed picking up on a certain tension that runs like a red thread throughout Freud's work—a tension which Freud himself makes increasingly explicit. On the one hand, Freud is aware of the importance and the centrality of the *Trieb* and the demand for defining and specifying it. Freud will repeatedly emphasize that the *Trieb* is not just another term among many in his work; it is, rather, an absolutely central concept and a cornerstone of psychoanalytic theory. On the other hand, Freud continuously runs up against the impossibility of giving the *Trieb* a final, definitive definition. As such, the *Trieb* is a concept whose definition continuously animates Freud's psychoanalytic theory, which constantly demands that he return to and revise it in light of fresh discoveries and insights in his work. In fact, one can see Freud return to and reevaluate the *Trieb* in some fashion at every significant twist and turn in his intellectual itinerary, and each time it takes on richer determinations.

A Brief History of Freud's *Trieblehre*

In a 1915 text dedicated specifically to reevaluating and reworking the *Trieb*, "Triebe und Triebschicksale,"[3] Freud asserts that the *Trieb* is an indispensable "basic concept," *ein Grundbegriff* (SE 14: 117/GW 10: 210). As such, it is an absolutely central concept on which psychoanalysis is founded and on which the advance of psychoanalytic knowledge depends (SE 14: 117/GW 10: 210). Almost a decade later, in a 1924 addendum to *Three Essays*, Freud will declare that the theory of the *Trieb*, the *Trieblehre*, is "the most important" part of psychoanalytic theory, but he will add that it is "at the same time the least complete portion" of it (SE 7: 168n/GW 5: 67n).

We see here again the tension that Althusser seeks to bring to our attention: somehow the *Trieblehre* is the most important aspect of psychoanalytic theory, yet it remains the least understood portion of it. How can the *Trieblehre* be both the focus around which psychoanalytic theory articulates itself, yet remain incomplete and its object without, as Althusser puts it, a "satisfying definition"? Freud himself alludes to precisely this problem in the sixth chapter of *Civilization and Its Discontents*: "Of all the slowly developed parts of psychoanalytic theory, the [*Trieblehre*] is the one that has felt its way the most painfully forward. And yet that theory was so indispensable to the whole structure that something had to be put in its place" (SE 21: 117/GW 14: 476). We can see here that for Freud the *Trieblehre* was indispensable for his psychoanalytic theory from the very beginning. Thus, despite not having a definitive account of it in the early days of psychoanalysis, Freud nonetheless felt the demand to put something forward like a placeholder, or a working hypothesis, such that the rest of psychoanalytic theory could continue to develop. This explains why Freud was brought back to refine the *Trieblehre* time and again. As his psychoanalytic theory continued to develop, more and more light was shed on the *Trieb* itself—allowing, or even forcing, him to rework his initial account of it.

This is why Freud is always compelled to tell the (hi)story of the *Trieblehre* every time that he seeks to rework his understanding of it. In several texts that were published toward the end of his career, Freud increasingly feels the need to recount the development of the *Trieblehre* to his readers. This happens most explicitly in chapter 6 of *Beyond the Pleasure Principle* and chapter 6 of *Civilization and Its Discontents*, but in other texts as well.[4] In these texts Freud divides the history of the *Trieblehre* into three successive phases.

The first phase of the *Trieblehre* roughly corresponds from Freud's earliest psychoanalytic works until around 1914. Freud explains in *Civilization and Its Discontents* that during these years the *Trieblehre* is modeled on Schiller's remark that "hunger and love are what moves the world" (SE 21: 11/GW 14: 476). Some ten years earlier in *Beyond the Pleasure Principle* Freud specifies that during this phase the *Trieblehre* is structured by an opposition between sexuality, the *Sexualtrieb*, and the so-translated "ego-instincts," the *Ichtriebe*—the latter of which represent the organism's drive for self-preservation (SE 18: 51/GW 13: 55). It is interesting to note here that Freud understands this as an opposition between two *Triebe* and not an opposition between *Trieb* and instinct. In *Civilization and Its Discontents*, Freud will go so far as to say that these two *Triebe* are antitheses. As such, sexuality qua *Sexualtrieb* represents a *Trieb* with aims and objects that often come into conflict and opposition with the *Ichtriebe*, that is, with the self-preservation of the organism.

The second major phase of the *Trieblehre* comes with Freud's gradual discovery of narcissism, which takes a prominent place in Freud's written work beginning with his 1914 text, "On Narcissism." With the discovery of narcissism Freud is forced to reevaluate his *Trieblehre* when he realizes that the ego itself can be cathected with libido, in other words, that the ego itself could become the object of the *Sexualtrieb* (SE 18: 52/GW 13: 55). Thus, according to Freud, the opposition between the *Ichtriebe* and sexuality was no longer viable because the *Ichtriebe* themselves were seen to be tinged with sexuality as well. (This is perhaps why Freud initially understood the *Sexualtrieb* and *Ichtriebe* to both be *Triebe* in their own right.)

The third phase of the *Trieblehre* comes with Freud's famous formulation of the *Lebenstrieb* and *Todestrieb*, which was first elaborated explicitly in his 1920 *Beyond the Pleasure Principle*. Having been confronted with the devastating and traumatic psychical effects World War I had on soldiers,

Freud was forced to begin reevaluating his theory of dreams, the pleasure principle and, as a result, his understanding of the *Trieb*. In short, Freud became increasingly dissatisfied with his theory of narcissism because it risked underemphasizing the dualistic and oppositional conflict at the heart of his *Trieblehre*. In order to defend the dualistic nature of the *Trieblehre*, Freud speculates that the opposition is no longer structured between hunger and love, the *Ichtriebe* and sexuality, but rather between the *Trieb* for life and the *Trieb* for death. With the introduction of the opposition between *Lebenstrieb* and *Todestrieb*, Freud now understands sexuality to be on the side of life because it brings the organism in combination with other objects and tends toward the reproduction of life itself, which is opposed to the organism's tendencies toward death and dissolution. Roughly speaking, then, to modify Schiller: the opposition is no longer between hunger and love, but love and death.

This is a complicated story, and there is much more to be said about each of these phases and the transitions and relations between them. However, with this very brief outline we can already see how much Freud struggles to structure his *Trieblehre* as a conflict between a sexual *Trieb* and some other type of *Trieb*. And although Freud describes each of these phases as successive stages in the development of the *Trieblehre*, it would be a mistake to understand this as a linear development in which each new phase comes to supplant and completely erase the previous ones. In both *Beyond the Pleasure Principle* and *Civilization and Its Discontents*, Freud seems to be full of hesitation in moving from one phase to the other. With each successive phase in this history, Freud will insist that certain indispensable elements of the theory cannot be left behind, that developments in the later phases are contained within the earlier ones, and that later developments contain insights that clarify and elucidate earlier formulations. As such, how are we to understand Freud's hesitation to completely abandon the earlier phases of the theory?

An answer to this question can perhaps be found in the *Trieb* itself. In "Triebe und Triebschicksale," Freud claims that the vicissitudes, *Schicksale*, of the *Trieb* in the individual are like that of a lava flow: with each eruption of libidinal energy the *Trieb* does not negate or erase what came before it, but overlays what came before it, creating layers of stratification over the life of the *Trieb* (SE 14: 131/GW 10: 223). Of course, in *Civilization and Its Discontents*, Freud famously declares that only in the psychical life investigated by psychoanalysis is it possible for earlier developments to be preserved and exist side by side with later ones (SE 21: 68–72/GW 14:

426–29). And we should understand the development of Freud's *Trieblehre* in much the same way: it is a series of developments that overlay each other, which can only be understood by looking at the whole picture, that is, all the stratified layers together, rather than, say, digging down to one specific layer of articulation at such and such a date and declaring it to be *the* definition of the *Trieb*. In other words, the *Trieblehre* is the very movement itself in Freud's development of the concept of the *Trieb*.

As such, the painful and painstaking development of the *Trieblehre* does not find an end, and certainly not in *Civilization and Its Discontents*. In 1932, two years after the publication of *Civilization and Its Discontents*, in the thirty-second of his *New Introductory Lectures on Psychoanalysis*, Freud once again returns to and underscores the importance, but also the incompleteness, of the *Trieblehre*. This time Freud describes the *Trieblehre* as psychoanalysis' mythology: "The [*Trieblehre*] is so to say our mythology. *Die Triebe* are mythical entities [*mythische Wesen*], magnificent in their indefiniteness [*großartig in ihrer Unbestimmtheit*]. In our work we cannot for a moment disregard them, yet we are never sure that we are seeing them clearly" (SE 22: 95/GW 15: 101). What is striking in this passage is that Freud seeks to align the mythological status of the *Trieblehre* with the mythical nature of the *Trieb* itself. In other words, the incompleteness of the *Trieblehre* is due to the indefinite nature, *Unbestimmtheit*, of the object around which it articulates itself—the magnificently indefinite *Trieb*. As such, the *Trieb* can never be seen clearly or in an unadulterated state—a point that Freud will implicitly and explicitly make time and again throughout his career.[5] In this way, there is something about the *Trieb* itself that resists rigid definition, that resists the final word, and yet still allows it, as Althusser points out, nonetheless to "function" conceptually in Freud's metapsychological theory.

This is why Freud himself never despairs over the indefiniteness of the *Trieb*. In fact, rather than turning out to be an inhibitory obstacle to psychoanalytic theory, that is, rather than dooming psychoanalysis to obscurantism, mysticism, or pseudoscientific pursuits, it is precisely this very indefiniteness of the *Trieb* that animates psychoanalytic scientificity. Without it, and without its indefiniteness, psychoanalytic knowledge would not, could not, advance. In "Triebe und Triebschicksale," Freud drives this point home by seeking to turn a popular view of science, which relies on a certain brand of (Cartesian) epistemological foundationalism, on its head: "We have often heard it maintained that sciences should be built up on clear and sharply defined basic concepts [*Grundbegriffen*]. In actual fact, no science, not even the most exact, begins with such definitions" (SE 14: 117/GW 10: 210). After Descartes, it is commonly (mis)understood that in order to guarantee scientific claims, the sciences should be built on an indubitable and unshakeable foundation. However, scientific pursuits, Freud argues, do not begin (or end, it must be said) with rigid, narrow definitions or immutable, unalterable foundational concepts. This would only serve to hinder scientific progress. While scientific work—and psychoanalysis is no exception—certainly seeks to establish these basic foundational concepts and doubtless seeks to make them more and more determinate and concrete, Freud vehemently resists the urge to oversimplify and overrigidify the basic concepts of psychoanalysis: "The advance of knowledge, however, does not tolerate any rigidity even in definitions. Physics furnishes an excellent illustration of the way in which even 'basic concepts' [*Grundbegriffen*] that have been established in the form of definitions are constantly being altered in their content" (SE 14: 117/GW 10: 210–11). For Freud, then, determination does not mean simplification, and definition does not imply rigidity because the basic concepts of psychoanalysis must "at first necessarily possess some degree of indefiniteness [*Unbestimmtheit*]" and "there can be no question of any clear delimitation of their content" (SE 14: 117/GW 10: 210).

Thus, we can see Freud implicitly pitting himself not only against the Cartesian, but also against a (later) Husserlian phenomenological understanding of scientific development. In the "Origin of Geometry," Husserl famously argues that scientific statements must be made "once and for all," *ein für allemal*, and its claims must "stand fast," *feststeht*, for there to be any scientific progress at all.[6] Otherwise, scientists would constantly have to start over from the beginning and no progress could be made. For Freud, on the contrary, the advance of scientific knowledge presupposes and depends on a certain openness—a certain indefiniteness—that allows the returning to and the altering of its basic foundational concepts.

As the historian of science, Alexandre Koyré, remarks about the modern scientific tradition in which Freud attempts to situate himself: "Modern science did not spring perfect and complete, as Athena from the head of Zeus, from the minds of Galileo and Descartes. On the contrary, the Galilean and Cartesian revolution—which remains, nevertheless, a revolution—had been prepared by a strenuous effort of thought" (Koyré 1968, 1). For Koyré, as for Freud I would argue, the scientific process itself is a struggle to keep the scientific revolution alive by "slowly and progressively forging for itself instruments and tools, new concepts, new methods of thinking" (Koyré 1968, 1). As such, Freud did not have the entire theory of psychoanalysis worked out in advance; however, its concepts were rigorous and open enough to correct themselves as further psychoanalytic discoveries and advancements were made, as blind spots were taken into account, and as prejudices were weeded out. In Freud's "Autobiographical Study," he returns to this idea, adding that any observational science "has no alternative but to work out its findings piecemeal and to solve its problems step by step" (SE 20: 58/omitted from the *GW*). In fact, Freud claims earlier in that same text that any portion of the "speculative superstructure" of psychoanalysis could and should be "abandoned or changed without loss or regret the moment its inadequacy has been proved" (SE 20: 32/GW 14: 58).

As such, the compulsion to hang on obstinately to certain formulations of the *Trieblehre* seems to hinder the movement of psychoanalysis. For Freud, what is said in psychoanalysis is not said "once and for all" but rather always open to refinement and revision. Without refinement and revision, psychoanalysis would stagnate, ossify, and lose its revolutionary impetus. (Remember that Freud aligns himself with Copernicus and Darwin—those scientific revolutionaries who he sees as upsetting and breaking with established knowledge, not simplifying or codifying it [SE 17: 139–141/GW 12: 7–8].) A complex concept, then, such as Freud's *Trieb*, demands a complex account of it, which evolves in tandem with the development of psychoanalytic theory and practice.

As we can see, the "impossibility" of defining the *Trieb*, to return to Althusser's vocabulary, is due to the impossible nature of the *Trieb* itself. In fact, its very "impossibility" is precisely what makes possible its functioning within Freud's theory. In other words, its imprecision is precisely its precision, so to speak, as a concept within Freud's psychoanalytic framework—that is, it is that which allows it to function within Freud's metapsychology despite the impossibility of defining it definitively. The reason that Freud has a problem defining the *Trieb* is because the *Trieb* itself *is a problem*—one that Freud takes seriously as being part of the nature of the thing itself. But whence, we might ask, this impossible nature of the *Trieb* in the first place?

Trieb as a Border—or Limit—Concept

In "The Discovery of Doctor Freud," Althusser seems to have an acute sense of the problem at work here. For Althusser, the impossibility of defining the *Trieb*, its magnificent indefiniteness, stems from the very "impossible difference" that the *Trieb* forms with the instinct: "This concept [*Trieb*] seeks its definition in an impossible difference with the instinct, that is, in a reality of the biological order. I say 'impossible' because for Freud the [*Trieb*] is profoundly tied to a biological reality from which it is distinct" (Dec. 103/217).

Althusser's acute sense of the problem here is marked by his unprecedented use of the term, "impossible difference," which he does not seem to use anywhere else in his work. Already in another one of the few works in which he discusses Freud's *Trieblehre* explicitly, a 1966 text titled "Three Notes on the Theory of Discourses," Althusser remarks that Freud situates his *Trieblehre* in a "differential" relation with the instinct (Althusser 1993d, 123; 2003, 42). What Althusser seeks to highlight here is that the impossibility of defining the *Trieb*, its indefiniteness, is due to the fact that it is always tied to the instinct—*to which* it is never completely reducible and *from which* it can never escape. In this way, the *Trieb* always necessarily depends on the instinct to define what it is and what it is not. In other words, the *Trieb* is always caught in a process of differentiation and identification with the instinct, making it impossible, as Freud would have put it, to "see it clearly." As such, Freud inevitably finds himself stuck in a movement of delineating the specificity of the *Trieb* by differentiating it from the instinct, while surreptitiously and almost within the very same gesture collapsing the *Trieb* back into the instinct.

Later in his own career, in "The Unfinished Copernican Revolution," Jean Laplanche will come to describe this tension as the "Copernican" and "Ptolemaic" movements in Freud's work, by which he seeks to thematize what he sees as Freud's revolutionary and reactionary tendencies (Cop. 60–62/xi). For Laplanche, as I have argued in the previous chapter, these movements can be characterized as Freud's breaking with and lapsing into a biologizing-instinctualizing understanding of the *Trieb*. In other words, there is both a revolutionary tendency in Freud's work to break with the instinct and a reactionary "temptation" to return to the instinct (FB 19, 76/25, 86).

As we have seen, the task for Laplanche becomes one of protecting the *Trieb* at all costs from any contamination whatsoever from the instinct, even in Freud's own work. This requires us as readers of Freud to go beyond him and continuously revisit his work in order to disentangle and further develop the revolutionary moments and distinguish them from those reactionary moments (Cop. 82–83/xxxiii–xxxiv; FB xi–xii, 3–4/6–10). Yet, Laplanche himself seems to point to a more complex problem at work here with his own paradoxical diagnosis of Freud's "temptation" for the instinctual.

According to Laplanche, Freud's temptation must be understood in certain places as: (1) a *fourvoiement*, a going-astray, a deviation, from his own original and revolutionary insight; *and* (2) in still other places it is to be considered as a *rabattement*, a folding-back, a collapsing into, a return to the instinct. Laplanche uses these two somewhat contradictory metaphors of coming and going interchangeably to describe Freud's temptation for the instinct. It is both a going-astray *and* a folding-back, a deviation *and* a return, a *fort and* a *da*.

For Althusser (as well as a certain Laplanche, which will we discuss in the following chapters), this paradoxical—and we might say "impossible"—*fort/da* that Freud plays with the *Trieb* and the instinct reveals something at work in the *Trieb* itself. In other words, the "temptation" for the instinct is necessary and internal to the work of the *Trieb* itself, which Freud traces in his psychoanalytic theory. After all, Althusser points out that Freud calls the *Trieb* a "limit-concept," *ein Grenzbegriff*, because it is situated between the domain of sexuality and the biological realm of the instinct.

In a text Althusser published a year after "The Discovery of Doctor Freud" in 1977, "On Marx and Freud," he returns again to this very problem. In this text, Althusser specifies that the *Trieb* is not only a limit-concept, a concept between two regions, but that it is itself the concept *of* the very limit between the biological and extra-biological. For Althusser, then, the *Trieb* itself is the (impossible) "difference" between the biological-instinctual domain and the extra-biological domain of sexuality (Sur. 121–2/242). In this way, the *Trieb* represents the limit at which the non- or extra-biological domain is supported by, leans on, "*étayé sur*," the biological-instinctual domain (Sur. 121–2/242).

In both "The Discovery of Doctor Freud" and "On Marx and Freud," Althusser points us to a well-known remark that Freud makes in 1915, in "Triebe und Triebschicksale," where the latter himself directly addresses this problem in these very terms. There, Freud writes: "If now we apply ourselves to considering mental life from a biological point of view, an instinct [*Trieb*] appears to us as a concept on the frontier between the mental and the somatic . . . [*als ein Grenzbegriff zwischen Seelischem und Somatischem*]" (SE 14:121–2/GW 10: 214).

This was, moreover, a point so nice that Freud had to make it twice. In his 1915 return to the *Three Essays*, Freud adds the following remark in the body of the first essay, echoing the remarks that were made in "Triebe und Triebschicksale": "The concept of [*Trieb*] is one of those lying on the frontier between the mental and the physical [*Trieb ist so einer der Begriffe der Abgrenzung des Seelischen vom Körperlichen*]" (SE 7: 168/GW 5: 67). For Freud, the *Trieb* is a concept lying on the frontier, a border-concept, *Begriffe der Abgrenzung*. In this way, Freud does not situate the *Trieb* in strict opposition to the biological, to the somatic, to the physical, to the instinctual, but in an impossible difference between certain biological and extra-biological forces. As a limit-concept, a border-concept, then, the *Trieb* always finds itself caught up in a movement in which it both breaks with and returns to the instinct—the process of which tinges the instinct with the *Trieb*. As such, the *Trieb* can never be understood purely on its own terms, since it is always torn from within; nor, however, can it be understood in pure opposition with the instinct, since the trace of the instinct can never be completely erased from it. No matter the amount of anti-instinctual hand-wringing, the *Trieb* will always necessarily be stained by its "impossible difference" with the instinct. And yet despite this impossible difference, it is precisely in this very border/limit that psychoanalysis finds—not some ineffable in-between about which nothing can be said or known[7]—but its scientificity, its *Grundbegriff*.

Part 2

Three Essays on Freud's Theory of Infantile Sexuality

Chapter 4

The Role of the Other in the Genesis of Sexuality

Throughout his career, Jean Laplanche continuously found himself struggling with and against Freud's problem of sexuality, as he always sought to defend the specificity of sexuality and to preserve the perversity of the *Trieb* against the instinct. This led him to experiment with and develop a number of different strategies for situating the *Trieb* with respect to the instinct—some of which we have already discussed in the previous chapters. However, in his magisterial 1970 text, *Life and Death in Psychoanalysis*, Laplanche puts forward arguably his most nuanced account of the *Trieb* and its relation to the instinct—one that seems at least implicitly to anticipate, but also to challenge, some of his later attempts to thematize this relation.

In *Life and Death in Psychoanalysis*, Laplanche zeros in on the *Three Essays* as the "resolutely innovative text," in which Freud puts forward his most concrete and determinate account of the *Trieb* (LD 8/19). Contrary to his more qualified and restrained claims about the *Three Essays* later in his career—in which he will gradually seek to prune the later revisions from the 1905 edition of the text—Laplanche declares in 1970 that the *Three Essays*, and not just the 1905 version, describes the *Trieb* par excellence (LD 8/19). This is because Freud seeks to model the *Trieb* on sexuality (in the Freudian sense): "It is sexuality that represents the model of every [*Trieb*] and probably the only [*Trieb*] in the proper sense of the term" (LD 8/20). For Laplanche, sexuality not only provides the model, *modèle*, for every *Trieb*, but it is the only *Trieb* properly speaking—a polemical and provocative claim, to be sure, since Freud himself will come to speak of many other *Triebe* throughout his work (e.g., *Ichtriebe, Lebenstrieb, Todestrieb,*

73

Selbsterhaltungstrieb, Bemächtigungstrieb, etc.). However provocative this may seem to certain readers of Freud's work, especially philosophical readers,[1] who have focused a great deal of their attention on Freud's *Todestrieb*,[2] Laplanche insists that unless any so-called *Trieb* meets the criteria of the *Trieb* par excellence qua sexuality as it is spelled out in the *Three Essays*, it is nothing more than an instinct and, therefore, not worthy of the name *Trieb*. In other words, anything that is not sexuality is not *Trieb*, and anything that is not *Trieb* must be an instinct. As such, Laplanche warns his readers to be forever suspicious of the instinct disguised as other so-called *Triebe* in Freud's work.

The primary symptom of this slippage in Freud's work for Laplanche is the former's unfortunate temptation for "dualistic" theories of the *Trieb*.[3] As soon as, and whenever, Freud seeks to posit two types of *Triebe* in a dualistic and oppositional manner against each other, he necessarily and surreptitiously dissolves the absolutely crucial, albeit implicit, distinction between *Trieb* and instinct. In so doing, the *Trieb* inevitably becomes all too instinctual in the process.[4] We can see, then, that for the Laplanche of *Life and Death in Psychoanalysis* it is not so much that Freud is able to give the best account of the *Trieb* in the *Three Essays* as much as it is the case that Freud is able to *properly situate the* Trieb *with respect to the instinct*. For Laplanche, the innovation of the *Three Essays* is not to have dismissed the instinct in favor of a dualistic *Trieblehre*, but rather to have taken the instinct and its relation to the *Trieb* seriously, however implicit Freud's account may be.

In *Life and Death in Psychoanalysis*, Laplanche explains that the relation between instinct and *Trieb* that Freud develops in the *Three Essays* is a "complex relation," *un rapport complexe*, which is made of an analogy, difference, and *dérivation* (LD 10/21–22). In this way, we cannot understand this relation simply in terms of an analogy between *Trieb* and instinct (as is the case in popular opinion), nor in terms of the strict opposition between them (as is the case in the anti-instinctual interpretations). It is not, then, as Udo Hock suggests, for Laplanche simply a matter of the *Trieb* "versus" the instinct (Hock 2007, 76). In order to understand sexuality, the *Trieb* must be understood in and through all three moments of the complex relation that it forms with the instinct: analogy, difference, and *dérivation*. In this way, the instinct plays an important structural role in every aspect of this complex relation: in their analogy (*Trieb* as instinct); in their difference (*Trieb* and instinct); and in their *dérivation* (*Trieb* from instinct). Thus, for Laplanche, the task of capturing this complex relation becomes one of articulating a way of thinking the *Trieb* that, in the terms we have been developing, takes seriously the problem of sexuality and the "impossible difference" between *Trieb* and instinct. In so doing, Laplanche arrives at a way of thinking the *Trieb* that is not dualistic—that is, not a strict binary opposition between two *Triebe*—but rather a *Trieb* split from the instinct and, as we will see in chapter 6, split from within by the instinct from which it arises.

In Between Analogy and Difference: The Four Component Parts of the *Trieb*

In order to begin specifying the nature of the *Trieb*, Laplanche begins as Freud does in the *Three Essays* by turning to popular opinion. As we have already seen, it is popular opinion itself that points out the analogy between *Trieb* and instinct when it attempts to define sexuality strictly in terms of the *Geschlechtstrieb* and model it on hunger. Although the analogy between these two terms is not, as we have seen, ultimately strong enough to contain the *Trieb* within the narrow confines of the instinct, Laplanche (like Freud) does not dismiss popular opinion's attempt to define sexuality in this way out of hand. Even if it does not ultimately prove to be an adequate account of the complexity and specificity of the *Trieb*, there is still something to this analogy worth taking seriously because the analogy between the *Trieb* and the instinct goes much deeper than popular opinion's own confused and confusing attempt to model sexuality on hunger.

Laplanche turns to Freud's "Triebe and Triebschicksale," in which the latter puts forward the most explicit definition of the *Trieb* in his work. There, Freud begins by analyzing the nature of the *Trieb* by breaking it down into its basic component parts. For Freud, any *Trieb*, properly speaking, is made up of four main components, which taken together define it: pressure (*Drang*), aim (*Ziel*), object (*Objekt*), and source (*Quelle*) (SE 14: 122–23/ GW 10: 214–16). Laplanche will take Freud's analysis a step further by explicitly demonstrating to the reader how each of these four component parts have their analogous counterparts in the instinct.

First, let us take the pressure. Freud describes the pressure, *Drang*, of the *Trieb* as a "motor momentum," *motorische Moment*, which can be understood as a "sum of force," *Summe von Kraft*, or the "measure of the demand for work," *Maß von Arbeitsanforderung*, made on the organism (SE 14: 122/ GW 10: 214). In other words, the pressure of the *Trieb* is the tension that builds within the organism, which demands that a certain amount and a certain kind of work be done in order to discharge this tension. According to Laplanche, Freud's characterization of the *Trieb* in terms of the pressure verges on tautology, since it is this very pressure, this demand for work, that animates the organism toward discharging the tension (LD 10/22). The term "*Trieb*" itself is a Germanic term that means "to push," and the pressure is nothing other than that which pushes the organism toward certain ends. Freud himself seems to say as much when he writes that the pressure is what is common to all *Triebe* and that it is their very essence, *Wesen*, since all *Triebe* are just a piece of activity (SE 14: 122/GW 10: 214).

Considered from this point of view, then, the pressure is completely analogous to the instinct. Take, for example, hunger. Hunger is an instinctual mechanism that builds a certain and specific tension in the organism that pushes it toward the ingestion and digestion of food. Just as in hunger, the pressure of the *Trieb* qua sexuality builds more and more tension within the organism and puts it to work, makes demands on it, in order to discharge this very tension. Structurally speaking, then, in essence, the *Trieb* is completely analogous to the instinct. Curiously enough, even though the pressure is almost tautologically defining of the *Trieb*—that is, it is its very essence or motor force—it alone cannot be defining of the *Trieb* as such because from this point of view it is indistinguishable from the instinct.

This pressure, Freud argues, always pushes the *Trieb* toward a certain aim, *Ziel*. The aim of the *Trieb*, and Freud is unequivocal here, is always satisfaction. All *Triebe* aim at satisfaction, and satisfaction is nothing other than the lowering of tension that builds up in the organism from the pressure. Once again, in terms of the aim, the *Trieb* seems to be completely analogous to the instinct. Both *Trieb* and instinct aim at satisfaction by discharging the tension building up in the organism. Even though they may share a structurally similar *Ziel*, this is not to say that the paths taken by the *Trieb* qua sexuality to achieve satisfaction are predetermined or decided in advance. As Freud himself argues, the activities through which the *Trieb* might be satisfied are variable and plastic, but nevertheless the goal is invariably satisfaction no matter how direct or circuitous the paths for achieving it may be (SE 14: 122/GW 10: 216). You may be, for example, a sadist, a masochist, a voyeur, or an exhibitionist, but in each of these instances the *Trieb* tends toward the same aim: satisfaction.

This helps explain why, as we saw in chapter 1, the *Trieb* cannot be defined solely in terms of the sexual aim. It is not only because there is no single activity decided in advance through which this satisfaction can be achieved, but also because there is nothing in the aim that separates the

Trieb from the instinct and would be defining of the *Trieb* as such. An instinct, such as hunger, might differ from the *Trieb* insofar as the pathways for sating hunger may be more rigid, determined, and limited; however, both the *Trieb* and instinct nonetheless share the same aim of lowering tension qua satisfaction. This means that the aim alone cannot be what is defining of the *Trieb*.

For Freud, all satisfaction must be realized in or through an object, *Objekt*, which is just "that in which or through which the *Trieb* is able to achieve its aim" (SE 14: 122/GW 10: 216). In "Triebe und Triebschicksale," Freud declares, echoing his remarks about soldering in the *Three Essays*, that the object is what is most variable about the *Trieb* and is not originally connected with it (SE 14:122/GW 10: 216). The object of the *Trieb* becomes, in this way, an object of the *Trieb* only and insofar as it makes pleasure possible. In other words, the object is, as we know, highly variable and must be soldered to the *Trieb*.

From the perspective of the object, the *Trieb* at first seems to take some distance from the instinct. An instinct has very specific and predetermined objects toward which it tends, while the object of the *Trieb* is only secondarily and surreptitiously soldered to it insofar as it makes pleasure possible. However, once again, the object of the *Trieb* alone does not ultimately distinguish it from that of the instinct. While the object of the *Trieb* may be variable and soldered to it as a consequence of making pleasure possible, the instinct also reaches satisfaction through some object, even if this object is determined in advance. In other words, both the *Trieb* and the instinct both require an object for satisfaction, and this object only becomes a satisfying object by virtue of its making satisfaction possible. There is nothing about having an object that makes the *Trieb* different than the instinct. In fact, as we have previously discussed, the distinction between *Trieb* and instinct becomes blurred when we consider that, for example, objects of hunger can also become objects of sexuality.

Trieb and instinct, then, are analogous, if not indistinguishable, at the level of pressure, aim, and object. As such, both in terms of its beginning (in the pressure) *and* its ends (in terms of the object and aim), the *Trieb* shares a common structure with the natural instinct. Freud himself seems to suggest as much when he claims that the source, *Quelle*, of all *Triebe* is a "somatic process which occurs in an organ or part of the body and whose stimulus is represented in mental life by [a *Trieb*]" (SE 14 123/GW 10: 216). In fact, Freud adds that *Triebe* are "*wholly determined* by their origins in a somatic source" (SE 14 123/GW 10: 216). The pressure, then, issues in some way from the source, which originates in some organ or part of the body, which Laplanche refers to as "a kind of biological X" (LD 12/25). And what we call or know of the *Trieb* is just the psychical representation of this "biological X." It is only from its representation in the psychical apparatus that we can know anything about the *Trieb*—its source, pressure, aim, and object. Since psychoanalysts do not have access to this biological substratum of the *Trieb*, it can only become known as it is represented in psychical life through psychoanalytic inquiry. But we have to ask at this point: Is that really any different from an instinct? Do we as human beings have immediate access to our instinctual impulses? Can we readily locate them and identify them? This does not seem to be the case, and we will show this in more detail in the following chapters. For now, let us turn to Laplanche's attempt to specify the *Trieb* with respect to the instinct.

The Difference between *Trieb* and Instinct: The Genesis of Infantile Sexuality

At every level of Freud's definition of the *Trieb*, the *Trieb* itself appears to be completely analogous to the instinct. This is a familiar pattern that we discussed at length in part 1—namely, each time the *Trieb* seems to go astray or deviate from the instinct, it nonetheless collapses back into it. According to Laplanche, this pattern is a direct consequence of Freud's attempt in "Triebe und Triebschicksale" to define the *Trieb* in abstract and general terms. For Laplanche, Freud's attempt to define the *Trieb* in a general way is necessarily biologizing and instinctualizing because it does not capture the specificity of the *Trieb*, and it is, therefore, no wonder that the *Trieb* begins to look like the instinct at every turn in the definition: "Treating every *Trieb* in general proceeds in a necessarily abstract fashion. Treating the [*Trieb*] generally is biologizing, giving an analysis that is *also* valid for instinctual behavior" (LD 13/26). To understand the specificity of the *Trieb*, then, we cannot rely on abstract definitions, as Althusser arguably already began to show us in chapter 3. Instead, Laplanche argues, we must do what psychoanalysts do best, that is, give a *genetic account* of the *Trieb*.[5] However, we must go back—not to its source, *Quelle*, which is not possible in psychoanalysis because we do not have access to the biological substrata from which the *Trieb* issues—but back to its origins, its genesis. In order to do this, Laplanche will follow the movement of Freud's *Three Essays* (which in some sense mirrors the movement of the *Trieb* itself) back to the origins of infantile sexuality in the second essay.

From Suckling for Nourishment to Infantile Sexuality

In the *Three Essays*, Freud argues that his psychoanalytic research and clinical work with patients continuously demonstrated that sexuality could be traced back to infancy (SE 7: 171–72/GW 5: 71–72). Furthermore, the idea that sexuality stretches all the way back to infancy is a theoretical possibility that Freud opens up through his confrontation with popular opinion in the first essay. For many and various reasons, which Freud outlines in the "The Sexual Aberrations" and many other places, popular opinion claims that the origins of sexuality are found in the physiological changes undergone by the human organism during puberty. In order to save the children, so to speak, from the contamination of sexuality, popular opinion declares that it is completely absent in childhood. If the end of sexuality is reproduction, then it stands to reason that this can only take place once the organism is capable of reproduction. And if the ability to reproduce marks the origin of sexuality, then it cannot be present in childhood (save for in aberrant, deviant, and naughty behavior). However, Freud has already shown that, even on popular opinion's own terms, reproduction cannot define sexuality as such. In this way, puberty and its supposed instinct for heterosexual intercourse and reproduction does not give us an adequate account of the origin of sexuality insofar as what is considered to be sexual extends well beyond these confines. By expanding our understanding of sexuality beyond the confines of puberty and the supposed instinct for reproduction, Freud puts forward one of, if not the most, provocative claims in the *Three Essays*—a claim that continues to provoke.

In the second essay of the *Three Essays*, "Infantile Sexuality," Freud describes the human infant born into a prolonged state of prematurational helplessness, or *Hilflosigkeit*—a term that Freud uses as early as his 1895 *Project for a Scientific Psychology* (SE 1: 318/N: 410) and as late as 1937's "Analysis Terminable and Interminable" (SE 23: 217/GW 16: 60). In this state, the infant is thrust into the world utterly unable to control even its most rudimentary motor functions and unable to accomplish even the most basic tasks to survive. It is born entirely ill-equipped to preserve its own life. Due to this state of complete and utter helplessness, the infant entirely depends on more capable others to help it meet its most vital needs. To paraphrase Winnicott: there would be no infant without the care relation.[6]

According to Laplanche, it is precisely in this relation of dependence with more capable others that Freud "locates," so to speak, the genesis of sexuality.[7] However, as we will see, what Freud finds is not an origin that is "locatable" in time or space, which could be definitively pointed to, as if such and such a moment constitutes *the* genesis of sexuality. Rather, as we will see, the genesis of sexuality is a continuous process of unfolding, deviation, splitting, and retroaction. If we can say that there is a genesis of sexuality, it is as complex as the relation between the *Trieb* and the instinct on which it is founded.

In *Life and Death in Psychoanalysis*, Laplanche turns our attention to Freud's paradigmatic example of infantile sexuality: sensual sucking. In the prolonged state of prematurational helplessness, the infant is unable to nourish itself because it cannot secure or even masticate its own food. Even if the infant by some miracle found itself in the presence of food, it could neither chew nor ingest it, since it only develops the physiological tools to do so much later in life. Of course, without nourishment the infant would simply die. Thus, the infant must rely entirely on the more capable others caring for it not only to procure its food, but also to provide it in such a way that it can be consumed by the underdeveloped infant. As we know, the infant's vital need for nourishment is met by suckling at the mother's breast or some substitute for it.

The infant's suckling for nourishment seems, at first glance, to be purely instinctual—in the sense that it is an innate, teleological, and functional behavior. The purpose of suckling is to provide the infant with a means of being nourished, which preserves its life—not because it is taught to suckle, and not because it learns to suckle—but as if it were a hardwired, pre-programmed, and automatic response passed down to it through heredity. An infant suckles because it must and because that is what it does (so long as the caregiver provides the infant with a source of nourishment).

Freud stresses the fact that suckling is initially tied exclusively to this vital need for nourishment. However, over time something curious begins to happen. Eventually the infant begins to suckle on objects that are not exclusively tied to the vital activity of nourishment. At some point, suckling appears to become detached from the vital function itself—the most common example of which is thumb sucking. This is what Freud comes to call, at a general level, "sensual sucking." And it is considered *sensual* sucking—which *differs* from suckling as an instinctual vital activity—precisely insofar as it no longer aims solely at satiating the vital need for nourishment. Instead, it aims at re-creating a certain kind of pleasure—a pleasure that was first introduced to the infant in the activity of receiving nourishment from its caregiver. Freud points out that in providing the infant with milk via the breast or some substitute for it, the caregiver inadvertently and inevitably stimulates the child's lips and introduces a surplus of pleasure over and above simply satiating the infant's vital need for nourishment (SE 7: 181/GW 5: 82). This surplus of pleasure comes about as a sort of side effect, *Nebenwirkung*, and becomes one that the child will constantly seek to renew and repeat (SE 7: 181/GW 5: 82). In seeking to continuously renew and repeat this newfound pleasure, it now aims at producing pleasure itself, *not just* preserving life (SE 7: 182/GW 5: 83). This is precisely what makes sensual sucking *sexual*—namely, it deviates from the instinctual need for nourishment and becomes a search for pleasure over and above the preservation of life. To put it in the Schillerian language that Freud adopts in other texts: love (or sexuality) comes about as a side effect of or deviation from hunger.

It is worth drawing our attention to the fact that popular opinion, seemingly despite itself, again almost hits the mark when it sought to model sexuality on the instinct of hunger. However, it does not seem to take this analogy seriously enough. For it is in this very instinct for nutrition, or hunger, that infantile sexuality emerges as a deviation from the vital instinct for nourishment in the care relation.

The Three Characteristics of Infantile Sexuality

Freud concludes his discussion of sensual sucking by summing up the three key characteristics that become defining of infantile sexuality as such (the first of which, it must be noted, was added to the *Three Essays* in 1915[8]): "Our study of thumb-sucking or sensual sucking has already given us the three essential characteristics of infantile sexual manifestation. At its origin it attaches itself to one of the vital somatic functions; it has as yet no sexual object, and is thus auto-erotic; and its sexual aim is dominated by an erotogenic zone" (SE 7: 182-83/GW 5: 83). Here we will discuss the latter two characteristics in detail, saving a focused and sustained discussion of the first for chapter 6. Suffice it to say that we can see the way in which infantile sexuality initially, as Strachey's translation has it, attaches itself to a vital somatic function. In the case of sensual sucking, we can see how this sucking for pleasure employs the very same instinctual mechanisms of suckling for nourishment for the means of securing extra-instinctual pleasure.

In fact, turning to the second characteristic, this is why Freud declares that infantile sexuality becomes autoerotic. Infantile sexuality no longer needs the other qua caregiver to produce autoerotic pleasures. Since, for example, sensual sucking is not directly tied to the vital activity of nourishment, the infant no longer needs the caregiver to provide it with the object of satisfaction (i.e., the breast, a substitute for it, or the milk). As a result, the infant can secure this peculiar satisfaction with recourse to objects in its immediate surroundings, including its own body.

This, however, as we will show at great length in the chapter 5, does not mean that infantile sexuality is altogether without an object; but rather, the pleasure-seeking activity does not need other people and is not directed toward them. Instead, the infant often takes parts of its own body, such as its thumb, as an object in its autoerotic quest for pleasure. It is crucial for us to highlight here that the infant's activity is not *initially* autoerotic from the outset, but rather it *becomes* autoerotic in the movement from suckling to sensual sucking, that is, from suckling for nourishment in the care relation to sucking on parts of its own body for pleasure.

This brings us to the third characteristic of infantile sexuality, which as Freud claims, is that infantile sexuality is dominated by an erotogenic zone. What this means is that the infant takes parts of its own body as a sexual object. In this way, the aim—in the sense of sexual aim qua activity through which sexual satisfaction is secured—of infantile sexuality is to stimulate the erotogenic zones, that is, those areas on the body that are receptive to stimulation (e.g., the lips, the anus, the genitals, the skin, etc.).

By taking an object on its own body as a sexual object, the infant is provided with two erotogenic zones in the same activity: for example, the lips *and* the skin of the thumb. Although these erotogenic zones seem to be in some way predestined to become the sites of pleasure—since they are physiologically fitted to receive or produce stimulation—they alone cannot account for the genesis of sexuality, a point we will expand on in more detail in the following chapter. This is because, as Laplanche claims, the role of the adult other is absolutely integral here: it is the caregiver who is largely responsible for introducing the infant to these erotogenic zones in the care relation. In the care relation the adult other must feed the child and, in so doing, stimulates its lips, which is not to mention all the ways in which the caregiver may stimulate other parts of the child's body during, for example, cleaning and bathing. This is an unavoidable and necessary consequence if the infant is to survive. In other words, there is no satisfaction of hunger without the introduction of stimulation, no survival without sexuality.

We can see that while both the sexual aim and the sexual object of infantile sexuality are there from the beginning (of infantile sexuality), they are only so in a secondary way. They are not innate since they only arise in the relation of dependence with the caregiver. It is the adult other who introduces stimulation to the infant and, in so doing, introduces it to the pleasures of, say, sensual sucking, which the infant seeks to renew and refind in its autoerotic activity. In this way, the infant depends on the adult other in order to survive, but it ends up with that plus something else—namely, infantile sexuality. In this way, Laplanche "locates," so to speak, infantile sexuality in an unfolding relation between the infant and the other.[9]

Chapter 5

Auto-Hetero-Erotism

Making Space and Time for the Object in Freud's Infantile Sexuality

As we have shown in the previous chapter, infantile sexuality finds its origin in the relation between the infant and its caregiver. Due to the infant's prolonged state of prematurational helplessness, the adult other must help the infant satisfy its most basic needs for survival. However, as we have seen, something peculiar happens in this care relation such that the infant's instincts begin to deviate from its self-preservative function toward a search for pleasure. By considering two of Freud's three characteristics of infantile sexuality, we have shown how the relation with the other plays a significant role in the genesis of infantile sexuality.

However, recent trends in Freud scholarship have vehemently argued that if we want to rescue Freud's theory of sexuality from himself and make it relevant today in light of contemporary queer theory and gender studies, we must read the other out of his theory of infantile sexuality altogether. As such, we will now turn our attention to arguably the strongest and most well-known version of this argument. However, against such a reading, we will seek to show that the relation to the other is inescapable and, indeed, necessary to understand the radicality and revolutionary nature of Freud's theory of sexuality. This will allow us to revisit the problem of sexuality in light of more contemporary concerns about sexuality and gender, by considering what are often understood to be the more "problematic" aspects of Freud's writings.

Completely Without Object?
Questioning the Status of the Object in Auto-Erotism

A Non-Oedipal Freud?

As if heeding Laplanche's call, in "The *Three Essays* and the Theory of Seduction," to return to the 1905 version of the *Three Essays*, editors Phillipe Van Haute and Herman Westerink, along with translator, Ulrike Kistner, have recently made the original 1905 edition of Freud's *Three Essays* available for the first time in English. Pushing some of Laplanche's later remarks about the various editions of the *Three Essays* to the extreme, their hope is that the original edition, which is free from what they see as many of the "problematic" aspects that come to plague the later versions of the text, will give anglophone readers a new chance to approach Freud. Sharing more contemporary concerns about Freud's work, yet wanting to salvage certain parts of it, the editors seek to put their 1905 version of Freud into constructive dialogue with contemporary queer theory and certain philosophers—in particular, Foucault and Deleuze—whom they see as dismantling the binary and heteronormative logics that Freud is often seen as championing (Van Haute & Westerink 2016, x). This rapprochement between philosophy and psychoanalysis seeks to mobilize a certain aspect of Freud's work against other aspects of it in order to challenge and, ultimately, as they claim, "deconstruct"[1] the normativity and normalizing logics of psychoanalysis.

In addition to providing readers with a detailed account of the polemical intervention made by Kistner's updated translation, Van Haute and Westerink provide a lengthy introduction to the text. This introduction is meant to give the reader all the requisite historical and theoretical background for understanding the importance of the 1905 version—a veritable how-to guide for reading the text properly. Echoing similar remarks made by Laplanche in his essay, "The *Three Essays* and the Theory of Seduction," Van Haute and Westerink want the reader to notice the striking differences between the original 1905 edition and the 1924 edition of the *Three Essays*. They are at pains to explain to the reader in great detail exactly what is not in the text: for example, the theory of the drives, the theory of narcissism, the developmental schema of infantile sexuality, Freud's interest in art and culture, and so on. However, what is most important for them is that the 1905 edition is free from any mention of the infamous and much maligned Oedipus complex[2]—which is to be understood here strictly as the heteronormalizing nuclear familial structure in which children are supposed to identify with the parent of the same sex and take a parent of the opposite sex as a sexual object, lest they develop a neurosis.

According to Van Haute and Westerink, again echoing remarks made by Laplanche, despite the fact that Freud presents a potentially revolutionary theory of sexuality in 1905, there is a reactionary tendency in Freud's work after its initial publication. In this way, Freud himself had, as the editors suggest, "difficulty in grasping the radical character of his own thinking," and unfortunately slipped back into, and even defended, the very popular opinion of sexuality he sought to challenge (Van Haute & Westerink 2016, lxxi). The most obvious and egregious example of this, according to Van Haute and Westerink, was Freud's regression into a heteronormative understanding of sexuality, which is entrenched in a distinction between the normal and abnormal. Of course, as we know, this is the very thing for which Freud took popular opinion to task in the "The Sexual Aberrations." However, according to Van Haute and Westerink, there is a certain pathologizing and heteronormative culture from which Freud could not free himself and which, in turn, completely undermines the "critical potential" of his work. "Despite the critical potential of his theory, Freud on several occasions falls back into the "popular opinion" that he rejects. . . . These passages . . . reintroduce a heteronormative perspective or re-establish a strict (and "natural") distinction between the normal and the pathological (in particular the perversions) . . . what is at stake is a certain mentality, a shared culture, from which Freud could not escape" (Van Haute & Westerink 2016, lxx–lxxi).

Van Haute and Westerink go on to identify the Oedipus complex as the theoretical linchpin for Freud's "heteronormative approach to sexuality" and his pathologization of the perversions (Van Haute & Westerink 2016, ix). They make similar remarks in the introduction to their edited volume, *Deconstructing Normativity?*, in which they seek to form an alliance with the most unlikely of all allies for reading the *Three Essays* in Michel Foucault (who himself candidly admits in an interview that he did not bother with the *Three Essays* when he wrote his famous *The History of Sexuality, Volume 1: The Will to Knowledge*,[3] a text that Van Haute and Westerink reference favorably).

> Psychoanalysis appears in this long history as a new technique of normalization which, according to Foucault, not by coincidence introduces the Oedipus complex at the historical moment, the end of the nineteenth century, when family life is discovered by

the juridical system as a locus of unwanted intimacies. . . . It is indeed oedipal thought that is at the heart of the Foucauldian critique of psychoanalysis. . . . According to Foucault, it is at exactly this point that Freud fails to initiate a break with the traditional *scientia sexualis* and actually continues its most fundamental ideas. (Van Haute & Westerink 2017, 3)

As is well known, Foucault's strategy in *The History of Sexuality, Volume 1*, is to put the novelty of Freudian psychoanalysis into question by continuously situating it within dominant historical trends, discursive practices, and biopolitical regimes of power-knowledge. Following Foucault, Van Haute and Westerink rhetorically ask whether it is any wonder that the Oedipus complex appears in Freud's work at the same time, historically speaking, family life becomes a site for juridical and psychiatric interest. As such, Freud's later work becomes synonymous with the apogee of practices that seek to "normalize" sexuality by constructing, defending, and continuing a specious (and naturalized) opposition between the normal and the abnormal, of which the Oedipus complex is the major symptom.

Inspired by Foucault's analysis and historicist critique of Freud, the pressing task for Van Haute and Westerink becomes one of reading, developing, and mobilizing the good, critical Freud who "deconstructs" normativity against the bad, normalizing Freud who slips back into popular opinion. If there is any hope of salvaging an unproblematic psychoanalysis, a critique of this supposed psychoanalytic heteronormativity needs to be aimed specifically at the Oedipus complex. As such, the 1905 edition of the *Three Essays* offers the editors the perfect point of departure for radically revising Freud's thought because the Oedipus complex is altogether, they claim, a "theoretical impossibility" in the 1905 version (Van Haute & Westerink 2016, ix). As such, Van Haute and Westerink spend a majority of their introduction arguing for and spelling out the "far-reaching consequences" of a non-Oedipal Freud—the key to which is a particular reading of Freud's theory of infantile sexuality and, more specifically, of one of its defining features, namely, autoerotism.

Auto-Erotism as Auto-Affection and the Destruction of the Oedipus Complex

By modeling its notion of sexuality on hunger, popular opinion defines sexuality in what Van Haute and Westerink want to call "purely functional terms"—or, what we have been calling a *natural instinct*. In this way, sexuality is said to serve a clearly defined self-preservative function that is predetermined in advance by nature, and this is nothing other than reproduction. In so doing, as Van Haute and Westerink highlight, popular opinion establishes a norm for sexuality (Van Haute & Westerink 2016, xvii). The moment sexuality is treated in purely functional terms, as a natural instinct for reproduction, it necessarily becomes heteronormative because heterosexual reproduction defines and determines the normal *sexual aim* and the normal *sexual object*. By contrast, anything that does not conform to this picture is considered to be a sexual aberration—that is, a perversion of the natural reproductive instinct and functional purpose of sexuality.

As we have seen, through his treatment of popular opinion, Freud shows that what is essential and constant in sexuality is neither the heterosexual object (which is only one object among many that can be secondarily "soldered" to it), nor the aim of reproduction (which is just one possible consequence of pleasure-producing activity). For Freud, the very fact that there are so-called inverts, perverts, and fetishists proves that—far from serving a functional purpose—sexuality does not have any naturally preprogrammed paths for securing satisfaction, nor does it have any naturally predetermined attraction toward certain objects. In fact, a quick survey of the field of these sexual aberrations reveals that many, many people are sexually attracted to many, many different objects in many, many different ways. Van Haute and Westerink argue that what this shows is that sexuality is altogether "nonfunctional" (Van Haute & Westerink 2016, xxvii). If the term *functional* implies that an activity has a natural, biological, self-preservative, vital, or instinctual purpose defined in advance, then sexuality is *nonfunctional* precisely insofar as it does not originally serve a self-preservative or reproductive function (Van Haute & Westerink 2016, xxvii).

By unsettling the relation between sexuality and its supposed functional purpose (and with it the very relation between normality and abnormality), according to Van Haute and Westerink, Freud begins to reveal a peculiar relation between sexuality and the object, which can only be seen in the 1905 edition of the text. For them, the fact that sexuality can become soldered to many different objects implies that the sexual object itself must be "contingent," meaning that it is entirely incidental to pleasure (Van Haute & Westerink 2016, lxii). What we were earlier calling "variability," Van Haute and Westerink call "contingency" in the strongest sense of the term, insofar as the object is seen to play no determining role whatsoever in sexuality. Because this soldering can take place with respect to any object, it is not considered to be integral to the nature of sexuality. Van Haute and Westerink are quick to trace the radical contingency of the object all the way back to the origins of infantile sexuality.

As we saw in the previous chapter, Freud himself claimed that sensual sucking was the paradigmatic example of infantile sexuality because it deviated from the vital instinct of nourishment. As such, it is a prime example of what Van Haute and Westerink call "nonfunctional pleasure." Thumb sucking cannot be considered functional, since it does not serve any predetermined self-preservative function; rather, it only seeks pleasurable satisfaction: an infant sucks its thumb not out of any need for nourishment but purely out of pleasure. Again, for Van Haute and Westerink, sensual sucking is considered to be *sexual* precisely because it is *nonfunctional*.

According to Van Haute and Westerink, the most striking aspect of sensual sucking is that the child can produce this pleasure on its own—that is, without any recourse to another person. Pleasure is derived from and produced by the infant's own body; after all, the infant sucks *its own* thumb. This is what Freud comes to call, following the sexologists of his time, "auto-erotism," which we already know from the previous chapter is one of the three fundamental features of Freud's theory of infantile sexuality. However, Van Haute and Westerink argue that Freud's conception of autoerotism, like many other terms that Freud borrows from his contemporaries, comes to break entirely with his predecessors' usage of the term (Van Haute & Westerink 2016, xlv). According to Van Haute and Westerink, Freud's use of the term "autoerotism" is more radical because it no longer refers solely to masturbation, taken in the narrow sense, but is expanded to any self-pleasuring of which the infant is capable.

More importantly, though, Freudian autoerotism is much more radical because it describes the "infantile experience of sexual pleasure" as being "completely without an object" (Van Haute & Westerink 2016, xlv). This supposed objectlessness of autoerotism is meant to be both obvious and shocking to the reader. It should be obvious because, of course, *auto*erotic pleasure would preclude the reference to an external object. Freud himself seems to say as much in the conclusion of the *Three Essays*, when he writes: "in childhood the [*Sexualtrieb*] is without an object [*objektlos*], that is, autoerotic" (RTE 82). (Whether or not Freud had such a strong reading in mind is, as we will see, at least debatable.[4]) However, it should also shock many readers of Freud to see the object disappear completely. After all, Freud often and in many different places speculated about there being some sort of primordial relation to an object. Freud will speak, for example, even in the 1905 version of the *Three Essays* of the important role that the breast or bottle plays in introducing the infant to the pleasures of sensual sucking. In this way, it seems that an object is necessary, at the very least, in introducing the infant to autoerotic pleasure. However, Van Haute and Westerink are quick to argue that while these objects may be important for introducing the infant to the pleasures of sensual sucking, the bottle or breast are themselves not considered to be integral in the activity of autoerotism. According to Van Haute and Westerink, the caregiver is somehow able to deliver milk to the child without stimulating the child's lips with the nipple of the breast or bottle, and it is the milk—and only the milk—that stimulates the child's lips. As such, Van Haute and Westerink go so far as to reduce the breast or bottle, which appear to play such a pivotal role in Freud's account of infantile sexuality, to "mere instruments in the discovery of autoerotic pleasure" (Van Haute & Westerink 2016, xlvi). As mere instruments of autoerotic discovery, the breast, bottle, and even the milk completely drop out of the picture in sensual sucking. This leads them to conclude that the presence or absence of the object is not at all integral to autoerotism (Van Haute & Westerink 2016, xlv–xlvi).

Since autoerotism, on this conception, has no need whatsoever for any object whatsoever—especially other people who are reduced to mere instruments for autoerotic discovery—infantile sexuality becomes, according to Van Haute and Westerink, completely "non-intersubjective" (Van Haute & Westerink 2016, xxvii). This nonfunctional, objectless, and nonintersubjective autoerotism rules out altogether the possibility of fantasy in the infantile sexual experience. Without an object, the infant simply has nothing to fantasize about: "Autoerotism as we find it in early infancy is not about sexual fantasies, since fantasy always implies an object" (Van Haute & Westerink 2016, xlv). At the very least, according to Van Haute and Westerink, fantasy requires that there is or was an object to fantasize about. Having no object, not even an imagined one, Van Haute and Westerink conclude that "neither imagination nor fantasy is among pleasurable infantile activities" (Van Haute & Westerink 2016, xlvn). Since autoerotism ultimately has nothing whatsoever to do with objects, alterity, others, or fantasy, emphasis is shifted away from the infant's psychical life to the infant's body alone: "[Autoerotism] is nothing but a physical-pleasurable activity originating from the 'drive' and the excitability of erogenous zones" (Van Haute & Westerink 2016, xlv). There is no longer space or time for the object, the unconscious, or fantasies in Van Haute and Westerink's autoerotism. The infant becomes completely isolated from others and objects, and the infant's body is nothing more than *a solipsistic pleasure-producing machine*. The autoerotic infant blissfully enjoys the physical pleasure it produces in and on its own body without recourse to anything other than its own erogenous zones.

Infantile sexuality, then, is no longer relational, intersubjective, or psychical, and the infant's body alone is the singular, isolated site of pleasure and sexuality. In this way, Van Haute and Westerink conceive of the infant as fully transparent, fully present to itself, and free from the risky and disruptive encounter with any object or other. The infant feels its needs and satisfies them without any recourse to anything outside. This leads Van Haute and Westerink to conclude that: "The paradigm for infantile sexuality, Freud writes, is the lips kissing themselves" (Van Haute & Westerink 2016, xlvi). In what follows, we will show that Freud, in fact, never wrote that the paradigm for infantile sexuality is the lips kissing themselves and wonder if and how this would even be a possibility for Freud. According their schema, however, autoerotism means that the infant touches itself, just as the lips can be seen as kissing themselves. As such, *autoerotism becomes pure auto-affection*; the infant is simultaneously that which touches and that which is touched, and there is no space or time for anything other.

Such a reading of autoerotism as auto-affection, in turn, paves the way for their destruction of the Oedipus complex as a theoretical possibility. Even on the most charitable reading of the Oedipus complex, it always involves the infant's sexual relation to either or both of its parents or caregivers. However, for Van Haute and Westerink, this is impossible because the infantile sexual experience is autoerotic, in their sense that it is nonfunctional, objectless, nonintersubjective, and without fantasy. Sure, the infant may relate to its caregivers, it may depend on them for care and survival; but like popular opinion, Van Haute and Westerink seem to argue that it is theoretically impossible for any of this to be sexual in any way (at least for the infant)—a curious argument, to be sure, because it seems to imply that the child's love for its parents either does not exist, is entirely natural and completely functional, or only occurs after puberty. Whatever the case may be, the child is absolved of any sexuality in the relation to its parents and is freed from the supposedly heteronormative constraints of the Oedipus complex. Having freed Freud and the child from the Oedipus complex and the normativity and normalizing function that they believe it implies, the authors claim to have opened space for rethinking Freud's work in line with contemporary discourses that seek to "deconstruct" heteronormativity and binary logics—to which Freud often supposedly falls prey.

From AutoErotism to Writing and Back to Auto-(Hetero-)Erotism

While it may serve to put Freud into an interesting conversation with Foucault and certain queer theorists, Van Haute and Westerink's critical and historicist approach to Freud's text also surreptitiously situates their 1905 Freud in another lineage of philosophical thinkers. Beginning arguably with Plato,[5] there are a whole host of philosophers who, when they dare to dirty their hands with autoerotism, treat it as a form of auto-affection. From Aquinas[6] to Kant[7] and up through contemporary examples like Thomas Nagel,[8] autoerotism is treated as a perversion that does not serve the divine, natural, instinctual, or functional purpose of reproductive sexual intercourse. Like Van Haute and Westerink, although perhaps to different ends, all these figures conceive of autoerotism as a deviation from the natural principle or order of sexuality, which is supposed to be directed toward a member of the opposite sex. In pleasuring oneself, in touching oneself, in affecting oneself, recourse to an other is avoided, thus violating the natural order of sexuality. Of course, this will lead these thinkers to denounce autoerotic behavior in various ways: as the violation of a law, as a sin, or at least as an abnormal perversion. While Van Haute and Westerink seek to use this very insight to "deconstruct" the same normativity that all these other thinkers seek to maintain, they share with these other thinkers the idea that autoerotism is auto-affection and, as auto-affection, a challenge to the supposedly natural (heterosexual) function of sexuality.

It is curious to note that, in their "deconstruction" of normativity, Van Haute and Westerink do not seem to mention Jacques Derrida. Of course, it is Derrida in *Of Grammatology* who argues that perhaps the most defining figure of this tradition of autoerotism as auto-affection is none other than Jean-Jacques Rousseau (G 154–55, 165/223–24, 235). What makes Rousseau of special interest here is that in struggling to maintain the pure auto-affection of autoerotism, he is led on his own terms, Derrida argues, to undermine, or deconstruct, the very purity of auto-affection that he seeks to posit (G 166/237). In so doing, Rousseau introduces a difference, or *différance*, into auto-affection such that it is always already a hetero-affection. In other words, auto-affection always presupposes some differential relation to alterity, that is, an object or an other. It is only with some minimal distance, delay, and division that auto-affection is even possible, necessarily exposing any auto-affection to alterity (G 166/237).

For Derrida, what makes Rousseau unique in some ways in the history of the metaphysics of presence, which is lurking in the background here, is that he is the first to try to thematize and systematize the subordination of writing to speech. According to Derrida, Rousseau will attempt to build an entire philosophical system on the suppression of writing, which he ultimately blames for the corruption of nature in general and human nature in particular. To combat this corruption of the purity of nature, Rousseau is led to introduce a new way of thinking about presence in terms of the subject's unmediated relation to its consciousness and sentiments (G 98/147). Derrida argues that Rousseau seeks to found and maintain this (self-)presence through the auto-affection of the voice. In other words, it is our ability to speak to ourselves that allows us to be present to ourselves: "Now *logos* can be infinite and self-present, it can be produced as auto-affection, only through the voice: an order of the signifier by which the subject takes from itself into itself, does not borrow outside of itself the signifier that it emits and that affects it at the same time. Such is at least the experience or consciousness of the voice [*la voix*]: of hearing-oneself-speak [*s'entendre-parler*]" (G 98/146). What guarantees the subject's unmediated self-relation to itself is the voice, *la voix*, and it is through *la voix* that the subject is present to itself. In hearing ourselves speak, in hearing our own voice, we are present to ourselves in the immediacy of the act of speaking/hearing, the *s'entendre-parler*. In hearing oneself speak, there is no space for mediation and no time for delay. There is no outside, no distance, no exteriority, no alterity: the signifier is heard at the very same time that it is uttered. In this way, *la voix* is pure auto-affection because there is no difference between the one who is affected and the one who is affecting. Auto-affection, then, is just the name for the subject's self-identity and self-presence in its immediate relation to itself in the *s'entendre-parler dans la voix*. For Rousseau, auto-affection is an immediate *self*-presence; there is no need/space/time for the other, which would only threaten to disrupt this natural auto-affection of *la voix dans la s'entendre-parler*.

According to Derrida, Rousseau's problem with writing is a necessary consequence of this very insistence on the primacy of *la voix* as the experience of auto-affection (G 146/98). Rousseau's focus on the voice excludes, or must exclude, writing because writing necessarily introduces mediation and distance in the act of signifying. In this way, writing threatens to interrupt, corrupt, and disrupt the immediacy of pure presence. We can see, for example, that in the empirical act of writing, one leaves a trace for some other who is not present. Even in writing a note for oneself, a trace is left by a self that is no longer present for another self that is yet to come. Thus, not only is there a spatiotemporal spacing, *espacement*—Derrida's term for the becoming time of space and becoming space of time—in between the empirically written characters, but there is an unavoidable *espacement* between the one writing and the other who reads. As Martin Hägglund points out, this *espacement* is another—and a crucial—way of conceptualizing what Derrida comes to call *différance*—the necessary movement of differing and deferral in the trace structure of writing (Hägglund 2008, 3). Writing becomes dangerous for Rousseau, in this way, because in exposing the signifier to the trace, to the outside, to the external, to *différance*, writing threatens to contaminate speech and destroy the pure self-presence and auto-affection of *la voix*.

Yet, Derrida points out, there is an unmistakable tension in Rousseau's commitment to the primacy of speech as pure presence and the subordination and suppression of writing: at the same time that Rousseau continuously decries the threats and evils of writing, he is also (necessarily) forced to rely on it as a palliative, corrective, or even protector of speech (G 144/207). When speech is not enough to protect nature/presence, writing comes to Rousseau's rescue. Derrida points out, for example, that Rousseau will famously claim that his *Confessions* must be written, so as to save them from any misunderstanding. This should raise an obvious question for us: if speech alone is what preserves the purity of presence and guarantees meaning, then why does Rousseau need to *supplement* speech with writing to ensure that he is not misunderstood?

Derrida, of course, seeks to underscore the significance of this term "supplement," which he borrows from Rousseau's own texts, and he seeks to show two seemingly incompatible and contradictory, yet intimately related, ways in which Rousseau deploys the supplement: (1) supplementation by addition; and (2) supplementation by substitution. On the one hand, then, Rousseau conceives of the supplement as a "surplus" that is added to or enriches another plenitude that, as plenitude, is already complete and sufficient (G 145/208). On the other hand, the supplement substitutes "in-the-place-of," *à-la-place-de*, or takes the place, "*tient lieu*," of something that is missing (G 145/208). In this case, it does not add but fills in. In other words, it compensates for something that is incomplete and insufficient.

What Derrida wants to emphasize here is that these two conceptions of the supplement provide two contradictory ways of understanding that which is being supplemented: on the one hand, that which is being supplemented is something that is merely added to, since it is already complete and sufficient; and, on the other hand, that which is supplemented needs a substitute because it is incomplete and insufficient. For Derrida, what Rousseau shows in oscillating between these two conceptions of the supplement is that presence always relies on a supplement to be what it is and, as such, is already itself incomplete and insufficient. This is what Derrida calls the "logic of the supplement," namely, the fact that what is self-present and self-identical necessarily depends on something other to be present and identical.

Through the logic of the supplement, we can see that what was supposed to be purely present and immediate is shown to be derivative and mediated (G 157/226). As such, something like pure presence never existed in the first place, since presence itself presupposes and depends on an other, a supplement, to be present to itself. And this is why Derrida will conclude that the supplement is just another name for *différance* (G 150/215): the supplement marks something that is already inconsistent in itself and, therefore, marked by difference and mediation. Furthermore, it is important for us to note that it is this difference and mediation that makes presence possible in the first place. As we can see, in order to be present to myself, for example, there must be both a moment of differing between myself and the me to which I am present. For Derrida, this means that in any self-relation or self-presence, there must be some movement of differing and deferral such that one can be present to oneself. In short, to be self-present *I* have to be present to *myself*.

The curious thing for Derrida, then, is not just that speech depends on writing as a supplement, but also that speech itself turns out to be structured by the very same trace structure as writing. In order to hear oneself speak, for example, there must be some minimal distance and delay, which would leave a mark, a trace, such that one could hear oneself speak. One speaks/hears oneself as an other who hears/speaks to oneself. In general, then, in order to affect oneself there must be some minimal distance/delay between that which is affected and that which is doing the affecting. Thus, what is supposed to be free from difference ultimately and necessarily presupposes and depends on it. As Derrida explains: "But what is no longer deferred is also absolutely deferred. The presence that is thus delivered to us in the present is a chimera. Auto-affection is a pure speculation" (G 154/221). Thus, the presence that we arrive at in Rousseau's auto-affection is a "chimera"—a presence already corrupted and already contaminated. In this way, Derrida claims, pure auto-affection, affecting oneself as self, is a "pure speculation."[9] But we have to be careful here. When Derrida says that auto-affection is pure speculation, this does not mean that there is no such thing as auto-affection or presence at all (G 166/236), but rather that there is no auto-affection or presence that is free from the contamination of *différance*. We still affect ourselves, and we do so all the time, which means that there is still auto-affection, and all experience presupposes this as a condition for its possibility (G 166/236). To experience anything at all, one must be present, but presence itself is only possible if there is some sort of internal division, delay, or distance already at work in this auto-affection (G 166/237). It is only with a privation of presence that presence becomes possible in the first place, since without this there would be no spacing for one to be present to oneself.

In this way, we could say that the exterior is already interior in the self-relation of auto-affection, the outside is already inside, the other already in the self.[10] In this way, we can say that every auto-affection is a *hetero-affection* because the *autos* always presupposes and depends on the *hetero* as its condition of possibility, and vice versa. In *On Touching* Derrida will put forward the term "auto-hetero-affection" to describe the fact that every auto-affection is structured by hetero-affection (OT 180/206). For in order to (auto-)affect oneself, one must (hetero-)affect oneself as other.

The Possibility of Pleasure: Autoerotism as Auto-Hetero-Erotism

According to Derrida, Rousseau is left scrambling to cover up this "catastrophe" of the logic of the supplement with more and more supplements in order to recover the supposedly lost purity of his auto-affection (G 41/61). While tracing this chain of supplements in Rousseau's work, which Derrida also calls the "problem of sexuality in Rousseau," Derrida is led to the theme of autoerotism in the former's work. As Derrida points out, Rousseau's treatment of autoerotism seems to split into two different, yet intimately related, directions. On the one hand, Rousseau seeks to situate himself in line with those philosophers for whom autoerotism is treated as an *unnatural* supplement to the natural heterosexual-reproductive function of sexuality. In attempting to bypass the other, autoerotism is a dangerous supplement, a perversion of the natural sexual function and, as such, a vice and an evil that must be avoided.

Yet, on the other hand, Derrida points out that in his *Confessions*, Rousseau gradually begins to treat autoerotism as a natural supplement that restores the purity of the subject and of nature itself. By renouncing a relation to the other in autoerotism, the spatial and temporal gap that separates oneself from the other begins to disintegrate. In this way, autoerotism becomes the most *natural*—because the most direct and sure—way of experiencing pleasure. One supposedly becomes fully present to oneself in touching and being touched by oneself. Of course, all of this begins to look a lot like what Van Haute and Westerink called autoerotism, namely, purely present auto-affection without the other. As such, despite their attempts at a "deconstruction," they, along with Rousseau, remain trapped in what Mauro Senatore describes as a "phenomenology"—that is, in other words, a predeconstructive understanding of autoerotism, which does not take seriously the "economic distribution between auto-erotism and hetero-erotism" (Senatore 2013, 252).

For Derrida, it is not a matter of pitting Rousseau's two conceptions of autoerotism against one another, but rather of seeing them as two sides of the same coin. We need to take seriously the fact that Rousseau's account of autoerotism is continuously frustrated—frustrated precisely by *différance*. No matter how hard Rousseau tries to preserve the purity of auto-affection through autoerotism, something always gets in the way: "Rousseau will never stop having recourse to, and accusing himself of, this onanism that permits one to be himself affected by providing himself with presences, by summoning absent beauties. In his eyes it will remain the model of vice and perversion. In affecting oneself by another presence, one alters oneself [*on s'altère soi-même*]" (G 153/221). In affecting oneself, one always and inevitably alters or corrupts oneself. The problem with autoerotism is that in touching oneself, one always touches oneself as an other. One alters oneself, corrupts oneself, *s'altère soi-même*, which necessarily introduces difference into the supposedly pure auto-affection of autoerotism (and which is not to mention the chain of fantasmatic others that haunt Rousseau's autoerotic activity and serve to further distance himself from himself). Thus, for Rousseau, auto-erotism is a vice and a perversion precisely because it is *self*-corrupting and *self*-othering. In other words, touching oneself always necessarily introduces a difference between the self who touches and the self that is touched: "In the structure of auto-affection, in the giving-oneself-a-presence or pleasure, the touching-touched operation welcomes the other in the small thin difference that separates acting from suffering [*qui sépare l'agir du pâtir*]. And outside, the exposed surface of the body, signifies, marks forever the division that puts auto affection to work [*qui travaille l'auto-affection*]" (G 165/235). Again, this does not mean that there is no autoerotic experience. But rather, for Derrida, and this is just a consequence of Rousseau's own writings, in order for there to be any autoerotic experience at all there must be some difference between that which touches and that which is being touched. In other words, autoerotic experience is necessarily divided within and against itself. Thus, when Derrida writes about Rousseau's chain of supplements that it is "difficult to separate writing from onanism" (G 165/235), it is not just because the empirical act of writing may contain some sublimated autoerotic quality in Rousseau's work, but because autoeroticism itself is structured by *différance*.

This is why Derrida will claim in *Of Grammatology* that there is no difference—or perhaps better said, *there is* a *différance*—between auto- and hetero-erotism: "between auto-eroticism and hetero-eroticism, there is not a border but an economic distribution. It is within this general rule that the differences are mapped out" (G 155/223). This is not to say that autoerotism and hetero-erotism are the same thing, but rather to say that they are two moments in the same self-differentiating process. Every autoerotism is a hetero-erotism, since every auto-affection is a hetero-affection. There is no opposition between them, only a difference in economic distribution, inflection, or emphasis. To touch oneself is always to touch oneself as an other because, as Derrida writes in *On Touching*, auto-affection is just hetero-affecting oneself, or being hetero-affected by oneself, *s'hétéro-affecter* (OT 53/67).

In her reading of autoerotism in Derrida's work, Ellie Anderson seeks to coin the term, taking Derrida's cue, "auto-hetero-erotism" to describe the fact that every autoerotism is always already hetero-erotism—that is, already structured by the other (Anderson 2017, 61). Yet, and here is the last Derridean twist, auto-hetero-erotism, as Anderson points out, also implies that all hetero-erotism is also structured by autoerotism. In other words, without autoerotism, hetero-erotism would not be possible. After all, one cannot touch an other without touching oneself in the process. In *On Touching*, Derrida explains that the self is indispensable in the self-other relation that defines hetero-erotism: "In the 'self-touching-you [*se toucher toi*],' the 'self' is as indispensable as you. A being incapable of touching itself could not bend itself to that which absolutely unfolds it, to the totally other who, as totally other like all others, inhabits my heart as a stranger" (OT 291/367). Touching oneself, *se toucher*, is always structured in such a way that the touching/touched never fully coincide in pure auto-affection. And the same is true of touching an other because to touch in general is always in some way to touch oneself, *se toucher*. One cannot touch anything without touching oneself and, by touching someone else, I am touching myself through the other. In this way, to touch an other, *toucher toi*, is always a *se toucher toi*—or, touching oneself touching an other. In this relation of *se toucher toi*, the *se*, oneself, is irreducible: in touching the other, one cannot but touch oneself (touching the other).

CAN THE LIPS KISS THEMSELVES?

To return to our discussion of the lips kissing themselves. We can see that if the lips were to kiss themselves, then they could only do so by kissing themselves as an other or as, what Freud calls, a "sexual object" in the expanded sense of anything that is soldered to the *Trieb*. It must be noted that nowhere in the *Three Essays* does Freud write that the model or paradigm of infantile sexuality is the lips kissing themselves.[11] What Freud does say in this regard is that *sensual sucking* in general is the "model" of infantile sexuality (RTE 40). In fact, Freud seems to indicate on those very same pages that such a situation—in which the lips are kissing themselves—is, if not impossible, nonetheless impossible without introducing some sort of object, other, or at least difference into the situation. Citing Kistner's translation,

> The child does not make use of an extraneous body for sucking, but prefers a part of its own skin because it is more convenient, because it makes it independent of the external world, which it is not yet able to control, and because in that way it provides itself, as it were, with *a second erogenous zone*, albeit one of an inferior kind. The inferiority of this *second zone* is among the reasons why at a later date the child seeks the corresponding parts—the lips—of another person. ("*It's a pity I can't kiss myself*," the child seems to be saying.) (RTE 42–43; my emphasis)

It sure is a pity but, according to Freud here, the child cannot kiss itself—a fact that even the child seems to register on some level. As such, the infant takes another object on its own body, like its thumb, as a *secondary* erogenous zone—that is, as a sexual object to kiss, suck, and so on. We can see here the differing and deferral that divides the child in its autoerotic activity: not only is there a spatial difference between the lips that suck and the thumb that is being sucked; but more fundamentally the infant is divided by that which is sucking and that which is sucked. As such, there is no reason to think here that the lips could not kiss themselves—or that the lips kissing themselves could not be the model of autoerotic infantile sexuality—but only if what we mean by this is that the lips take themselves as an object because the lips can only kiss themselves if they are kissing themselves as an other. After all, when we say that the lips kiss *themselves*, there are two terms: the lips and themselves. The lips becoming present to themselves in the activity of kissing reveals the work of *différance* structuring this auto-hetero-erotic activity.

In fact, without this differential structure at the heart of auto-hetero-erotism, pleasure itself would not be possible in the first place. An erogenous zone only becomes an erogenous zone when it is touching/touched as an other. Take the skin, for example, which is a potential erogenous zone that stretches over our entire body and is in constant contact with itself. However, the skin only becomes an erogenous zone, that is, only produces pleasure when it is touched in such a way that it is touched as an other. Without this minimal distance or delay no pleasure would be produced. If autoerotic activity were pure auto-affection, that is, if the touching and the touched completely coincided without any trace of difference, then my skin would always be in a state of producing pleasure because it is always in contact with itself. The twist here, however, is that if the skin were always producing pleasure, it would produce no pleasure because there would be no way to differentiate pleasure from nonpleasure. Freud himself is adamant, in all his variations on the pleasure principle, that pleasure is produced as a lowering of tension—or perhaps better said: in the differential relation and movement between pleasure and unpleasure. In other words, pleasure is only thinkable and experienced within some sort of differential relation. As such, pure auto-affective pleasure, pure autoerotism, would be impossible because there would be no space or time for any affection or pleasure to take place.

We can see how this auto-hetero-erotism is already at work in Freud's 1905 *Three Essays*. In the passage cited above, Freud shows that in (auto-hetero-affective) sensual sucking, a differential relation to an object is already opened up in which the child takes itself as an object by sucking its own thumb. This is something Freud will later find important enough to reiterate in his "Autobiographical Study," in which he plainly states concerning the *Triebe* of infantile sexuality that "they find their object for the most part in the subject's own body" (SE 20: 35/GW 14: 61). And this is precisely what makes the "sexual function" of infantile sexuality, according to Freud, "auto-erotic" (SE 20: 35/GW 14: 61). As we can see, Freud readily acknowledges that infantile sexuality has both a "sexual function" and an "object." However, as we have shown, this is not because he betrays his early insights from the 1905 *Three Essays*, but because it cannot be otherwise. Just because infantile sexuality is initially and primarily, as Freud claims, detached from the genitals and reproduction, does not mean that infantile sexuality does not serve any function at all. Discharging tension, seeking pleasure, securing satisfaction, or whatever you want to call it, is still an important function for the organism. Furthermore, it is a function that would be impossible to conceive without being structured on a complex differential relation with some sort of object, even if that object is to be found on the organism's own body.

The taking of oneself as a sexual object in autoerotism is what opens the possibility of—or even animates—the finding of an external object later in life, that is, in Freud's terms, seeking out the lips of another. This is precisely what the child will seek out later in life by soldering to other objects. This perhaps provides us with a heterodox way of understanding what Freud may have meant by the "diphasic" nature of object choice. Of course, Freud often conceives of the "choice" of object qua soldering of the *Trieb* to an object as happening, as the term suggests, in two phases. The first takes place during childhood in which we are sexually attracted to, among other things, our caregivers. The other phase takes place after puberty when we are attracted to less incestuous objects. However, we can see that there is something like a diphasic choice of object already at work in infantile sexuality and the autoerotic relation. After the initial relation to the instinctual object is disrupted the child must then find other objects to which to solder, including autoerotic objects. Thus, while the relation to any given sexual object might be contingent after all, the relation to an object itself is irreducible in Freud's theory of sexuality because autoerotism is always structured and only made possible by its relation to an object.

We could say, then, that autoerotism is nothing other than a hetero-erotic relation in which the object is oneself, that is, in which one hetero-affects and is hetero-affected by oneself, *s'hétéro-affecter soi-même*. This is why Freud will later conclude in the *Three Essays* that the finding of an object is always the refinding of it because soldering to some object in a hetero-auto-erotic relation is just a refinding of the auto-hetero-erotic object, even if the former is a substitute (or, a supplement) for the latter. For better or worse, we cannot escape the other, even in our autoerotic activity, and the infant cannot escape the object, its caregivers, or even perhaps the Oedipus complex.

The Problem of Sexuality Revisited: A Brief and Modest Defense of the Oedipus Complex Based on Freud's Idea that Sexuality Is a Problem

The purpose of staging Derrida's deconstruction of autoerotism as auto-affection against Van Haute and Westerink's more Foucauldian-inspired historicist critique of Freud is not to go back and champion some sort of normalizing and pathologizing function for the Oedipus complex. Rather, the aim is to take very seriously Freud's problem of sexuality when reading his work. In fact, we will seek to show that, by taking this problem of sexuality seriously, Freud's Oedipus complex might furnish us with the tools necessary to challenge the very normativity it supposedly defends.

In their latest rereading of Freud's 1905 version of the *Three Essays*, *Reading Freud's Three Essays on the Theory of Sexuality: From Pleasure to Object*, Van Haute and Westerink move beyond the first two essays of the 1905 version, engaging with some of the material in the third essay and the subsequent editions of the text. However, this move is meant primarily to reinforce their conclusions about the *Three Essays*, as already spelled out in their earlier works. In fact, much of the third essay and the subsequent editions are again repeatedly dismissed simply as being "heteronormative" (Van Haute & Westerink 2021, 47, 67, 69, 106). Furthermore, they confirm yet again that the *Three Essays* gradually becomes a "defense of popular opinion" (Van Haute & Westerink 2021, 79).

Ultimately, Van Haute and Westerink remain committed to playing up certain aspects of what they see as the good Freud—aspects that are amenable to contemporary discourses about sexuality, especially Foucault's wayward criticisms of psychoanalysis and contemporary concerns about gender and queer theory (Van Haute & Westerink 2021, 108–13). In fact, they go so far as to wonder whether Freud could be considered a queer theorist *avant la lettre* (Van Haute & Westerink 2021, 109). They do so all while attempting to dismiss what they view as the more *problematic* aspects of Freud's theory of sexuality. Yet, Van Haute and Westerink take it as a matter of fact that these contemporary discourses themselves represent a definitve improvement on Freud's ideas about sexuality. They do not at all seem concerned with the ways in which Freud himself might offer challenges to such contemporary discourses, nor do they seem to question the ways in which such discourses themselves might, in fact, depend on or reinforce what Freud called popular opinion, which we will discuss in more detail in the conclusion.

For now, let us focus on the ways in which Van Haute and Westerink's method of reading Freud, while certainly allowing them to adeptly bring important tensions in Freud's work to light, nonetheless forces them to conclude that these tensions will remain forever unresolvable within the so-called Freudian paradigm (Van Haute & Westerink 2021, 6). Of course, as we have shown, Van Haute and Westerink must conclude that they will remain "unthinkable" in Freud, since they have strategically left him bereft of any of the theoretical tools that he developed to address such issues. As such, they claim that the problems plaguing Freud's texts and psychoanalysis as such can only be resolved with a change of paradigm (Van Haute & Westerink 2021, 107). A new paradigm? Sure, but does Freud not already furnish us with some of the key elements of this supposedly new paradigm once we take sexuality seriously as a problem?

Freud's announcement in 1915 that even heterosexual attraction toward a member of the opposite sex is a problem because it is not self-evident and cannot be accounted for in chemical (and, thus, instinctual, functional, etc.) terms is meant to be much more than a call for a *mere critique* of popular opinion. For Freud then declares that this is "a problem that *needs elucidating*." As such, part of the problem for Freud is that it is not enough just to critique popular opinion or, in Van Haute and Westerink's terms, heteronormativity. (In fact, as we have shown, popular opinion itself does a decent job of doing this on its own—provided that one listens to what it has to say.) Simply critiquing popular opinion's explanation of reproductive sexuality as a natural instinct still leaves us with two huge and daunting questions: namely, (1) How—seemingly against all odds—does polymorphous infantile sexuality end up imitating in such a large number of cases something like what we call normality, even at the cost of neuroses and psychoses, and so much so that it appears to be natural to the vast majority of people?[12] (2) Why—against all the evidence to the contrary and all the internal contradictions upon which it depends—do people remain so obstinately attached to popular opinion?

This is precisely the problematic to which the Oedipus complex and the supposedly heteronormative aspects of Freud's texts respond. It provides a theoretical framework for thinking the ways in which a human child—overdetermined by its nonfunctional, polymorphous infantile sexuality—may *or may not* desire a heterosexual object and reproduction.[13] For Freud, it is not enough simply to point out that heteronormativity is a contingent development or that heterosexuality is not necessarily endemic or innate to sexuality as such. Yes, things could have been and could be otherwise. But we still need to account for how that norm is still nonetheless being produced, maintained, reproduced, and desired, despite the fact that it is not naturally founded. In fact, it is precisely *because* it is not naturally founded or decided in advance that we need to account for how and the conditions under which this process of normalization takes place.

It should go without saying that Freud did not invent, for example, the patriarchal society that attempts to establish and impose, however effectively, the nuclear familial structure and heterosexuality as norms. Of course, Freud himself was no stranger to oppressive sexual morality. In fact, he famously wrote numerous texts decrying the restrictive sexual morality of his time,[14] advocating for the sexual liberation of women,[15] and defending so-called perversions from needless and harmful forms of what we would now call normalization.[16] The novelty of Freud's studies is precisely that they take the oppressive nature and the deleterious effects of these norms seriously—seriously enough to listen to what his patients had to say about them.

As Juliet Mitchell points out in her excellent essay, "Psychoanalysis and Women," Freud's psychoanalytic studies take place within a patriarchal society and seek to describe that very system—a system which seeks to normalize, among other things, heterosexuality (Mitchell 1990, 339–40). It is no wonder, then, that the explanatory mechanisms Freud developed to understand these processes *appeared* to be patriarchal and heteronormative; he was, after all, attempting to describe how our patriarchal and heteronormative society functions and the psychical effects it produces on us in reproducing itself. However, this does not mean that Freud is necessarily a proponent or defender of a patriarchal and heteronormative society. As Mitchell claims, the power of Freud's analyses is not so much that it calls into question the normativity of a given social formation as a contingent historical development. Rather, what Freud does is give us the tools to understand—and this is perhaps why he is so troubling to us—how we all consciously and unconsciously reproduce the (hetero)normalizing society of which we find ourselves a part, even when we are critiquing it, and even when we think we are outside of it. However, this is something that we must take seriously if we wish to challenge such structures.

With the Oedipus complex, for example, Freud is attempting to register and provide us with an account of how our sexuality is structured by our relations with others in the families and societies into which we are born. Thus, to throw out the Oedipus complex simply because infantile sexuality is not inherently heteronormative or reproductive would be to ignore the fact that children are born into some sort of kinship structure and often in, as many feminists and queer theorists argue, a patriarchal society. In other words, dismissing the Oedipus complex fails to take seriously the ways in which this patriarchal society continues to reproduce itself through the heteronormativity of the nuclear familial structure, and it risks surrendering any means by which we could begin to understand the far-reaching psychical effects such a society has on us. (The Freudian twist, of course, is that no matter how restrictive a heteronormative and patriarchal family or society may be, it never fully represses the polymorphous aspect of our infantile sexuality, which becomes manifest in many ways, including in the form of neuroses.)

Furthermore, when Freud notes the deleterious effects of the Oedipus complex on his patients, it is not because he wants to normalize them by forcing them conform to some ideal heterosexual schema of psychical development. He is not the forerunner of conversion therapy. Quite the contrary. Freud's practice of psychoanalysis is meant to give patients, their suffering, their unconscious, and their infantile sexuality an opportunity to speak in a world that seeks to shut them up (Ramos 2022). Moreover, it seems misleading to treat Freud's attempt to take seriously, listen to, and alleviate the suffering of his neurotic patients simply as an attempt to normalize their sexuality—a project, as we have shown, Freud explicitly rejects as only causing them more harm. And it seems tokenizing to treat the neurotic's suffering as a challenge to normativity—as thinkers like Foucault often seem to do.

As such, we might borrow a Derridean way of phrasing this from Michael Naas: *yes*, to a critique of popular opinion, *but* we still need to give an account of it; or perhaps, *no* to heteronormativity, *and yet* we need to take it seriously (Naas 2008, 88). This is ultimately the force of Derrida's deconstruction as I have tried to outline it above—namely, deconstruction is not just a destructive or critical method (Naas 2008, 88); it is perhaps not even a method at all (Naas 2008, 140). Whatever the case may be, it always requires much more than merely putting into question or showing the contingency of a given binary opposition (Naas 2008, 28, 88). In a word, showing that the opposition between normality and abnormality is contingent, or that it is not natural and could be otherwise, does not explain how that opposition, *given its very contingency*, is nonetheless possible, takes hold, and still, it must be said, structures to an extent the very ways in which we think about and experience certain phenomena like sexuality. All of this is not to reinforce or shore up the opposition between them, but to take it seriously.

For example, although the distinction between the normal and the abnormal may or may not be "natural," it is difficult to imagine a psychoanalytic project that completely washes its hands of such a distinction. What would psychoanalysis be without an understanding of the difference between the neuroses and normality? After all, there do seem to be some qualitative differences between, say, the obsessional neurotic who constantly suffers from obsessive thoughts about contamination and, as a consequence, religiously washes their hands so much so that they cannot function in their daily life and the person who fastidiously keeps their workstation clean. Such a distinction seems absolutely crucial to clinical work and, as Freud put it, "changing neurotic misery into common unhappiness" (SE 3: 305/GW 1: 312). And we can say all of this while still admitting that the line between these two terms is very blurry: in other words, that the normal is tinged with the neurotic and that the neurotic is widely diffused and, as a result, normal in itself. However, not only is there clinical and theoretical value to these sorts of distinctions, it also does not seem like we can escape them anyway. They appear to structure the very ways in which we (are able to) think about these matters, just as we still have been unable, after decades of trying, to get rid of that pesky natural instinct when thinking about the *Trieb* in Freud's theory of sexuality.

With all of this in mind, we might wonder, then, how Freud's confrontation with popular opinion in the first essay already gives us the tools necessary to rethink the supposed normativity of his later work on his own terms. We might wonder, for example, not how the Oedipus complex changes (or normalizes) Freud's theory of sexuality, but how Freud's theory of sexuality, in turn, informs our interpretation of the Oedipus complex itself. In other words, how does a reading of the Oedipus complex change when we take Freud's theory of sexuality, in all of its rigor, seriously? As such, the challenge of Freud's work becomes not so much pruning the supposedly bad Freud from the good Freud or pitting them against each other; but rather, it is to follow the *Trieb* wherever it leads without anticipating where it should go or assuming what it should be in advance, even (and perhaps especially) when it begins to contradict popular contemporary discourses concerning sexuality. This is the challenge that one is left with when we take Freud's problem of sexuality seriously.

Chapter 6

Perversion and Pervertibility of the Instinct

Infantile Sexuality as Derivation-Deviation-Drifting from the Instinct

Having confirmed the necessary and inescapable role of the other in the care relation and the genesis of sexuality, we can return to Laplanche's discussion of infantile sexuality in *Life and Death in Psychoanalysis*. We will now turn our attention to the remaining characteristic of infantile sexuality—the attachment, *Anlehnung*, of infantile sexuality to a vital somatic function. For Laplanche, this *Anlehnung* is an concept that Freud himself unfortunately left underdeveloped in his work. Furthermore, according to Laplanche, the translation of this term *Anlehnung* into English is another moment in which we have unfortunately been led astray (LD 16/30; FB 59/73).

As a result, in his own work and in his translation of Freud's work, Laplanche seeks to raise the term *Anlehnung* to the dignity of a concept, by emphasizing the crucial role it plays in the genesis and nature of infantile sexuality (FB 29/38). Laplanche is at pains to point out that *Anlehnung*, which Strachey prefers to translate as "attachment," should be translated into French as "*l'étayage*." According to Laplanche, the word *Anlehnung* is better captured in French by *l'étayage*, because the meaning is something along the lines of a support or a propping, a propping up or a leaning-on (LD 16/30). In this way, infantile sexuality is not so much attached to the instinct, but rather infantile sexuality initially leans, or props itself, on the vital instincts: "What Freud describes is a phenomenon of support [*appui*] of the [*Trieb*], the fact that nascent sexuality leans itself on [*s'étaye sur*] another process that is both similar and profoundly divergent: the sexual [*Trieb*] leans itself on [*s'étaye sur*] a non-sexual, vital function. Or, as Freud formulates it in terms that defy all additional commentary, upon a 'bodily function essential to life' " (LD 16/31). To return to our example of sensual sucking, we can now see how the *Trieb* initially leans on the vital instinct of suckling for nourishment. It first props itself, or is propped up, on the vital activity of suckling for nourishment, only to become detached from it in its search to renew and repeat the pleasure of sensual sucking with objects that are not related to the vital function of nourishment. Thus, what is initially the nonsexual activity of suckling for nourishment (which is non- or, perhaps, presexual precisely insofar as it is initially tied exclusively to the vital need for nourishment) is sustained by and then gradually detaches itself from this vital activity. In other words, infantile sexuality comes into being by leaning-on the vital function of suckling and then hijacks it in its search for extra-instinctual pleasure.

In this way, borrowing Laplanche's language in *Life and Death in Psychoanalysis*, we could say that there is a *dérivation* of infantile sexuality from the instinct: infantile sexuality is derived, emerges, or comes from the instinct itself. Of course, in French, when we hear the word *dérivation*, we hear both a derivation in the genetic sense as well as a deviation. *Une dérivation* in say, plumbing or in circuitry is a diversion or a bypass. That is, it is the diversion of a fluid or a current from its initial pathway into another. It can also mean "to drift" in the sense of drifting from a certain pregiven pathway into another. Thus, we can say that infantile sexuality is defined by a *dérivation* from the instinct—in the fullest sense of it being derived from, but then also deviating and gradually drifting from the instinct. The genesis and movement of infantile sexuality is, then, a derivation-deviation-drifting from the instinct.

This is why Laplanche declares that infantile sexuality is a perversion of the instinct. From the Latin word *pervertere*, *perversion*, means to "turn away," meaning that infantile sexuality is that which turns away from, is turned away by, or turns itself away from the instinct. Of course, as we know, perversion usually carries with it the connotation of a norm. Colloquially speaking, perversion is often thought of as something deviant, something unnatural, that strays from established norms or accepted customs. However, according to Laplanche, the perversion at stake here in Freud's theory of infantile sexuality is much more radical than such colloquial usages of the term (LD 23/29). This is because Freud's theory of infantile sexuality completely destroys the idea that there is some innate, internal norm governing sexuality because *infantile sexuality is constituted by/*

as a perversion—a perversion, precisely, of the vital instincts (LD 23/40). Since infantile sexuality is that which by nature deviates and drifts from the instinct, there cannot be any innate norms or inherent teleology governing it (LD 23/40). (Of course, there are certainly norms imposed on sexuality, to be sure, but these always come from without, not from the nature of infantile sexuality itself.)

It is crucial at this juncture for us to stress that what is perverted in infantile sexuality is not some supposed sexual instinct. In other words, infantile sexuality does not deviate from the ends of, for example, the *Geschlechtstrieb qua* heterosexual instinct for reproduction, which supposedly arises during puberty. Instead, as Laplanche writes,

> What is perverted is still the instinct, but it is as a vital function that it is perverted *by* sexuality. Thus, the two notions discussed at the beginning of this chapter—instinct and [*Trieb*]—are seen once again to meet and separate. The [*Trieb*] properly speaking, in the only sense faithful to Freud's discovery, *is* sexuality. Now sexuality, in its entirety, in the human infant, lies in *a movement which diverts* [dévie] *the instinct, metaphorizes its aim, displaces and internalizes its object, and concentrates its source on what is ultimately a minimal zone, the erotogenic zone.* (LD 23/40)

In this passage, like Althusser, Laplanche remarks on the fact that the instinct and *Trieb* cannot help but continue to meet and separate. They are always intermingling and intertwining. This is manifest in the complex relation between the two and movement from suckling for nourishment to sucking on objects that serve no vital function. In this way, infantile sexuality is the diversion of the instinct from its predetermined aim, deflecting it from its predetermined object, internalizing and then metaphorizing this now lost instinctual object in the process. The infant inevitably and necessarily loses the instinctual object in this process because, for example, the breast, bottle, and caregiver are not always present when the child needs or wants them. When the infant begins sucking its thumb, it is seeking to refind this object and the pleasure that comes along with it in its autoerotic activity. However, this new object that the infant finds is not the original object, but rather some other satisfying substitute object, which Laplanche specifies is: "not the lost [instinctual] object, but its substitute by displacement; the lost object is the object of self-preservation, of hunger, and the object one seeks to re-find in sexuality is an object displaced in relation to that first object" (LD 20/35). For Laplanche, we see in this movement a metonymical displacement from the object of nutrition, the milk, to the breast, which provided the milk, to the thumb and, finally, the fantasmatic breast (LD 19/35). The aim of satisfaction—which was initially part of the vital, instinctual function of preserving life—turns into a perverse aim in itself. In other words, sensual sucking is still suckling; but sensual sucking is *sexual* precisely insofar as it does not aim at the instinctual ends of suckling laid down by heredity in the vital activity of nourishment. It *becomes* sexual precisely insofar as it diverts from those ends and seeks satisfaction in a displaced and refound substitute object.

We can say, then, that infantile sexuality becomes a relatively *autonomous* search for pleasure in relation to the instinct from which it arises. *Relatively* autonomous since, even though it aims at something other than its original instinctual ends, it still nonetheless relies on the same physiological mechanisms as the instinct to get there. It repeats the instinct, but it aims at something else—pleasure via extra-instinctual objects. As such, infantile sexuality is split from the instinct and, moreover, split between, on the one hand, the natural instinctual foundation on which it leans and from which it derives and, on the other hand, its extra-instinctual search for pleasure. In this way infantile sexuality qua perversion is a repetition with a deviation, a *dérivation*.

The Weakness of the Instinct

Although in chapter 1 of *Life and Death in Psychoanalysis*, Laplanche shows that infantile sexuality finds its origin or genesis in the perversion of the vital instinct in the care relation, he begins chapter 2 by immediately putting the genetic aspect of this account into question. According to Laplanche: "The very term 'genesis' evokes the notion of an emergence, the possibility of a linear understanding of what is later by what precedes it" (LD 25/45). The terms *derivation, emergence*, and *genesis* seem to imply that we can understand the structure, the movement, or even the logic of sexuality as an evolution from the instinct. In other words, it is as if we could give a chronological account of this process as a linear development from instinct to infantile sexuality. However, as Laplanche reminds us, things are not so simple. In psychoanalysis, since we do not have access to the biological substrata, all we have access to is infantile sexuality, which has already come to pervert and, as a result, obfuscate the entire vital order from which it is said to emerge: "Therein lies the whole *problem* of the 'vital order' in man and of the possibility, or rather, impossibility of grasping it 'beneath' what has come to 'cover' it over" (LD 25/45; emphasis added). The problem here is that in order for sexuality to be at all, that is, for it to have come into being, it must have already perverted the natural instincts from which it derives-deviates-drifts. This makes it impossible to recover some supposedly "pure" instinct and study it in its "pure" state. As such, Laplanche concludes that infantile sexuality is more important and deserving of our attention than this vital order: "On the other hand, to that very extent, it is the later which is perhaps more important, and alone allows us to understand and to interpret what we persist in calling the prior" (LD 25/45). For Laplanche, it is only through sexuality that we are able to grasp anything *après-coup* about the structure, movement, or logic at work in the instinct itself. Our understanding of the instinct can only be reconstructed or reverse-engineered out of our understanding of infantile sexuality, which has already come to distort the instinct in the perversion of the latter.

However, the very fact that infantile sexuality "emerges" from the vital instincts does nonetheless tell us something about the very nature of the vital instinct itself. In the never-delivered 1933 *New Introductory Lectures on Psychoanalysis*, Freud colorfully and concisely illustrates the underlying logic at work here for rethinking the nature of the instinct from the standpoint of infantile sexuality. In the thirty-first lecture, titled "The Dissection of the Psychological Personality," Freud claims to model his metapsychological theory on what I would call a sort of negative crystallography, in which the mind is to be studied like the breaking apart of a crystal. Freud writes: "If we throw a crystal to the floor, it breaks; but not into haphazard pieces. It comes apart along its lines of cleavage [*Spaltrichtungen*] into fragments whose boundaries, though they were invisible, were predetermined by the crystal's structure" (SE 22: 59/GW 22: 64). For Freud simply observing the crystal in its seemingly natural state, that is, its stable and ordered state, reveals little if anything about the crystal's actual structure, which in this state remains "invisible." (Of course, we have to remember that Freud was writing before technological advancements made it possible to view the crystal's structure in this state.) Although the result of throwing the crystal to the floor may initially appear as a random and chaotic mess, it nonetheless breaks, according to Freud, in a systematic and ordered manner along its "lines of cleavage." These lines of cleavage, *Spaltrichtungen*, these weak spots, as it were, are themselves always contained within and constitutive of the composition of the crystal. They are determinative of its very structure.

In this way, the crystal (although it appears stable and coherent before it is broken) was never whole to begin with; it was always composed of and by weak spots, which make it breakable in the first place. In other words, its fault lines and weak spots are already inscribed into its very structure; it contains its structural inconsistencies within it. The manner in which the crystal breaks is, then, nothing but the symptom of the inconsistencies structuring the crystal.

Expanding this illustration beyond Freud's application in this lecture, this is what I would call the Crystal Principle, according to which the mechanics, dynamics, and structure of an object (not only a physical object such as a crystal, but psychical processes and any theoretical object under investigation) can be understood in and though its weak spots, which determine the very mechanics, dynamics, and structure of that object.

Implicitly following Freud's Crystal Principle, Laplanche argues that the perversion of the instinct in the genesis of sexuality tells us something about the instinct itself. What it shows, according to Laplanche, is that instinct itself is "weak" and "premature": "What is 'perverted' by sexuality is indeed the function, but a function which is somehow weak or premature" (LD 25/45). Because the function, the vital instinct, is perverted in the genesis of infantile sexuality, we can say that the instinct itself must in some sense be *pervertible* for this perversion to take place. Laplanche equates this pervertibility with weakness, insofar as the infant's vital instincts are not strong enough to carry out its own aims without giving rise to the extra-instinctual forces that come to hijack these very functions.

Dehiscence: Split Infant, Split Instinct

For Laplanche, the prematurity and weakness of the instinct seems to be a direct result or reflection of the infant's own prematurity and weakness. Recall that Freud finds the infant born into a prolonged state of prematurational helplessness, in which the infant is unable to satisfy its most basic needs for survival. What this means for Laplanche is that the human being is structured by a "fundamental imperfection" or "a dehiscence" (LD 25/40).

Medically speaking, a dehiscence is the splitting open of a wound. In surgery, for example, a dehiscence occurs when the initial incision reopens and separates. The wound represents a weak spot from which it is later liable to reopen. The term *dehiscence* has botanical connotations as well. Dehiscence is the process by which a seed emerges or bursts from a seed pod. In such a case, we can see that the weak spot in the pod from which the seed emerges is part of the pod's very structure.

Of course, Laplanche is more than likely borrowing this term from his mentor, Jacques Lacan. In fact, in one of his most well-known *écrits*, "The Mirror Stage as Formative of the Function of the I," Lacan uses this term to describe infantile helplessness: "However, in man this relationship to nature is altered by a certain dehiscence at the very heart of the organism, a primordial Discord betrayed by the signs of malaise and motor incoordination of the neonatal months" (Mirr. 96/78). For Lacan, infantile helplessness introduces, or stems from, a "dehiscence," a fundamental split, a "primordial Discord" in the organism itself, which completely alters its relation to nature and from which the organism is never able to recover. Because of this dehiscence, the infant is never able to form a unity with its vital needs, their satisfaction, or the other who satisfies them.

What Lacan makes clear later in his career, is that this condition of helplessness must be supported not only by the other, but also by language. In his 1960 "Subversion of the Subject and Dialectic in the Freudian Unconscious," Lacan writes: "And while the somatic *ananké* of man's inability to move, much less be self-sufficient, for some time after birth provides grounds for a psychology of dependence, how can that psychology elide the fact that this dependence is maintained by a universe of language? Indeed, needs have been diversified and geared down by and through language to such an extent that their import appears to be of a quite different order, whether we are dealing with the subject or politics" (Subv. 687/811–12). The fate, *ananké*, of the prematurely born, powerless, and helpless infant is that it finds itself born with instinctual needs that constantly push and pull it, but it is too weak to do anything about them. Although these instinctual needs threaten to tear the infant apart from within, the infant is not strong enough to satisfy them. Overwhelmed by these needs, the infant must *demand* that some other come satisfy them and grant it some temporary relief from them. Of course, the infant, as the *infans*, as the one who is unable to speak, initially articulates, so to speak, this demand through erratic gestures, cries, screams, and so on, to which the other qua caregiver must give significance. The caregiver must—and does so without realizing it—"interpret" these various demands; for example, such and such a cry is interpreted as the child being hungry, needing their diaper changed, and so forth. Regardless of whether the caregiver is correctly interpreting these demands, they nonetheless provide meaning and significance to them.

As such, when the infant issues demands, they are then reflected, so to speak, back to the infant in the process of explicit and implicit, verbal and nonverbal, signification from the caregiver. We can see, then, how the infant's needs necessarily, and from the beginning, pass through language. By issuing the demands, the infant seeks to "translate" and "express" its needs to the caregiver who then attempts to satisfy the need and gives it significance in the process.

However, it is precisely this "expressive" idea of communication that Lacan seeks to challenge. Far from simply "translating," "expressing," or "communicating" a specific need to the caregiver through their cries, language only comes about secondarily through the other as they give the infant's demands any meaning. As Phillipe Van Haute puts it in his wonderful book-length study of Lacan's "Subversion of the Subject": "More specifically, the relation between these two orders cannot be thought of as a relation of expression; the symbolic is not the translation of a pre-given natural order. On the contrary, for Lacan language is like an alien body that grafts itself onto the order of the body and of nature" (Van Haute 2002, 25). Left to its own devices, the infant's needs remain nothing but a teeming multitude of chaotic, unsatisfiable dictates made upon the infant, and its demands are nothing other than meaningless cries for help. It is only with the intervention of the caregiver that these needs and demands begin to "mean" anything at all. As such, the caregiver "grafts" language onto the child and its instinctual needs.

In this way, the instinctual needs, which are too weak, and the infant, who is born too premature, get inextricably caught up in the extra-instinctual process of signification, from which it can never free itself. The infant's demands, which pass as its first attempts at articulating its needs, come to work on the need such that it shapes and reshapes the need itself, which creates a split or discord within the need (and the infant itself). In "Subversion of the Subject," Lacan writes: "Yet it is impossible, for those who claim that discordance is introduced into the needs assumed to exist at the subject's origins by the way demand is received, to neglect the fact that there is no demand that does not in some respect pass through the march of the signifier [*les défilés du signifiant*]" (Subv. 687/811). When the infant formulates its needs through the demand, it must pass through what Lacan calls "the march of the signifier," *les défilés du signifiant*. In so doing, the need inevitably and necessarily gets caught up in the procession of the signifying process, the chain of signifiers, which precedes and determines the demand through which the need must pass. Of course, for Lacan signifiers only find their "meaning" in their differential relation to other signifiers. Signifiers, in other words, like the child's prelinguistic demands, do not have any meaning on their own; they do not represent something "signified"—in the sense of a thing that would satisfy the need. Due to the infant's prematurity, we can imagine that the child has no clue what its needs are—let alone what to call them or what would ultimately satisfy them (a problem from which we all still perhaps suffer). In this way, there never is, was, or could be a simple "translation" by the infant of its needs that could then be "communicated" to the other through its demands.

Furthermore, the adult other's own "interpretations" of the infant's demands are never an exact one-to-one translation of the need or the demand, nor does the adult other just simply satisfy the child's need in answering the demand. We can think about all the extra significance the adult other, consciously and unconsciously, verbally and nonverbally, brings with it in meeting the child's demand: for example, love, affection, desire, and so on. In this way, the child's demands are only given significance by passing through the march of the signifying process in the infant's calling out to the other, who is already themselves a split subject caught up in this signifying process as well. As such, the signifiers pass through two subjects who are not present to each other or to themselves: neither knows, or can know, exactly what they or the other wants or what is being communicated in this care relation. There is never a closed circuit of communication between two fully present subjects.[1]

While at times Lacan seems to portray this as a somewhat linear process (for example, needs *pass* through the march of the signifier) it is important to insist that Lacan is primarily concerned here with a *logical process* rather than a linear chronological development.[2] We can think, for example, of the fact that for Lacan the infant qua purely biological being, a purely natural thing, never existed in the first place because the infant is always already caught up in the extra-instinctual process of signification. Not only is the infant's place in the familial kinship structure, its place in the socio-symbolic, already carved out by the adult others who speak about the child before it is even born; but for its need to even become a need at all it must always have been issued through the demand. The prelinguistic demand is what retroactively gives the need any signification by passing through the march of the signifier, and retroactively constitutes the need in the process.

Since the need must always "pass," or always already passes, through the extra-instinctual signifying process in the form of a demand, an extra-instinctual remainder is always left over. In other words, once needs are "articulated" in the form of a demand and given significance by the other, an excess of signification always remains. For Lacan, this is the origin of desire. In a 1958 *écrit*, "The Signification of the Phallus," Lacan formulates this in terms of an equation: desire is what is left once we subtract the need from the demand (desire = demand − need) (*Sign*. 579–580/690–91). That is, desire is the remainder that is left over after the child's need is "met." When needs take on extra-instinctual significance in the form of the demand, the need is outstripped and leaves behind a remainder of signification in the process. As we can see, the infant's needs always are, were, and forever will be split from within because it is only through the demand that the need becomes a need . . . plus something else that disrupts the need from within. As Alenka Zupančič puts it in *What Is Sex?*: "The concept of [*Trieb*] (and of its object) is not simply a concept of the deviation from a natural need, but something that casts a new and surprising light on the nature of human need as such: in human beings, any satisfaction of a need allows, in principle, for another satisfaction to occur, which tends to become independent and self-perpetuating in pursuing and reproducing itself. There is no natural need that is absolutely pure" (Zupančič 2017, 87). In this way, the purely instinctual is never pure and never was to begin with. The instinct is always already caught up in an extra-instinctual process that makes satisfying the need possible, but also splits the instinct from itself. In other words, articulating the need simultaneously and surreptitiously disarticulates the need, breaks it apart, and indicates the split or discord within it. We could say, then, that language is a supplement grafted on to the infant that reveals the dehiscence already splitting it and its instinctual needs from within.

The Weakness of the Reproductive Instinct: Complicating the Opposition between Adult and Infantile Sexuality

Human beings are not only born so weak and premature that they are unable to sustain their own life, but also the life of the species. As we know, human beings do not reach reproductive maturity until much later in life during puberty. It is also with puberty, we are told, that the supposed instinct to reproduce sets in. However, the problem is that infantile sexuality predates the advent of puberty and, as a result, comes to complicate this simple developmental schema. As Laplanche explains: "What psychoanalysis teaches us is that in man acquired sexuality—the intersubjective, thus, pulsional *sexuel*—comes, and this is really strange, before the innate. The [*Trieb*] comes before the instinct, the phantasm comes before the function; and when the instinct arrives, the seat is already occupied" (Pul. 22/22). For Laplanche, what psychoanalysis shows us is that, when it comes to sexuality, "acquired sexuality" (which is roughly synonymous with what Laplanche calls elsewhere "infantile sexuality" or simply the "*Trieb*") comes *before* so-called innate or instinctual sexuality (which, if such terms make sense anymore, is roughly synonymous with the *Geschlechtstrieb*, natural sexual instinct, or normal adult sexuality). In other words, sexuality precedes the instinct: "There is a sexual instinct, which is pubertal and adult, but it 'finds its place occupied' already by the infantile *Trieb*" (Pul. 25/25). Long before the so-called heterosexual instinct for reproduction emerges during puberty, infantile sexuality is already at work and has already taken the libidinal throne. In fact, as Adrian Johnston puts it, what Laplanche is calling here the innate comes "too late"—in the sense that infantile sexuality already structures the libido before puberty and the advent of the reproductive function (Johnston 2018b). As such, puberty often arrives too late and the reproductive instinct, like any other human instinct, is too weak to override the *Trieb* qua infantile sexuality and steer the organism toward the so-called instinctual function of reproduction, according to which the organism is supposedly preprogrammed.

However, we have to ask ourselves how much this idea of lateness, this schema of precedence, and the opposition between infantile and adult sexuality make sense even on Laplanche's own terms—at least in the terms that we have been developing in this chapter. After all, should the term *sexual instinct* itself not be a contradiction in terms, given Laplanche's own insistence on marshaling the two terms and holding them apart (Pul. 11–12/12)? How can there be such a thing as a "sexual instinct" if sexuality is defined as that which breaks from the instinct? In other words, why does he insist on calling heterosexual intercourse and reproduction sexual at all, if it is merely instinctual? It seems, then, that Laplanche himself was also unable to resist the "temptation" of the instinct.

Strachey's Infelicitous Translation?

Despite our own hardwiring over the term *Geschlechtstrieb*, as discussed throughout our study, we have so far followed Laplanche and popular opinion's lead, assuming it is a natural instinct for heterosexual intercourse that sets in during puberty. Yet, it is important for us to remark that this term, *Geschlechtstrieb*, nonetheless still contains the *Trieb* within it. At a very basic level, then, we have to wonder how we could have ever considered this *Geschlechtstrieb* to be an instinct in the first place. After all, it is a *Geschlechts-Trieb*.

In her "Translator's Introduction" to the recently revised translation of the 1905 edition of the *Three Essays*, Ulrike Kistner makes an important intervention in, and contribution to, debates swirling around Freud's *Three Essays* in general and the translation of the term *Trieb* in particular. With her translation, Kistner seeks, among other things, to distance herself form Strachey's potentially misleading translation of "*Trieb*" as "instinct." Kistner openly declares herself on the side of the anti-instinctual interpretation of Freud's work, claiming to remain much more faithful to Freud's German by rendering *Trieb* into English as "drive."

Furthermore, in order to bring to light certain nuances and subtleties in Freud's innovative use of language, which may have been otherwise obscured in previous translations, Kistner explains to the reader that Strachey silently collapses two other key terms in his translation—"*Geschlechtstrieb*" and "*Sexualtrieb*." (It is worth noting that Strachey does this not only in the *Three Essays*, but also, it seems, throughout the entire *Standard Edition*.[3]) Strachey decides to translate both terms as "sexual instinct."

According to Kistner, Strachey's translation unfortunately obfuscates the distinction between these two terms, which is a distinction between adult sexuality (*Geschlechtstrieb*), which she translates as "genital drive," and infantile sexuality (*Sexualtrieb*), which she translates as "sexual drive" (Kistner 2016, lxxxi–lxxxii). This is a distinction that Freud seems to make clear in the absolutely crucial passage we cited earlier in which he postulates the soldering of the *Trieb* to an object. In this passage Freud deploys three variations on the word "*Trieb*" in the same paragraph to articulate what exactly is at stake in this concept of soldering. Here we will cite Strachey and Kistner's translations respectively, in order to show what Kistner hopes to bring to light in her translation.

> It has been brought to our notice that we have been in the habit of regarding the connection between the sexual instinct [*Sexualtrieb*] and the sexual object as more intimate than it in fact is. Experience of the cases that are considered to be abnormal has shown us that in them the sexual instinct [*Sexualtrieb*] and the sexual object are merely soldered together—a fact which we have been in danger of overlooking in consequence of the uniformity of the normal picture, where the object appears to

Perversion and Pervertibility of the Instinct | 121

form part and parcel of the instinct [*Trieb*]. It seems probable that the sexual instinct [*Geschlechtstrieb*] is in the first instance independent of its object; nor is its origin likely to be due to the object's attractions. (SE 7 147–48/GW 5: 46–47)

Our attention is drawn to the fact that we imagined too close a connection between the sexual drive [*Sexualtrieb*] and the sexual object. In cases that have been considered abnormal, our experience teaches us that the sexual drive [*Sexualtrieb*] and the sexual object are merely soldered together—a fact we risk overlooking due to the uniformity of the normal configuration, where the drive [*Trieb*] appears to carry the object along with it. We are thus instructed to loosen the bond that we had imagined between drive and object. The genital drive [*Geschlechtstrieb*] is probably independent of its object initially, and its origin is likely not owed to the object's attractions. (RTE 10–11/ GW 5: 46–47)

What Kistner attempts to bring to our attention in her translation is not only Freud's use of the term "*Trieb*" (and not *Instinkt*), but also that Freud employs three variations on the German term "*Trieb*" here: *Trieb*, *Sexualtrieb*, and *Geschlechtstrieb*. Furthermore, it is important to highlight the significance of Freud's use of the word "*Sexualtrieb*" here in this passage. This is only the third time that Freud has used the term "*Sexualtrieb*" up to this point in the text, which appears for the very first time on the previous two pages in the German edition. Kistner argues that this is only further evidence that Freud is making an important distinction between the *Geschlechtstrieb* and the *Sexualtrieb* (Kistner 2016, lxxxi). Still further, this is the first time that the term "*Sexualtrieb*" is used in direct relation to the term "*Geschlechtstrieb*" in the *Three Essays*. In fact, it also worth noting that this is only the fourth time up to this point (including the two aforementioned references in *Three Essays*) that Freud has used the term "*Sexualtrieb*" in his published work at all.[4] Thus, there seems to be an important shift going on in the text here as Freud moves from the *Geschlecht*—of the *Geschlechtstrieb* to the *Sexual*—of the *Sexualtrieb*. In fact, Strachey's choice to collapse both terms into a single word seems to betray Freud himself on a fundamental level, since Freud was convinced that many mistaken objections to his theory were ultimately due to a "confusion between 'sexual' and 'genital' [*Verwechslung von 'sexuell' und 'genital'*]"—a point that Freud makes clear in the *Three Essays* itself (SE 7: 180/GW 5: 81). Thus, it seems to be no accident that Freud employed these two different terms here, and there must be something at stake in his doing so.

It seems that in moving from *Geschlecht*—to the *Sexual*—Freud is, at the very least, seeking to take some distance from popular opinion, signaling that he is now putting forward his own claims about sexuality under the heading of the term "*Sexualtrieb.*" The term *Geschlechtstrieb* itself is, of course, an amalgam of two German words *Geschlecht* and *Trieb*. (Both of which have proven to be absolute nightmares to translate from German into other languages.[5]) In our case, the former, *Geschlecht*, is often colloquially understood as sex and/or gender; it can mean either or both (and many other things) depending on the context. However, in this case, following Kistner's translation, it could be translated more literally along the lines of "genital." Let us recall that for popular opinion, sexuality is all about the genitals. The *Geschlecht*—of the *Geschlechtstrieb* is everything, and it marks the instinctual teleology at work in it. The ends of the *Geschlechtstrieb* are determined in every way by the genitals: its aim is *genital* union and an orgasm (which itself takes place in the *genitals*); and its object is someone of the opposite sex (which is, again, defined in terms of their *genitals*). As such, the *Geschlecht*—of the *Geschlechtstrieb* stands in here for popular opinion's emphasis on the genitals. However, as we know, Freud wants not only to deemphasize the role that genitality plays in the *Geschlechtstrieb*, but also popular opinion's focus on the ends (i.e., the aim and object).

If the *Geschlechtstrieb* is defined by its emphasis on genitality and its attraction toward a predetermined object, then the *Sexualtrieb* seems to be that which does not have its object determined in advance and is only secondarily soldered to it. In fact, Freud argues that: "Experience of the cases that are considered to abnormal has shown us that in them the [*Sexualtrieb*] and the sexual object are merely soldered together." Here, the *Sexualtrieb* and "the cases that are considered to be abnormal" (i.e., the sexual aberrations) are equated in the same sentence. In this way, we can assume that the term "*Sexualtrieb*" is used here to describe Freud's theory of sexuality according to which the *Trieb* is secondarily soldered to its object.

By collapsing these two German terms into the same English word, Strachey seems to commit a fateful error, as he covers up a significant conceptual difference that Freud begins to tease out when he attempts to put popular opinion's definition of sexuality strictly in terms of the *Geschlectstrieb* into question and move beyond it, even at the level of technical vocabulary. As such, Strachey is guilty, at least at first glance, of distorting a certain key Freudian insight by obfuscating an important distinction that is made here between the *Geschlechtstrieb* and the *Sexualtrieb*. If the *Sexualtrieb* is precisely that which comes to complicate and put into question the *Geschlechtstrieb*, then why translate them with the same word?

STRACHEY'S FELICITOUS TRANSLATION?

Yet again, we see Strachey's translation being vilified for betraying Freud's deepest insights into the nature of sexuality. By translating both terms as "sexual instinct," Strachey mistakenly collapses the distinction between the *Geschlechtstrieb* and the *Sexualtrieb*. In so doing, for lack of a better phrase: Strachey is guilty of "instincting" and "genitalizing" the *Trieb*, that is, turning the *Trieb* altogether into a genital instinct. In this way, Strachey ultimately commits the same error as popular opinion by turning sexuality itself back into a sexual instinct dominated by the genital (quite literally doing so in the text). Providing such a biologizing-instinctualizing-genitalizing translation goes against the letter and supposedly the spirit of Freud's text.

However, it is interesting to note how Kistner's own reasons for criticizing Strachey's translation seem, in some sense, to mirror popular opinion. Similar to popular opinion, albeit perhaps to much different ends, Kistner argues that the *Geschlechtstrieb* should be understood as the "adult" sexual instinct for reproduction that comes about with the advent of puberty, while the *Sexualtrieb* should be understood as infantile sexuality that extends well beyond these confines (Kistner 2016, lxxxi–lxxxiii). There is, of course, plenty of textual evidence that this is the case, which we have already discussed in great detail. Yet, Kistner's criticisms of Strachey risk overlooking a potentially crucial double movement at work here in Freud's theory of sexuality, which is revealed in Strachey's translation (however mistaken it may be).

We can see that by collapsing the *Sexualtrieb* into the *Geschlechtstrieb* Strachey also simultaneously collapses the *Geschlechtstrieb* into the *Sexualtrieb*. In this way, the two poles of the supposed instinct/*Trieb*, adult/infant, opposition are brought together in the same term "sexual instinct"—an almost ingenious, albeit paradoxical, formulation, which forces us to take both aspects of this movement into consideration. To take up the previous phrasing again, however awkward it may be: in instincting and genitalizing the *Trieb*, there is also a *Trieb*-ing of the instinct and the genital itself. In other (still approximate) terms: by instincting and genitalizing the sexual, Strachey also sexualizes (in the Freudian sense) the genital-instinctual. As we will show, what this means is that puberty and its supposed instinct for heterosexual reproduction can no longer account for not only the origin of sexuality, but also does not take into account everything at stake in heterosexuality or reproduction. In fact, the genius of Freud's theory of sexuality is that he not only seeks to expand the concept of sexuality beyond the confines of some supposed adult heterosexual instinct for reproduction, but he also seeks to problematize and throw that very "adult" instinct into question.

In the first,[6] second,[7] and third[8] essays of the *Three Essays*, among other places,[9] Freud rules out the idea that puberty or some natural instinct can magically explain everything that is at stake in so-called adult heterosexual intercourse and reproduction. Certainly, we all agree that there are undeniable physiological changes in the organism that occur during puberty—specifically, changes that allow the organism to be capable of reproduction. Saying that puberty alone cannot explain everything at stake in heterosexual intercourse and reproduction is not to deny that the organism undergoes significant changes during puberty.[10] Rather, the point is to take very seriously the problem of sexuality. For if sexuality is not entirely reducible to chemical, hormonal, biological, or instinctual models, then how can we account for the fact that people nevertheless desire to reproduce? We can no longer simply turn around and claim that it is through instinctual means brought about by puberty.

In a short, less-cited text published in 1913, "The Claims of Psycho-Analysis to Scientific Interest," Freud seeks to address this very concern. For Freud, once we rule out puberty as the origin and sole factor determining heterosexuality and reproduction, we must consider all manifestations of sexuality, including so-called normal adult sexuality as just another vicissitude of infantile sexuality: "[Infantile sexuality] includes the germs of all those sexual activities which in later life are sharply contrasted with normal sexual life as being perversions, and as such bound to seem incomprehensible and vicious. *The normal sexuality of adults emerges from infantile sexuality* by a series of developments, combinations, divisions and suppressions, which are scarcely ever achieved with ideal perfection and consequently leave behind predispositions to a retrogression of the function in the form of illness" (SE 13: 180–81/GW 8: 409; emphasis added). For Freud, what we call normal adult sexuality is, in fact, the outcome of certain "developments, combinations, divisions and suppressions" *of infantile sexuality itself*—and a precarious outcome at that—one that can just as easily deviate into perversion and neurosis. Again, we see the distinction between the normal and the abnormal, between childhood and adulthood, begin to blur and break down. What we have come to call normal adult sexuality is just one manifestation of infantile sexuality among many. As such, normal adult sexuality is just as perverse as any other manifestation of sexuality, including what is often labeled the sexual aberrations, because they share the same perverse origins in infantile sexuality.

What this means is that the *Geschlechtstrieb* itself (the *Trieb* for heterosexual intercourse and reproduction) must somehow be much more perverse than the framework of popular opinion allows (or wants) us to think. This is why Freud concludes in the passage cited above from the *Three Essays* that: "It seems probable that the [*Geschlechtstrieb*] is in the first instance independent of its object; nor is its origin likely to be due to the object's attractions." What this means is that *the Geschlechtstrieb qua Trieb must also be secondarily soldered to its object as well*. And this is perhaps one of the most important concerns animating Freud's discussion of sexuality, since it is just another way of articulating the problem of sexuality that he mentions in that crucial 1915 footnote, which we will quote here again: "Thus from the point of view of psychoanalysis the exclusive sexual interest felt by men for women is also a problem [*ein Problem*] that needs elucidating and is not a self-evident fact based upon an attraction that is ultimately of a chemical nature" (SE 7: 146n /GW 5: 44n). The question we must ask ourselves is: if the attraction toward the heterosexual object cannot be explained chemically or, in other words, by an innate natural instinct, then how is it the case that the *Trieb* becomes soldered to a heterosexual object in the first place? Since all manifestations of sexuality, including heterosexual attraction, are just one perversion among many, they cannot be given an instinctual explanation, which would only lead us down the series of problems that, for example, come to plague popular opinion.

Unlike Kistner and Laplanche, then, who conceive of the infantile *Sexualtrieb* as *opposed to* the "normal" "adult" *Geschlechtstrieb*, Freud sees the desire to have heterosexual intercourse, reproductive sex, or a child as being just one development—and a precarious one at that—of infantile sexuality. It is just one perversion among others, but one that seems to produce a statistical majority and mimic whatever we have come to call normal adult sexuality.

Of course, our personal experience should be enough to prove Freud's point that heterosexuality and reproduction cannot be entirely explained by nor completely limited to puberty and some heterosexual instinct for reproduction. On the one hand, as we all know, puberty does not definitively guarantee that one will desire heterosexual intercourse or to reproduce. It is not difficult to find examples of people who have gone through puberty and in no way conform to popular opinion's *Geschlechtstrieb*. On the other hand, the desire to reproduce and, perhaps better said in Freudian parlance, the desire to have a child, seem to be independent not only of puberty, but also of the drive for heterosexual copulation. It may come as a great surprise to some that there are plenty of people who are otherwise unable or do not desire to reproduce, yet still desire to have a child. As such, the desire to have a child can often be found completely independent of heterosexuality or the ability to procreate. Furthermore, anyone who has seen children playing at house or children playing with baby dolls will observe that the desire to have a child—this supposedly adult desire to reproduce—can set in well before puberty.[11] In fact, many children who have not undergone puberty will explain that they want to have a family and children when they grow up. Thus, puberty and the supposed instinct for heterosexual intercourse and reproduction cannot fully account for the desire to have a child. This means that *there must be some accompanying psychical and libidinal shifts in the individual's sexuality toward those aims, which cannot be explained, as Freud points out, merely by puberty or an instinct.*

It is absolutely crucial to note that this also means that the other side of the supposed opposition between the normal/natural/adult and unnatural/perverse/infantile is not left unaltered either because infantile sexuality itself becomes somewhat less perverse than many, such as Laplanche, are at pains to maintain. For if the vicissitudes of infantile sexuality could lead to something like heterosexual copulation and reproduction, then the former itself must be capable of reproducing the so-called normal. By putting the distinction between the instinct and *Trieb* into question in his theory of sexuality, Freud ends up altering both sides of this supposed binary opposition. What is considered to be natural becomes perverse, but what is perverse itself also becomes natural.

Strachey's translation, in its own complicated way, captures Freud's problematizing of this very opposition. By collapsing "*Sexualtrieb*" and "*Geschlechtstrieb*" into the same term in his translation, Strachey is able, felicitously, to capture the very movement of Freud's text, which is nothing other than this double movement at work in his theory of sexuality—namely, that instincting the *Trieb* also means *Trieb*-ing the instinct, and vice versa. As such, his translation, like any other translation that seeks to give solutions to these problems, will always be problematic, not because it is a bad and unfaithful translation but precisely because the terms themselves stand in for a necessary conceptual problem. In other words, no matter how hard we try to keep these terms apart, they keep coming back together, contaminating each other, complicating each other, and disrupting each other because they are structured by their impossible difference—an impossible difference that cannot help but continue to produce sexual problems.

Complicating the Care Relation: The Instinct Leaning on Sexuality

If the desire to reproduce, to have a child, is not instinctual, then we also have to wonder whether the desire to care for the child is purely instinctual. We have already shown that the caregiver's intervention to satisfy the child's needs introduces extra-instinctual processes and structures of signification, which as extra-instinctual could be considered sexual. This is not to even begin discussing the sexual pleasures—that is, the extra-instinctual stimulation and satisfaction—that takes place in the care relation between the infant and caregiver, which Laplanche calls seduction and certainly focuses on in his own work.[12] This is also not to mention all the ways in which the caregiver also derives extra-instinctual pleasures from the infant (e.g., the stimulation of the breast in breastfeeding, the living out of fantasies via children, etc.), which Laplanche also speaks about in his own work (Laplanche 1989, 126–27). However, even more fundamentally, if so-called adult sexuality is just one vicissitude of infantile sexuality among many, then it turns out, as we will now show, the entire care relation as a whole is supported by sexuality. As such, *not only does infantile sexuality lean on the instinct, but also that the instincts themselves must be propped up by sexuality.*

This is certainly a bizarre claim, to be sure, because we are often told that nothing is more instinctual than a mother's love and care for her infant. However, to employ a familiar line of questioning that Freud deploys against popular opinion in the first essay, we might ask: if this care relation were purely instinctual, purely natural, then how can we account for the fact that there are some people who, although they cannot or do not desire to reproduce, nonetheless desire to care for and raise children? Furthermore, how can we account for the fact that many people who do reproduce have no desire to care for their child? For example, we can think of those that choose to put their children up for adoption or the phenomenon of postpartum depression, in which a mother—who supposedly has some ingrained maternal instinct, a natural motherly love for her child—is capable of neglecting her child or even go so far as to kill it.[13] Are we to conclude from this that these particular women who put their children up for adoption or who suffer from postpartum depression are simply aberrant? No, because following Freud's logic in the first essay of the *Three Essays* and the Crystal Principle, we can see that these so-called deviations from the supposed natural maternal instinct reveal something about that instinct itself—namely, that it alone is not enough to guarantee that a mother will care for her infant. As such, this instinct must be supplemented, or propped up, by a desire to do so. And this desire is sexual by its very nature precisely because it is extra-instinctual insofar as the instincts themselves are too weak to guarantee that a mother will care for her child. Ultimately, without the (sexual) desire to care for the child, the supposed instincts for care alone would not be enough to sustain the care relation and, by extension, the infant itself. The caregiver's instinct for care and the infant's vital instincts *both* rely on extra-instinctual forces and factors for the care relation to happen in the first place and for the infant to survive. Without sexuality the instincts themselves would not, could not, exist.

Trieb as the Self-Differentiation of the Instinct

In the so-called genesis of sexuality, what we are left with is a temporality in which a "before" or an "origin" is continuously perverted in the very process of its unfolding. Sexuality is always caught up in its impossible difference with the instinct through a process of continual emergence in which it is always departing and returning to the instinct—that is, in which the instinct supports and is supported by sexuality. In this way, sexuality is in a continuous process of constructing and restructuring its origins after the fact, *apes-coup*. While from a certain perspective, so to speak, the instinct is the origin of sexuality (because sexuality is that which derives-deviates-drifts from the instinct), we can also see now that sexuality is at the origin of the instinct (because without the former the latter would not exist). In this twisting, reversing, and complicating of the origin, what comes "after" turns out to be the origin of the origin.

On the one hand, the adult inevitably and necessarily stimulates the child and introduces it to the sexual pleasures of, say, sensual sucking in the care relation. This is unavoidable. Even more fundamentally, the care relation itself is already pervaded or structured by sexuality. This is also unavoidable. The infant relies necessarily on the sexual intervention of the other in order to prop up its instincts in the care relation. As such, sexuality itself becomes the *condition of possibility* for the instinct, without which the weak instinct would not be enough to guarantee the infant's survival.

On the other hand, sexuality seems to become the *condition of impossibility* of the instinct, as it comes to irrevocably contaminate (or pervert) our weak instincts. As Laplanche shows, it becomes impossible to distinguish extra-instinctual sexuality from the so-called natural instinctual foundation from which it arises. We can see that the natural instinct of hunger, for example, becomes perverted and, thereby, sexual: food is often consumed (or not consumed) in ways that deviate from or even go against self-preservation itself, which is not to mention all the ways in which food is incorporated into sexual acts. In this way, nourishment itself—just as we have already shown is the case with reproduction—also becomes a by-product or a side effect of sexuality. Going against Laplanche's later claims that sexuality must come from without, entirely from the seduction of the other, we can see that the instinct itself, the supposedly non-, or rather presexual always had/has the potential to be perverted, to be contaminated or tinged by sexuality. In other words, it is/was always *pervertible*.

In one and the same movement sexuality becomes the conditions of possibility and impossibility for the instinct. In other words, being weak, premature, and pervertible means that there is no—nor was there ever—a pure instinct, which is then subsequently corrupted by sexuality. The instinct was always imperfect, and it can only become perverted precisely because it is itself weak, premature, and pervertible. As such, Laplanche himself writes,

> The entire instinct with its own "source," "pressure," "aim," and "object," as we have defined them; the instinct, kit and caboodle with its four factors, is in turn the source of a process which mimics, displaces, and denatures it: the *Trieb* [*L'instinct tout entier avec lui-même sa "source." sa "poussée," son "but," et son "objet" tels que nous les avons définis, l'instinct, armes et bagages avec ses quatre facteurs, est à son tour source du processus qui le mime, le déplace, et le dénature: la pulsion*]. (LD 22/39)

It is important to emphasize here that the instinct is the source of its own undoing in the process which comes to mimic, displace, and denature *itself* [*se dénature*], which Laplanche calls the *Trieb*. The *Trieb*, then, is just the continuous process of the instinct perverting itself. Thus, what we were calling the perversion of the instinct, that is, the derivation-deviation-drifting of infantile sexuality from the instinct is nothing other than the work of the *Trieb* internal to the instinct perverting and denaturing itself.

On the one hand, as we have shown, the *Trieb* is split from within: it is split between the natural instinctual foundation from which it emerges, but never escapes, and the perverse search of extra-instinctual pleasure. On the other hand, the instinct itself is structured by dehiscence, as it is split from within and divided against itself because it is made possible by and gives rise to the extra-instinctual. As such, *Trieb* and instinct, or perhaps *Trieb*-instinct, become two moments or points of inflection, that while irreducible to each other, nonetheless remain part of the same self-differentiating process in which the instinct *se dénature*, is denatured or denatures itself. However, it is important for us to remark that the self-denaturing of the instinct is part of the nature of the instinct itself. Perhaps, then, we could say that infantile sexuality qua *Trieb* is the auto-hetero-perversion of the instinct— in the sense that it is the self-differentiated and self-differentiating nature of the pervertible instinct that gives rise to the very *Trieb* that perverts it.

Conclusion

No Exceptions

By taking Freud's confrontation with popular opinion seriously, that is, by taking popular opinion as seriously as Freud himself did, we were led to the seemingly paradoxical claim that sexuality is an innate perversion. This is because the *Trieb*, that through which sexuality becomes manifest, is in all cases only secondarily soldered to the object. Tracing sexuality all the way back its origins in infancy, we discovered that infantile sexuality emerges, so to speak, in the care relation as a perversion of the vital instincts, that is, as derivation-deviation-drifting from the instinctual object and soldering to extra-instinctual substitute objects. In this way, the *Trieb* comes to name the self-differentiating process whereby the pervertible, weak instinct undoes itself and gives rise to the extra-instinctual forces known as infantile sexuality that pervert those very instincts. By hijacking the functional purpose of the instinct and breaking with the supposed inherent teleology of it, infantile sexuality diverts toward new aims and objects. As such, we said that infantile sexuality has what we might call a "weak directionality," insofar as it still has a directionality; it still tends toward aims and objects, even though the routes it takes to get there may be circuitous and always open to exchange and sublimation. In fact, what we discovered is that infantile sexuality is so perverse that it can, through various vicissitudes, come to mimic what popular opinion called the "*Geschlechtstrieb*," or what Laplanche and others have insisted on calling "instinctual," "pubertal," or "adult" sexuality.

On the one hand, then, when it comes to sexuality, whatever is considered to be normal and natural turns out to be quite perverse, that is, just another perversion of the instinct. On the other hand, what was considered to be abnormal and perverse ends up being itself natural, that is, part of the very nature of sexuality. Since sexuality is, by its very nature, a perversion of the instinct, there is no exceptional form of sexuality, as every manifestation of sexuality is just one vicissitude of infantile sexuality among others.

For example, what popular opinion, Laplanche, and others consider an "adult" sexual instinct no longer enjoys its privileged status as an exception to infantile sexuality. This is not meant to gloss over the fact that, from a certain perspective, so-called adult heterosexuality might constitute something like a statistical majority. However, by treating sexuality as a problem, Freud forces us to consider how heterosexual intercourse, reproduction, and child rearing—although they seem to be natural and, moreover, to constitute a statistical majority—nonetheless turn out to be much less "straight" than we often think. On the one hand, the vicissitudes resulting in heterosexual intercourse, reproduction, or child rearing are so circuitous and complex that they often come into direct conflict not only with the subject's well-being and self-preservation, but also their own supposed heterosexuality. On the other hand, the libidinal and psychical shifts necessary for reproduction and child rearing to take place extend well beyond puberty and the supposed instinct for heterosexual intercourse and reproduction—so much so that those who are not considered heterosexual adults can nonetheless desire to have and raise children.

Furthermore, this nonexceptionality of sexuality is so radical that not even asexuals, who consider themselves to be exempt from sexuality as such, seem to be able to escape the clutches of sexuality. Sure, the asexual might not conform to popular opinion's definition of sexuality in terms of the *Geschlechtstrieb* or pursue pleasure in ways that we often think of as sexual. However, to be alive at all, to have survived their prolonged state of prematurational helplessness, the asexual must have also passed through the care relation in which their vital instincts were perverted. This is not to mention how Freud's expanded concept of sexuality includes much more than intercourse or masturbation, but perhaps all forms of extra-instinctual pleasure.

However, in many contemporary discourses concerning sexuality we still discover trends that seek, on the one hand, to treat sexuality as such like an exception or, on the other hand, to grant one's own sexuality exceptional status. For example, Lacanian-inspired philosophers have sought to turn sexuality itself into a point of departure for making broad philosophical claims. As such, human sexuality is often treated as an exception to the rest of nature—a privileged position from which general claims about nature and ontology can be made.[1] For example, in a text that is, without a doubt, highly influential for this work, *What Is Sex?*, Alenka Zupančič claims that sex is a position from which, and perhaps the only position from which, one can understand the fundamental conflict undergirding reality (Zupančič 2017, 4). Zupančič goes so far as to claim that sex is a "concept that formulates a persisting contradiction of reality," "not as an ultimate reality, but as an inherent twist, or stumbling block, of reality" (Zupančič 2017, 3). For Zupančič and others, sexuality bequeaths a sort of Hegelian project—one of understanding how, to paraphrase Hegel himself, Substance becomes sexual, that is, how nature, or reality itself, must be structured in order for something like sexuality to have emerged from it in the first place. Slavoj Žižek, as a paradigmatic example, seems to take the denaturing of the instinct in the genesis of sexuality as a point at which we can understand the very denaturalization of nature itself.[2] In light of Freud's theory of sexuality, however, we might ask: if by its very nature there is no exceptional sexuality, does it make sense to then turn around and treat sexuality itself as a privileged perspective from which we can make general claims about nature and ontology? It at least does not go without saying how sexuality can be such an exceptional place for doing so.

For what it is worth, Freud seems to take the opposite approach in his own work. For example, in his "The Question of a *Weltanschauung*," Freud will explicitly claim that psychoanalysis itself is "unfit" to construct a *Weltanschauung* for itself, so it accepts that of the modern natural sciences (SE 22:158–59/GW 15: 170–71). As a modern natural scientist, then, Freud sought to situate himself in a tradition that conceives of nature as inherently nonteleological, so it should not surprise us that Freud's research leads him to the conclusion that sexuality—itself natural and a nonexceptional part of nature—is also nonteleological. In fact, we can see the stakes of this position in a brief debate that unfolded during a meeting of the Vienna Psychoanalytic Society. In a 1911 meeting of the Vienna Psychoanalytic Society, Freud was challenged by one of his colleagues, Rudolf Reitler, who claimed that Freud himself held too "teleological" of a view of infantile masturbation in the 1910 version of his *Three Essays*. In the passage under scrutiny, Freud writes: "It is difficult to overlook Nature's purpose of establishing the future primacy of sexual activity exercised by this erotogenic zone [i.e., the genital zone] by means of early infantile masturbation, which scarcely a single individual escapes" (SE 7: 188).[3] We can see that Reitler is certainly justified to criticize Freud here for upholding a teleological view of infantile masturbation. In fact, Freud seems to fall prey here to the very logic that popular opinion employs in order to define the norm of sexuality in terms of the *Geschlechtstrieb*—namely, that because a statistical majority seems to conform to a certain practice, it must then be natural. By following Freud's own logic, which we have described in detail in chapter 1, we can see that just because a vast majority of people are unable to "escape" genital masturbation during childhood does not imply that it is "Nature's purpose." Such an idea would fly in the face of Freud's entire theory of sexuality as we have spelled it out above. And this is perhaps the risk in using sexuality as a privileged position from which to make general claims about nature, since errors in our understanding about a concept as complicated and confusing as sexuality could, then, seem to generate errors in our understanding of nature, whether teleological or not.

Under the duress of Reitler's criticism, Freud promises to strike the passage from the subsequent editions of the *Three Essays*, and he does so, taking with it any claims that he makes about nature as such or its purpose.[4] However, there is one aspect of Reitler's criticism of which Freud will not let go. After acknowledging his criticism, Freud turns around and charges Reitler himself for putting forward an understanding of nature that is too "anthropocentric" and too "teleological" in his own account of infantile masturbation.

> Reitler seems to me to take too anthropocentric a view of the way in which Nature pursues her aims—as though it were a question of her carrying through a single purpose, as is the case with human activity. But so far as we can see, in natural processes a whole number of aims are pursued alongside one another, without interfering with one another. If we are to speak of Nature in human terms, we shall have to say that she appears to us to be what, in the case of men, we should call inconsistent [*inkonsequent*]. For my part, I think Reitler should not attach so much weight to his own teleological views. (SE 12: 247–48/GW 8: 337)

According to Freud, Reitler attempts to model nature on the human search for utility, presupposing that Nature pursues a single aim that is planned out and determined in advance. As such, Reitler's teleological understanding of infantile masturbation presupposes, subtends, or implies a teleological conception of nature. However, if we were to take Reitler's anthropological model of nature seriously, then we would have to say that nature is, instead, "inconsistent" precisely insofar as, according to the modern natural sciences, nature is nonteleological. The question, then, becomes: if nature does not assign purpose to sexuality, why is it still nonetheless the case that scarcely a single individual can escape infantile masturbation?

The difference here between Freud, on the one hand, and Zupančič and company, on the other, is subtle. This is especially so because Zupančič and those like her have been developing very nuanced readings of the psychoanalytic theory of sexuality, on which the present study has drawn. Furthermore, Zupančič and others have used the psychoanalytic theory of sexuality to describe nature in terms that look very similar to what here Freud is calling "inconsistent" qua nonteleological. Nonetheless there is a difference, and the difference lies in the questions each project is led to ask and pursue. Freud is led to a much different set of questions than those concerning what sexuality might tell us about the fundamental nature of nature and ontology. As we have argued, the main concerns animating Freud's psychoanalytic project have to do with the fact that, despite sexuality being inherently nonteleological, we nonetheless have to account for how sexuality comes to take on what we have been calling a "weak directionality." At a general level, the questions guiding Freud's project seem to be: How, despite the nonteleological or inconsistent nature of the *Trieb*, does anyone become attracted, or soldered, to anyone or anything? And why, for that matter, despite the fact that sexuality can come to tinge any human activity, do individuals often seem to pursue pleasure and satisfaction through highly specific acts? And, moreover, how can we account for all of this within the framework of the inconsistent and nonteleological nature of nature while considering sexuality itself as a problem?

In other contemporary discourses there has also been a renewed interest in naturalism; or perhaps better said, there has been a renewed interest in challenging the very naturalizing gesture that has historically and traditionally entrenched a hierarchy between the natural and the nonnatural—a gesture for which Freud is often condemned by such discourses for repeating.[5] Across many different disciplines, there has been a movement to put traditional explanations of nature into question because they are arguably responsible for shoring up the naturalistic ideologies that justify oppressive hierarchies and social structures.[6] The rallying cry for these various disciplines has been to dismantle these "problematic" naturalistic assumptions by *denaturalizing them*.[7]

By "denaturalizing," it is often meant that we should be skeptical of and contest any naturalistic discourse precisely because it always risks treating social structures as natural, in the sense of timeless, unchanging, unalterable, or guaranteed by some supposedly inviolable and incontestable law of nature. Often, to denaturalize is to point out that any given social structure is not natural in this way, but rather produced by human beings. As such, denaturalizing seeks to complicate the picture of nature as the guarantor of and justification for normative hierarchies. They are not natural in the sense of being timeless and unalterable because they have a history in the development of human society. By showing that any so-called natural category is itself constructed and nonnatural, the binary between, say, the normal and the perverse loses its supposed natural foundation and opens up opportunities for change.

For our purposes, we can see how this denaturalizing gesture is applied to sexuality.[8] Contemporary critical theorists, often under the heading of "queer theory," argue that certain sociohistorical structures and discourses have been put in place to make it seem as if heterosexuality is natural. Denaturalizing sexuality, then, becomes a radical gesture insofar as, on the one hand, it contests the natural status of heterosexuality and, on the other hand, it grants an exceptional status to nonnormative sexualities. As exceptions, then, those with nonnormative sexualities seem to enjoy a sort of privileged access to epistemology,[9] temporality,[10] politics,[11] or even secret forms of pleasure.[12] At the very least nonnormative sexualities have the possibility, by their very nature as nonnormative, of not only challenging heteronormativity, but also of becoming exempt from the problematic logic and practices of heteronormativity.

However much these discourses might question the natural status of the heterosexual norm by denaturalizing sexuality, we might still be left with a number of questions in light of our present study. It must be said that the point of questioning this denaturalizing gesture is not, just as was the case at the end of chapter 5, to reestablish or justify a normative conception of nature or any oppressive systems such a naturalistic ideology might undergird. But rather, the point is to emphasize that things are much more complicated. For such a conception of sexuality as perversion challenges not only the normativity that is often at stake in the naturalizing gesture, but it also calls into question the radicality of the denaturalizing gesture itself. We have already seen how in seeking to uphold a (heterosexual) norm concerning sexuality, the popular opinion of Freud's time did violence to itself at its own hands and undermined its own normative framework both theoretically and practically. Theoretically speaking, as we demonstrated in great detail in chapters 1–3, popular opinion's definition of sexuality in terms of the *Geschlechtstrieb* and the aberrations of that *Geschlechtstrieb* falls apart on its own terms. Practically speaking, heteronormativity is never enough to completely repress infantile sexuality altogether, which we demonstrated in chapters 4–6.

Like Freud, queer theorists also seek to challenge this heteronormative popular opinion, but we might still wonder whether this denaturalizing gesture might itself constitute a new form of popular opinion. For if the very nature of sexuality as such is perversion, how much sense does it make to treat certain sexualities as exceptional due entirely to their deviation from a norm? To borrow a more colloquial way of expressing this problem: if all of sexuality is denaturalized and, thus, considered to be "fluid" and on a "spectrum," then it seems that this fluidity would also apply to the norm of hetero*sexuality*. On this conception, heterosexuality would become much less "straight" insofar as it, like other sexual "orientations," always contains the fluidity within itself to deviate. If, however, this fluidity were only to apply to queer, nonnormative sexualities, then the binary between the normal/natural/instinctual and the nonnormative remains intact.

In fact, whatever critical purchase the denaturalizing gesture of queer theory might have, it risks becoming just as one-sided as popular opinion because it nonetheless seems to presuppose the very binary between normality and abnormality, only to privilege the other side. Despite their differences, both sides of this contemporary version of popular opinion find themselves locked in the same logic: in one way or another, and for one reason or another, they uphold a heterosexual norm around which to articulate their position and to defend their exceptionality. We can see this in the very term *queer* of queer theory, which presupposes and depends on a heterosexual norm around which to articulate its nonnormativity and exceptionality. Without the heterosexual norm, what would it mean to be queer? Furthermore, we might even wonder why a queer theorist would challenge heteronormativity in the first place, since it seems that nonnormative sexualities—precisely because they are exceptions to the heterosexual norm—are granted privileged access to better forms of epistemology, temporality, politics, and pleasure. Would abolishing heteronormativity not also dissolve the binary and, along with it, the exceptional status of queerness in the process?

Furthermore, the denaturalizing gesture also seems to merely shift the binary to the natural qua Nature with a capital *N* and the nonnatural qua sociohistorically constructed. After all, the rhetorical force of the denaturalizing argument resides in opposing denaturalized social constructions to Nature qua external guarantor of the law and norm. However, in pitting nonnatural and denaturalized human constructions against Nature, it surreptitiously deploys an age-old conception of human beings as an exception, as superior to—or at least different and removed from—Nature. While it may, at face value, serve to reverse the hierarchy between the natural and nonnatural, it nonetheless presupposes and leaves the binary between them intact. Like popular opinion, then, it ends up trading one binary and one problem for another.

Freud's theory of sexuality, on the contrary, provides us with a way of challenging both of the one-sided aspects of the naturalizing and denaturalizing gestures by showing the dual movement at work in sexuality, which is nonetheless one and the same movement. On the one hand, the perverse effects of sexuality remain internal, but never completely reducible, to the natural instinct from which it arises. On the other hand, sexuality qua relatively autonomous derivation-deviation-drifting from the instinct reveals that the instinct itself was always structurally pervertible, insofar as the possibility for perversion is already part of the very nature of the instinct itself. However, we must once again emphasize the dual movement at work here in the auto-hetero-perversion of the instinct: human nature is pervertible, and perversion itself is part of human nature. In other words, human nature itself is inconsistent, insofar as it produces itself and its perversion in the auto-hetero-perversion of the vital instincts. We have to take both aspects of this movement seriously—especially if we want to critique, challenge, and dismantle those traditional naturalizing gestures but, more importantly, if we dare to go beyond the framework of problematization itself.

As Derrida notes in a response to some questions about the relation between deconstruction and childhood during a conference held in 2003, the word "problem"—taken from the ancient Greek noun "*problêma*"—can be understood not only as an obstacle that confronts us, but also as a shield or something that is meant to cover and protect us (Cixous & Derrida 2019, 151). Derrida plays on the more defensive connotations of "*problêma*" in order to claim that the tradition of problematization itself constitutes a shielding—a building up of a fortress even—against what is truly disturbing, that is, precisely what cannot itself be problematized (Cixous & Derrida 2019, 151–53). According to Derrida, the gesture of problematization is, then, a gesture of mastery that seeks to censure, cover up, and cover over what resists problematization (Cixous & Derrida 2019, 151–52).

Continuously pointing out problems and compulsively problematizing them provides us with a security measure or insurance against that which cannot be mastered by problematization (Cixous & Derrida 2019, 153).

We can think of the ways in which we often take ourselves to be immune from the very problems that confront us if we simply point them out. For example, we can imagine the ways in which continuously pointing out problems concerning sexuality serves to further consolidate and protect our own sexual exceptionality and exempts us from the problems of the world. This is the case, for example, with the religious zealot who—by following the Word of God and engaging only in heterosexual intercourse after marriage for the sole purpose of procreation—is supposedly exempt from sin and the moral degradation of society brought about by the proliferation of sexual perversions. However, this might also be the case for a certain brand of queer theory that seeks to protect itself from the ills of heteronormative society by engaging in an endless process of critique, constantly pointing out the problems associated with heteronormativity and always seeking to weed out anything that smacks of heterosexuality.[13] We might even wonder how this constant preoccupation with problematizing sexuality is, indeed, just a symptom of the problem of sexuality, that is, the ways in which the so-called normal/natural and abnormal/perverse are constantly intertwining and intermingling in their impossible difference. In this way, religious zealots are always worried that their heterosexuality will be contaminated by perversion, while certain queer theorists try to prevent queer sexuality from being tainted by heterosexuality.

Yet, for Derrida, no matter how necessary, reassuring, and even valuable the gesture of problematization may be, there remains something that nonetheless pulls us beyond the problem and problematization (Cixous & Derrida 2019, 151). However, following after that which cannot be problematized is a serious and risky affair because to do so we must be willing to surrender our defenses: "The most *serious* is what one cannot even problematize. These are the questions that cannot even take the form of a problem. And thus to which we are exposed without a shield" (Cixous & Derrida 2019, 151; my emphasis). On the one hand, we must take seriously that there is something that cannot be problematized, something threatening that cannot be captured by the problem, something recalcitrant that resists problematization and, as such, elicits our defensive gesture against it. On the other hand, at the same time, we should realize that there is nonetheless something beckoning and pulling us beyond the problem itself, if we are able to resist attempts at mastering it.

Curiously enough, by taking the problem of sexuality seriously, Freud himself seems to be urging us beyond the gesture of problematization and the drive to master the problem of sexuality. In so doing, Freud seeks to uncover what was so disturbing about sexuality, endeavoring to show us how and why it becomes a problem for us in the first place. For what is it about sexuality that makes it such a problem for us? Why does popular opinion, for example, end up producing such a "problematic" response to that problem? And why, for that matter, does that lead to the entire "problematic" of problematizing popular opinion, which is put forward by, among others, certain psychoanalysts and the call for denaturalizing sexuality?

By raising these questions and pursuing them, we gradually dissolve the calcified layers of the problematization of sexuality, which eventually brings us back to what Derrida would call here "childhood." This is childhood, as Derrida reminds us, in the sense of *infans*, a state in which we were weak, caught off guard, and left completely unable to speak before the demanding and polymorphous question of sexuality (Cixous & Derrida 2019, 152–53). For, as we have seen, this a question that touches a weak spot. It is a question that is so overwhelming and powerful, so shifting and complex, so disturbing and irrepressible, that all we could do (both individually and collectively) was put up shields against it—a gesture that has been repeated for millennia. However, by confronting the weak spot of sexuality—or, our weak spot that is sexuality—we seek to shed our *problêma*, and without the safety of our exceptionality or our attempts to problematize one pole of the natural and nonnatural distinction, we are left completely helpless before the disturbing nature of sexuality. What this might mean for the future of theories and practices concerning sexuality, we do not yet know.

Notes

Preface

1. See, for example, Paul B. Preciado's influential work, *Can the Monster Speak?* This text is considered by many to be one of the most thoroughgoing criticisms of psychoanalysis in recent memory from the perspective of gender and queer theory. Yet, toward the end of the text, Preciado makes impassioned pleas for psychoanalysis to get with the times, so to speak—that is, to perform a conscientious self-critique and, moreover, to look toward a future that takes into consideration scientific advances and contemporary gender and queer theory (Preciado 2021, 85–98). The present work before you hopes, in some way, to contribute to this self-critique. However, Preciado's work addresses the psychoanalytic theory of sexuality (and gender) through their personal experience of analysis, while wrestling with a few French (mostly Lacanian) theorists. They do so while certainly mentioning Freud along the way, but not once citing him. This is not meant to take away from Preciado's provocation; rather, the present study only humbly claims that Freud's own theory of sexuality already anticipates and furnishes many of the key elements for such a self-critique of psychoanalysis.

2. Thanks to the late Phillipe Van Haute, Herman Westerink, and Ulrike Kistner, this text is presently enjoying a sort of renaissance with the recent and important publication of the 1905 version of the text in English (Freud 2016).

3. As we will see in chapter 5 of what follows, in their own work, Van Haute and Westerink use this 1905 version of the *Three Essays* to develop a peculiar strategy for reading Freud. They seek to play up certain aspects of what they see as the good Freud of 1905, who is more or less in line with contemporary gender studies and queer theory, against the bad Freud of the subsequent versions of the text who is said to be at odds with such contemporary theories. They attempt to get Freud to speak the language of queer theory, while condemning the supposedly controversial and problematic aspects of his theory of sexuality. However,

the purpose of the present study is, as stated, to let Freud speak for himself and see, instead, what sorts of challenges his theory of sexuality may present to these contemporary discourses.

4. Some, most notably Jean Laplanche, argue that Freud was often "tempted" by the biological and, thus, teleological (FB 19, 76/25, 86). In other words, that despite his occasional attempts to treat sexuality as nonteleological, he nonetheless unfortunately collapsed back into a teleological understanding of it time and again throughout his career. However, as we will show in what follows, this teleological reading of Freud is, at the very least, thrown into question once we take seriously Freud's endeavor to treat sexuality itself as a problem.

5. From his work prior to the discovery of psychoanalysis, to the early days of psychoanalysis itself, through his metapsychology, and beyond to his second topography, Freud can be seen situating himself in line with the tradition of the modern natural sciences. His "Autobiographical Study" does a wonderful job of sketching this trajectory. See also his "Question of a *Weltanschauung*," in which Freud explicitly situates the project of psychoanalysis within the scientific *Weltanschauung* (SE 22: 158–59/GW 15: 170–71).

6. Breaking with the ancient and Scholastic traditions, Sir Francis Bacon, the father of the modern empirical sciences and scientific method, claims that we must throw out final causes as an explanatory mechanism for understanding natural phenomena (Bacon 2000, 102–3). On the rationalist side of the modern tradition, no one goes further than Spinoza in attempting to rid teleology from our understanding of nature. See part I of his *Ethics* and, especially, the accompanying Appendix to part I (Spinoza 1985, 408–46). For a wonderful historical perspective on this aspect of the modern natural sciences see Alexandre Koyré's *Metaphysics and Measurement*, especially the first essay, "Galileo and the Scientific Revolution of the Seventeenth Century." In this brief, but illuminating essay, Koyré chronicles the history of the scientific revolution that he credits mainly to Galileo. Although Koyré famously focuses much of his attention on Galileo's mathematization of nature, we can see that part of what is at stake in the history that he sketches is overcoming Aristotle's natural philosophy and with it his account of (final) causality and the ways that human beings spontaneously interpret nature through their experience of it.

Introduction

1. For example, in his "Autobiographical Study," Freud writes of his later tendencies for speculation that: "Even when I have moved away from observation, I have carefully avoided any contact with philosophy proper" (SE 20: 59/GW 14: 86). For an in-depth analysis of Freud's complicated and complex relation to phi-

losophy, and especially Plato, see Elizabeth Rottenberg's excellent *For the Love of Psychoanalysis*. Rottenberg masterfully complicates Freud's own purported ambivalence to philosophy, showing a deeper connection between psychoanalysis and philosophy than Freud himself was willing to admit (Rottenberg 2019, 68–71; 81–98).

2. Freud repeatedly claims that philosophers would disagree with his conception of the unconscious. According to Freud, philosophers view the very term "unconscious" as either logically untenable or a category mistake. See, for example, among other places: "The Ego and the Id" (SE 19: 14/GW 13: 240). However, in other places, Freud will also credit certain philosophers for anticipating his idea of the unconscious; for example, see Theodor Lipps (SE 23: 286/GW 17: 147); Schopenhauer (SE 14: 15/GW 10: 53); and Nietzsche (SE 14: 15–16/GW 10: 53). Yet, Freud will ultimately claim that this very proximity forced him to avoid philosophy altogether, going so far as to say that he deprived himself of "the great pleasure of reading Nietzsche" in order not to "hamper" his psychoanalytic project. As Elizabeth Rottenberg shows, it would be a mistake, though, to understand Freud's refusal to read philosophy as a sort of insatiable drive for originality; in fact, Freud often vociferously condemned those who he saw as having a need for originality (Rottenberg 2019, 72–76).

3. See, for example, Jonathan Lear's book-length introduction to Freud, *Freud*, which is symptomatic of this gesture. In the first chapter, Lear informs the reader that his book is "unusual" as a philosophical text because it is "a philosophical introduction to a *non-philosopher*" (Lear 2005, 22). He then goes on to list all the reasons why Freud is not a philosopher but is still nonetheless important for philosophy.

4. One exception, as Alexandre Matheron shows, could be Spinoza. Matheron goes so far as to claim that Spinoza is the only philosopher to give a non-genital-centric theory of sexuality (Matheron 2020). This, as we will see, is a central concern for Freud in the *Three Essays*. Furthermore, it is curious to note that both Spinoza and Freud remain committed to nonteleological conceptions of nature. We should wonder what role this plays in their respective and related discussions of sexuality.

5. There is some notable debate about the connotations of this term in the preceding passage between ancient scholars, which as it turns out have even spilled into a Colorado courtroom (Clark 2017). However, given what Plato has to say about nonprocreative acts later in the text, in this case we are siding with Finnis and George, who claim against Nussbaum that "*tolmêma*" is not morally or legally neutral. It is interesting, though, that the debate over this term also sparked a debate about the role of nature in this passage and the rest of the dialogue (Clark 2017, 19–23). At any rate, Plato's conception of nature, it seems, is not unaffected by how he understands sexuality.

6. Interestingly, outside of the two specific instances at stake here, Plato also briefly mentions procreation in Book VI, in which he outlines several strategies and

guidelines for married couples to reproduce the best children possible (Plato 2001, 772E–773E; 775C–D; 783D–785B).

7. The present study, of course, takes quite a bit of inspiration from Alenka Zupančič's wonderful text, *What Is Sex?* However, over the course of her argument, it becomes clear that, while intimately related, the question "what is sex?" is different than the question "what is sexuality?" This will lead us to much different investigations, which we will explain in more detail in the conclusion.

8. I am considering the definitional dialogues to be the ones in which Socrates appears to be asking his interlocutor for a definition of a given virtue by asking the "what is . . . ?" question. Following Benson, I consider the following dialogues to be of the definitional sort: *Charmides, Euthyphro, Hippias Major, Laches,* Book I of the *Republic, Lysis, Protagoras, Gorgias,* and perhaps the *Meno* (Benson 1990, 126n).

9. For example, although the question "what is sexuality?" and the way that Freud arrives at it begins to look a lot like the Socratic "*ti esti*" question, and while the question is productive, and not merely rhetorical, much like Socrates's question, it is important to keep in mind that Freud's investigation will not end in *aporia*. For Freud, as we will see, psychoanalysis gives us a method for discovering what sexuality is, even if this is an unending and ever-evolving process. While psychoanalysis will demand that we develop a new logic to think about sexuality, which breaks with traditional ways of thinking about it, Freud's investigation will not be aporetic in the Socratic sense of the early dialogues.

10. As Joan Copjec points out, the child's intellectual curiosity in these sexual matters is not born from some innate principle of sufficient reason, and the problem of sexuality is not just one problem among many. It is not one that we want to solve because we simply have a drive to know: "the sexual questions of children cannot be prompted by the principle of sufficient reason, by a belief that there is a reason for everything, since this principle cannot be assumed to be innate and has no doubt not yet been acquired at this age. The queries, then, do not open a disinterested investigation, prompted by reason, into the way things work, but are, rather, self-interested. They bear directly on the child herself and are prompted by her experience of sex" (Copjec 2010, 65–66). As such, there is something unique and uniquely pressing about the problem of sexuality—the origins of which would deserve a much more rigorous treatment than is possible within the scope of the present study.

11. Even a cursory reading of Aristophanes's famous speech in the *Symposium* will show that Freud may have missed the mark when criticizing this "poetic fable" as being another instance of popular opinion. After all, Aristophanes allows for a much more diverse spectrum of sexuality, including homosexual attractions as being part of human nature. And yet, the deeper point Freud seems to be making here is that both popular opinion and the poetic fable conceive of sexuality as something defined in advance by nature. This is the problem that they share in common.

Chapter 1

1. Jonathan Lear, for example, in his philosophical introduction to Freud, titled *Freud*, argues that Freud uses the designation "popular opinion" in an effort to goad our intellectual narcissism to go beyond the vulgar beliefs of what Aristotle would have called "the many" (Lear 2005, 74–75). Similarly, in the introduction to their 1905 edition of the *Three Essays*, Phillipe Van Haute and Herman Westerink, claim that Freud's "rhetorical strategy" is to distance himself from the established body of knowledge that constitutes popular opinion Van Haute & Westerink 2016, xv). While both of these statements are true to a certain extent, reducing popular opinion to a mere rhetorical device or strategy fails to take into account the necessity of Freud's confrontation with popular opinion and its importance in the development of his theory of sexuality.

2. Harry Oosterhuis, whose views on this matter are the most virulent and extreme, goes so far as to accuse Freud of stealing and plagiarizing Albert Moll's work on sexuality (Oosterhuis 2020). Oosterhuis claims that Freud's depiction of popular opinion is a vulgarized version of Moll's (and others') theories, which he then critiqued in order to put forward his "own" theory of sexuality. For Oosterhuis, it is not popular opinion that is vulgar, but rather it is Freud's own views on sexuality, which were mere vulgarizations of his contemporaries and for which he did not give them enough credit.

3. See Jonathan Lear's comments on popular opinion in *Freud* (Lear 2005, 74–75), or Richard Wollheim's comments in *Sigmund Freud* (Wollheim 1981, 116).

4. Even during Freud's own lifetime, certain psychoanalytic trends often sought to reestablish popular opinion within a psychoanalytic framework. One can see this in Freud's vicious and vigorous polemics with Adler and Jung in "On the History of the Psychoanalytic Movement." There, Freud laments the fact that his two former colleagues had embraced a watered-down version of the psychoanalytic theory of sexuality in order to make it more palatable to the general public—that is, the very popular opinion that Freud continuously combated. However, instead of making psychoanalysis more palatable, according to Freud, all that Jung and Adler succeeded in accomplishing was a sacrifice of "the hard-won truths of psychoanalysis" (SE 14: 58/GW 10: 103). Being readily accepted by the public meant that they had lost all the true and hard-fought psychoanalytic insights into sexuality. For Freud, the psychoanalytic theory of sexuality would always necessarily, and by virtue of its very articulations and declarations, stir up the resistances of the general public precisely because it sought to challenge this very popular opinion. Any so-called psychoanalytic theory of sexuality, like those of Jung and Adler, that sought to side-step these resistances would only be putting forward a bastardized, or even nonpsychoanalytic, theory of sexuality.

5. Take the case of the father in Freud's 1920 case study, "The Psychogenesis of a Case of Homosexuality in a Woman," whose resistances and attempts to suppress his daughter's so-called deviant and degenerate homosexuality led him into a hostile confrontation with her—a confrontation that resulted in her attempted suicide. One sees Freud go on in that case study to report, among other things, the severe injurious effects that the young woman incurs in her own confrontation with the popular opinion of sexuality that is embodied in her father.

6. See also, for example, already as early as in his 1898 short essay, "Sexuality in the Aetiology of Neuroses," Freud argues that we must create a place in "public opinion" for sexual discourse, in which those who talk about sexuality will not be met with resistance. Toward the end of chapter 4 of *Civilization and Its Discontents*, Freud points again to something similar to what he had earlier called "civilized" sexual morality (SE 21: 104–5/GW 14: 463–65). Freud, of course, also begins famous and important texts such as *The Interpretation of Dreams*, *The Psychopathology of Everyday Life*, and *Jokes and their Relation to the Unconscious* by investigating something like the popular opinion of dreams, parapraxes, and jokes.

7. One needs to look no further, for example, than a text like "'Civilized' Sexual Morality and Modern Nervous Illness," an article published just three years after the first edition of the *Three Essays*, in order to see just how much weight Freud ascribes to popular opinion. There, popular opinion finds its guise under the heading of a "'civilized' sexual morality" that imposes strict prohibitions on sexuality. In this text, Freud spends some thirty-odd pages vehemently decrying both the theoretical inadequacies of popular opinion qua "civilized" sexual morality; and he is at pains to bring attention to the widespread "social injustices" that it, in turn, produces on everyone in society.

8. Some have convincingly argued that Freud clearly has in mind the authoritative scientific and medical discourses concerning sexuality, as Freud continuously wrestles with and distances himself from his contemporaries in the *Three* Essays. See, for example, Lear's comments in *Freud* (Lear 2005, 74–75); Jean-Michel Quinodoz's comments on popular opinion in *Reading Freud: A Chronological Exploration of Freud's Writings* (Quinodoz 2005, 57–59); and Van Haute and Westerink's comments in their introduction to the revised 1905 edition of the *Three Essays* (Van Haute & Westerink 2016, xxvii–xx). It has also been suggested that Freud is primarily concerned with certain religious doctrines and institutions—the very same ones that come to preoccupy him in his later works such as "'Civilized' Sexual Morality" and *Civilization and Its Discontents* (see, for example, Bompard-Porte 2019. Still others have contended that by "popular opinion" Freud simply means the average, everyday person's spontaneous ideas about sexuality. For example: Jonathan Lear in his philosophical introduction to Freud likens the designation "popular opinion" to Aristotle's appeal to the "beliefs of 'the many'" (Lear 2005, 74–75), and Gayle Salamon, in *Assuming a Body*, claims that Freud seeks to marshal his scientific knowledge against the errors of popular opinion, or what is commonly believed (Salamon 2010, 14–15). Freud himself is

often at pains to point out, for example, in his essay "On the Sexual Theories of Children," that parents, his patients, and even children all have their own ideas about, or theories of, sexuality (SE 9: 212/GW 7: 174). Furthermore, it is also clear that Freud has in mind a certain philosophical tradition starting with Plato, whose "poetic fable" Freud will explicitly tie to popular opinion at the opening of the *Three Essays* (SE 7: 136/GW 5: 34).

9. See, for example, his letter to an American mother, which was written in 1935 (Freud 1951). There Freud claims that psychoanalysis is not in the business of curing patients of their homosexuality but working through their neurotic illnesses. Freud famously claims in this letter that homosexuality is not the indication of some innate mental defect or degeneracy.

Chapter 2

1. In her *For the Love of Psychoanalysis*, Elizabeth Rottenberg demonstrates the way in which Laplanche is led to protect, in a somewhat paradoxical manner, the perversion of sexuality from philosophy. She demonstrates how and why Laplanche must protect sexuality from, on the one hand, Plato's vitalistic Eros and, on the other hand, from Hegel and Heidegger's philosophy of death (Rottenberg 2019, 95). There is a "strangely paradoxical way," she points out, that Laplanche is forced to protect the perversity of sexuality from a subsequent perversion of sexuality by philosophy—a perversion of perversion is, it seems, one perversion too many.

2. For example, in *Totem and Taboo*, Freud repudiates the idea that there could be an "innate instinct" that would account for the revulsion toward incestual relations (SE 13: 122, 124/GW 9: 148, 151). The term used there is "*Instinkt*." Later in the text, it is worth also noting that in his discussion of Trotter's "group instinct" or "herd instinct" Freud leaves the term "*instinct*" in the English original. Yet, Freud explicitly opts for the German term "*Trieb*" in the title of that section: *Herdtrieb*. It is not clear whether this means that Freud found the words interchangeable or whether he is seeking to make a distinction of some sort between Trotter's herd instinct and his own *Herdtrieb*.

3. Since I try to consistently employ the word *Trieb* to denote the concept that Freud develops under the heading of this term (and not *drive* or *instinct*), I have decided to leave this title in the original French so as not to introduce confusion by suddenly inserting the word *drive* into the discussion. However, I still cite the relevant passages in the English edition.

4. Although it is not used as often as the term "*Trieb*," Freud nonetheless wrote the word "*Instinkt*" in some form or another many times throughout his work. Alex Holder claims that the term "*Instinkt*" only appears in five of Freud's texts, and in four out of the five times in reference to what Freud calls an "instinct in animals" (Holder 1970, 19). While Holder is correct that Freud does often use

this term in relation to what he calls an "instinct in animals," Freud can be seen to use the word in more (con)texts. Its usage stretches from texts as early as "Sexuality in the Aetiology of Neuroses" all the way until *Moses and Monotheism*. Moreover, there seem to be a number of ways in which he used it more or less systematically, which I have grouped into four categories.

1. Animal Instinct: Outside of the instances that we have already cited where he uses the term "*Instinkt*," Freud most often employs the idea of an instinct, the instinctual, or an instinctive impulse when referring to what he calls an "instinct in animals," which occurs in the following works: "The Unconscious" (SE 14: 195/GW 10: 294); "Thoughts for the Times on War and Death" (SE 14: 293/GW 10: 345); "An Infantile Neurosis" (SE 17: 120/GW 12: 156); *New Introductory Lectures on Psychoanalysis* (SE 22: 106/GW 15: 113); and *Moses and Monotheism* (SE 23: 100, 133/GW 16: 207–8, 241).

2. Reactive Instincts: In his earlier works, Freud occasionally uses the term to describe lower or base instincts in "The Sexual Aetiology of the Neuroses" (SE 3: 278/GW 1: 509); instincts for fear in *Studies on Hysteria* (SE 2: 87/GW 1: 143); instincts for cleanliness in *The Interpretation of Dreams* (SE 4: 239/GW 2: 245) and also motherhood in the same text (SE 4: 252/GW 2: 258); and instinctive movements in "Delusions and Dreams in Jensen's *Gravida*" (SE 9: 29/GW 7: 54). It is also used to describe the mind's instinctive aversion to pain in "On Transience" (SE 14: 306/GW 10: 359). There are also instincts for heroism in "Dostoevsky and Parricide" (SE 21: 178n/GW 14: 401n) and "Thoughts for the Times on War and Death" (SE 14: 296/GW 10: 351). And there is mention of an instinct for/of understanding in "Inhibitions, Symptoms, and Anxiety" (SE 20: 168/GW 14: 201).

3. Instinctive Resistances to Psychoanalysis: Freud also uses the term systematically to describe instinctual or instinctive resistances to psychoanalysis or psychoanalytic theory: *Interpretation of Dreams* (SE 4: xxvi/GW 2: x); *Three Essays*: (SE 7: 164/GW 5: 64); *Introductory Lectures on Psychoanalysis* (SE 15: 16/GW 11: 8); *Introductory Lectures on Psychoanalysis*: (SE 15: 219/GW 11: 219); and "Dreams and Telepathy" (SE 18: 204/GW 13: 172).

4. Citing the Work of Others: The other set of instances occur when Freud is quoting others either in German, like Frazer in *Totem and Taboo* (SE 13: 123/GW 9: 150); Dr. Eduard Hitschmann in *Psychopathology of Everyday Life* (SE 6: 124/GW 4: 137); or Alphonse

Maeder's theory that dreams are similar to the innate instincts for play found in animals and children (SE 5: 579/GW 3: 585n). He also cites a number of Frenchmen who use the French cognate "*instinct*": E. Gley in French *Three Essays* (SE 7: 143n/GW 5: 42n); in the *Interpretation of Dreams* when citing Maury (SE 4: 73/ GW 2: 77); in *Totem and Taboo* when citing Reinach (SE 13: 113/GW 9: 137); and Gustave Le Bon in *Totem and Taboo* (SE 18: 79–81/ GW 13: 84–86). Citing the Italian, Angelo Conti, in "Leonardo da Vinci and a Memory of his Childhood" (SE 11: 109/GW 8: 180). He also cites a German translation of Norwegian playwright Henrik Ibsen's *Roseholm* in "Some Character-Types Met with in Psycho-Analytic Work" (SE 14: 327/GW 10: 384). And last, he cites a number of anglophone figures—some of which we have already pointed out—like Garth Wilkinson in "A Note on the Prehistory of the Technique of Analysis" (SE 18: 264/GW 12: 310).

5. Here I cite the original French text only. The English translation of this passage seems to indicate that Freud never wrote the word *official* (Lacan 1999b, 708), when it seems more likely that what Lacan meant was that Freud never wrote the word *instinct*. At any rate, this seems to be the passage in question to which Laplanche refers.

6. The status of this opposition becomes a problem for Laplanche in much the same way that we claimed sexuality becomes a problem for popular opinion. In certain places, Laplanche seems to maintain a hard-and-fast opposition between the *Trieb* and instinct in order to keep them separate and to protect the former from being contaminated by the latter. However, in other places, there are many instances in which Laplanche's understanding of the *Trieb* and the instinct begins to undermine, blur, or even deconstruct this very opposition. What becomes clear in reading his work, however, is that for Laplanche the threat of the instinct is always lurking around every corner, and one must always remain suspicious of a *rabattement* or a *fourvoiement* to/from the instinct. This is what leads Laplanche to try to prune Freud's texts and constantly seek to separate a bad instinctual Freud from the good perverse Freud. Ultimately, Laplanche's determined attempt to keep the instinct and *Trieb* separate in Freud's work inevitably leads him into a sexual problem of his own—the symptom of which is that he eventually, later in his career, posits an opposition between a so-called adult *sexual instinct* and the (infantile and polymorphously perverse) *Trieb* (Pul. 22, 25/22, 25). Also see: (Laplanche 2008a, 101; 2008d, 198; 2011b; 2011d). In order to keep the *Trieb* free of the instinct and to preserve the perversity of (infantile) sexuality, Laplanche is forced to claim—much like popular opinion, it must be said—that heterosexual copulation and reproduction is a sexual instinct that is opposed to the *Trieb* of (infantile) sexuality proper. We will return to a detailed discussion of this in chapter 6.

7. From here on out, I will keep the title of this important work in the original French. In English, the title of the work has been translated as *The Temptation of Biology: Freud's Theories of Sexuality*. Such a tendentious translation unfortunately risks turning, from the very outset, what is a complex problem that Freud encounters in his study of sexuality into a mere idiosyncratic quirk on Freud's part to be tempted to favor biology over his own psychoanalytic insights. As we will see, the French term, *fourvoiement*, means something along the lines of a "going-astray." We will argue that much more than a misguided temptation for biology, it was sexuality itself that constantly sent Freud toward and away from biology—an insight Laplanche himself acknowledges in the text.

8. Laplanche will, however, come to endorse a certain brand of qualified pansexualism, which he sees as challenging this sort of vulgar pansexualism that desexualizes sexuality. See, for example, his interview with Cathy Caruth (Caruth and Laplanche 2001), and the last chapter of *Life and Death of Psychoanalysis*.

9. Such is the case with, for example, Melanie Klein and her followers (FB 110–11/123–24), for whom, according to Laplanche, certain fantasies come prepackaged with the infant from birth (FB 12–13, 45, 52, 75/19, 54, 61, 86). If such fantasies are innate, then all of fantasmatic life and, thus, sexuality as such risks becoming instinctual.

10. As Laplanche quips, echoing Freud who echoes Charcot: "but that doesn't prevent self-preservation from existing [*mais cela n'empêche pas l'autoconservation d'exister*], and that doesn't prevent us from referring to it in order to have a view of what psychoanalysis (and sexuality) is in the human being" (FB 111/124).

11. For the difficulties of translating *Trieb* into English, see, for example, Abensour (2014), Kistner (2016), and Solms (2013). For the difficulties and influences of the translation of *Trieb* into French, see, for example, Quinodoz (2011), Laplanche and Pontalis (2009), and Bourguignon (1989).

12. It is worth mentioning at the outset here that this is a translation choice that Freud himself is never reported as having repudiated. Bruno Bettelheim, in his text *Freud and Man's Soul*, ascribes this to Freud's voluntary ignorance of how his work was being translated into English (Bettelheim 1984, 80). According to Bettelheim, Freud had no interest in the anglophone, especially American, world and did not care how his book would have been translated for such a crude and undereducated audience. (*Freud and Man's Soul* is pervaded by a derisive attitude toward American intellectual life and scholarship; see, for example, but certainly not limited to, chapters 5 and 6 of this work). These claims, however, have been rather easily refuted (Davidson 1983). In fact, in the present case, Freud had no need to repudiate the translation of "*Trieb*" as "instinct" because he can be shown to have implicitly supported this translation choice on an etymological and theoretical level. For example, in his own translation work, when translating the work of James Jackson Putnam from English into German, Freud renders the English word "*instinct*" into German as "*Trieb*." This seems to be further corroborated by

the fact that Freud likewise renders the French cognate of *"instinct"* (*"instinct"*) into German as *"Trieb."* In this way, Freud himself, it seems, at least implicitly, found the term *instinct* (and its cognates) capable of capturing what is at stake in the German term *Trieb*.

13. See the footnote above on Freud's usage of the word *"instinct."*

14. See, for example, Adrian Johnston's *Time Driven: Metapsychology and the Splitting of the Drive* (Johnston 2005, 156–69); Dylan Evans's *An Introductory Dictionary of Lacanian Psychoanalysis* (Evans 1996, 46–49); and Holder's "Instinct and Drive" excerpt from the *Basic Psychoanalytic Concepts on the Theory of Instincts* (Holder 1970, 21). Ulrike Kistner argues that the source of this particular distinction between *Trieb* and instinct has primarily grown out of a French, and specifically Lacanian and Laplanchean, psychoanalytic reading of Freud's texts (Kistner 2016, lxxx).

15. See, for example, Teresa de Laurentis's article, "The Stubborn Drive" (de Laurentis 1998, 852n.). De Laurentis's case is especially interesting because after lambasting Strachey's supposed mistranslation translation of "*Trieb*" as "instinct," she then explicitly decides to use both "*instinct*" and "*drive*" more or less interchangeably in the rest of her article to talk about the *Trieb*.

16. See Solms (2013), Kistner (2016, lxxx), and Whiteside (2006).

17. See Laplanche and Pontalis's *Language of Psychoanalysis* (Laplanche and Pontalis 2009, 360).

18. See Lacan's "Subversion of the Subject and Dialectic in the Freudian Unconscious" (Subv. 803/680).

19. Not only, according to Strachey, was the word *drive* used as a noun in this context not to be found in *The Oxford English Dictionary*, it would also be impossible to find an adequate adjectival form of *drive* that could capture the German word *Triebhaft* (Strachey 1953, xxv–xxvi). To do so would require yet another neologism. This is a problem that commentators and translators of Freud's work have continued to struggle with: drivenness? drive character? perhaps, drive-al? drive-ual? None of these neologisms, or any other for that matter, prove to be elegant enough for Strachey's portrayal of Freud as a turn-of-the-century "English man of science," which the former hoped to convey in his translation. For an excellent account of this aspect of Strachey's translation see Elizabeth's Rottenberg's *For the Love of Psychoanalysis* (Rottenberg 2019, 180–82).

20. By allying translation with hermeneutics later in his career, in texts such as "Psychoanalysis as Anti-Hermeneutics," Laplanche seems to situate translation in such a way that it becomes opposed to the work of psychoanalysis. Ultimately, according to Laplanche, translation works on the side of *repression* (Laplanche 1999a, 250; 1996, 9), sedimenting translations over the unconscious, distorting it, suppressing it, shutting it up (Laplanche 1999a, 252; 1996, 10), and it is the work of psychoanalysis to undo precisely these translations. For more on Laplanche's understanding of the relation between translation and analysis see Ramos (2022).

21. In an early article, "Interpreting (with) Freud," Laplanche sets out to sketch the basic methodological considerations guiding and animating his return to Freud, a return to which he will return again and again. With the publication of this article, the question of method—of *how* precisely to return to Freud, of *how*, moreover, to interpret Freud—becomes the privileged point of departure for his engagement with Freud's work. In this article, Laplanche seeks not only to elaborate on Freud's method of psychoanalytic interpretation—underscoring its singularity and originality—but also begins to articulate the specificity of his own approach to Freud's work. For Laplanche, these two projects are, and will continue to be, inextricably and necessarily woven together: to return to Freud—to interpret Freud [*with Freud*]—*demands a method of interpreting Freud's work that is in accord with the latter's own method of interpretation*. As he puts it in *Le fourvoiement biologisant chez Freud*: "Interpreting Freud with Freud at the level of *exigence* is to decompose, to adapt *mutatis mutandis* Freud's very rules of dissolution, in order to go eventually to the things and recompose them otherwise right before our eyes, precisely from the *exigence* of the object" (FB 6/13). See, again, Ramos (2022).

22. For Laplanche and his translation team's extended discussion on the topic see Bourguignon (1989, 11–12).

23. Freud, as we will see, decided to drop this preface from 1915 onward. As such, it is not published in the 1924 edition and, therefore, did not find its way into the *Gesammelte Werke*. This is why the GW is not cited here.

24. The only "new research" that Freud introduces to the 1910 edition is a quick reference to a case study carried out in the intervening years between the publication of the first and second edition: that is, the case study of Little Hans (SE 7: 193–94n/GW 5: 94n), in which Freud tries to back up claims he made about infantile sexuality with some "direct" observation. How direct this observation truly was is certainly an interesting question, since Freud himself did not conduct the case study himself. Freud famously guided Little Hans's father in the psychoanalytic treatment of the young boy and received all his information about the case from the father.

25. See Strachey's note: SE 17: 7n.

26. For example, in light of essays such as "Triebe und Triebschicksale," a full paragraph is added in which Freud declares that the *Trieb* is a "concept lying on the frontier between the mental and the somatic" (SE 7: 168/GW 5: 67). This phrasing is taken almost verbatim from "Triebe und Triebschicksale."

27. We can see that for Freud even though the war neuroses presented psychoanalysis with a difficult problem, he never shied away from the important role sexuality played in the development of neuroses. See, for example his remarks in his "Autobiographical Study," in which he claims: "The war neuroses, they said, had proved that sexual factors were unnecessary to the aetiology of neurotic disorders. But their triumph was frivolous and premature" (SE 20: 54/GW 14: 80). The fact

that he returns to champion the lasting importance of this text at a time when the war neuroses are threatening the psychoanalytic theory of sexuality, only provides more evidence for the importance of sexuality in psychoanalysis.

28. Of course, the reference to Plato's Eros here harkens us back to Freud's "far-reaching" speculation in *Beyond the Pleasure Principle*, which was largely written in 1919 and published in 1920, where the hypothesis of *Lebenstrieb* and *Todestrieb*, life and death drives, Eros and Thanatos, are posited for the first time. Although the life and death *Triebe* never appear explicitly in the *Three Essays*, Freud's reference to Plato here indicates that it was playing a major role in his thought at the time.

29. In 1924, Freud also points readers to his 1924 article, "The Economic Problem of Masochism" (1924), seeming to indicate his attempt to square the *Three Essays* with his famous second topography (SE 7: 158n/GW 5: 57n).

Chapter 3

1. For Althusser, the specific problems that psychoanalysis confronts in specifying the *Trieb* have to do with the specificity of psychoanalysis as a scientific practice. In the academic year 1963–1964, roughly a decade before he wrote "The Discovery of Doctor Freud," and about one year before he invited Lacan to begin giving his annual seminars at *l'École normale supérieure* (after the latter's infamous "excommunication" from the IPA), Althusser himself held a seminar at the ENS addressing Lacan and psychoanalysis. During this period, Althusser tried vigorously to combat what he saw as certain ideological, that is, psychological importations of Freud's work into France. This was mostly due to what he—and notably Laplanche for very similar reasons (Laplanche and Leclaire 1981)—saw as the predominant influence of Georges Politzer's *Critique des fondements de la Psychologie* in France, especially in the work of Merleau-Ponty and Sartre (Althusser 1996d, 12; 1996c, 33–4n). (The texts in particular under both Althusser and Laplanche's scrutiny are Sartre's *The Transcendence of the Ego*, the sections of *Being and Nothingness* on existential psychoanalysis [Sartre 1943, 602–21], Merleau-Ponty's Introduction to Hesnard's *L'œuvre de Freud* [Merleau-Ponty 1982], and Merleau-Ponty's *Phenomenology of Perception* [Merleau-Ponty 2002, 182–85].) As such, Althusser initially found a worthy ally in Lacan, whose own polemics against psychological interpretations of Freud's work are well known. See, for example, Martin Murray's *Jacques Lacan: A Critical Introduction*, in which he seeks to document the importance of Lacan's opposition to psychology in the development of his work (Murray 2016, 88–89).

2. Psychoanalysis presents Althusser with the perfect example of the ways in which a science is formed in and through its putting into question and breaking with ideology, which retroactively constitutes ideology as ideology in this very

process (Althusser 1996d, 49–50; 1996c, 79–80). With Freud's discovery of the unconscious, not only is the specificity of psychoanalysis made manifest as a science whose precise object is the unconscious, but also the methodological shortcomings, undetermined presuppositions, and ideological underpinnings of nonpsychoanalytic disciplines, especially psychology, are laid bare. In the second session of *Psychoanalysis and the Human Sciences*, titled "Psychoanalysis and Psychology," Althusser advances his major thesis concerning the scientificity and specificity of psychoanalysis. For an excellent discussion of the way in which Althusser takes up the problematic of science and ideology, and how the sciences are shown to break with and retroactively constitute ideologies, see David Maruzzella's article, "The Two Bachelards of Louis Althusser" (Maruzzella 2019).

3. We have chosen to leave this title in the German original because Strachey's English translation as "Instincts and Their Vicissitudes" only invites the very problems of translation that we have already discussed and complicated.

4. See, for example, chapter 5 of the "Autobiographical Study."

5. See, for example, Freud's claim in "The Ego and the Id" that *Triebe* are always fused together into "alloys," that is, never found completely independent and in a pure state (SE 19: 41/GW 13: 269).

6. In the "Beilage III" to his *Die Krisis der europäischen Wissenschaften und die transzendentale Phänomenologie: Eine Einleitung in die phänomenologische Philosophie*, which later became known as and published in English as the "Origin of Geometry," Husserl declares that scientific development depends on its pronouncements being made "once and for all" (Husserl 1976, 362/373). According to Husserl, if the utterances of science do not remain in this way, then there could be no scientific progress. Otherwise, the beginning and every intermediary step would continuously have to be returned to and reactivated—a painstaking, exacting, and paralyzing project for science. No one could continue any scientific work if they were always starting over from the beginning. This, of course, for Husserl will lead to the problematic sedimentation of future utterances over the original discovery, which needs to be recovered and rescued in order to provide the true significance and meaning of any given science. This and only this is the true scientific gesture for transcendental phenomenology.

7. There is a certain strain of feminist criticism of psychoanalysis, relying heavily on the work of Luce Irigaray, that seeks to find a sort of negative theology in the border or the "in-between." In this way, the border becomes something undecidable and about which nothing can be known other than it is fluid and blurred (Irigaray 1993; 1980). See, for example, Ann-Marie Priest's, article, "Woman as God, God as Woman: Mysticism, Negative Theology, and Luce Irigaray" (Priest 2003) or Fanny Söderback's "Liminal Spaces: Reflections on the In-Between" (Söderbäck 2017). In both cases, the authors seek to use Irigaray to carve out an ineffable in-between about which nothing can be said, and it is this ineffability that makes the in-between a place of radical undecidability. Yet, it seems that the very gesture

of making a claim about something's undecidability predicates something about it (i.e., precisely its undecidability), making it at least in some ways knowable. Paradoxically, its undecidability and unknowability are known about it.

Chapter 4

1. Elizabeth Rottenberg traces Laplanche's own struggle with and against philosophy in her *For the Love of Psychoanalysis* (Rottenberg 2019, 81–87).

2. Laplanche himself always had a penchant for provoking the philosophical reader of Freud on matters concerning the *Todestrieb*. See, for example, Laplanche (1992a; 1992d; 1999a; 2020a; 2020b; 1996). He certainly set out to shock his philosophical contemporaries who, influenced either by Hegel or Heidegger, focused much of their attention on the repetition and death involved in the *Todestrieb*. See, for example, Derrida's *Life Death* seminar or Deleuze's *Difference and Repetition*.

3. Freud, of course, for example, in his *Beyond the Pleasure Principle*, will famously try to reformulate his *Trieblehre* in terms of the eternal battle between two opposing kinds of *Triebe*, namely, *Lebenstrieb und Todestrieb*. In his zeal to combat and oppose Jung's so-called monistic theory of the *Trieb*, Freud seems to force his own hand, as he declares that the only true psychoanalytic understanding of the *Trieblehre* must be dualistic (SE 18: 52–53/GW 13: 57).

4. For Laplanche, Freud will make two huge mistakes when he attempts to structure his *Trieblehre* in dualistic terms—that is, as two *Triebe* opposed to each other. On the one hand, for Laplanche, Freud is just plain wrong to declare what he calls the *Todestrieb* to be a *Trieb* at all. Laplanche quite provocatively argues that the *Todestrieb* cannot be a *Trieb*, since it does not meet the criteria of the *Trieb* qua *Sexualtrieb*, as it is spelled out primarily in the earlier editions of the *Three Essays*. After all, Laplanche argues, how could the *Todestrieb* be a *Trieb*, if it has a rigid, inherent teleology toward death decided in advance? According to Laplanche, all of Freud's somewhat convoluted and contradictory musings on the death drive all presuppose that there is some teleological aim for death determined in advance. In this way, the *Todestrieb* becomes inherently teleological and, as such, instinctual. (And thus, perhaps Strachey was right yet again when he translated this term as "death *instinct*.") On the other hand, in *Beyond the Pleasure Principle*, Freud also mistakenly subordinates sexuality to some great cosmological force, Eros, or to the *Lebenstrieb* and, in so doing, Laplanche argues, Freud also turns sexuality back into an instinct—and even worse an instinct for coupling, which should remind us of popular opinion. For Laplanche, the symptom of this confusion in Freud's work is his backpedaling on Aristophanes's myth in the *Symposium*. If in the *Three Essays* Aristophanes's "poetic fable" stands in for the most egregious form of popular opinion, why does it return favorably in *Beyond the Pleasure Principle* (Pul.

22/27–28)? For Laplanche, it is obvious that it is because popular opinion's sexual instinct has returned thinly, if at all, disguised in Freud's ruminations beyond the pleasure principle. Ultimately, Freud's attempt to go beyond the pleasure principle leaves him with two instincts—one for life and one for death. See Laplanche's article, "La pulsion de mort dans la théorie de la pulsion sexuelle" (1992b; 2020c), his article "La soi-disant pulsion de mort: une pulsion sexuelle" (1999b; 2015b), as well as some of his concluding remarks to *Le fourvoiement biologisant chez Freud* (FB 105–9/117–22).

5. In *Civilization and Its Discontents*, Freud goes so far as to equate psychoanalysis with the genetic explanation of psychical phenomena: "The idea of men's receiving an intimation of their connection with the world around them thorough the immediate feeling which is from the outset directed to that purpose sounds so strange and fits in so badly with the fabric of our psychology that one is justified in attempting to discover *a psycho-analytic—that is, a genetic—explanation* of such a feeling" (SE 21: 65/GW 14: 423).

6. Winnicott claims, "I once said: 'There is no such thing as an infant,' meaning, of course, that whenever one finds an infant one finds maternal care, and without maternal care there would be no infant" (Winnicott 1965, 40n.). Of course, this is not just limited to mothers, unless the term *mother* is a placeholder for anyone who intervenes to take care of the infant.

7. When taking Freud's idea of *Nachtraglichkeit*, or *après-coup*, into consideration, it becomes impossible to locate a specific moment when sexuality emerges. For a discussion of *Nachtraglichkeit* and Freud and Laplanche's complication and problematization of the physical and temporal "locatability" in psychoanalysis, see Rottenberg (2019, 26–34).

8. The reason that it is so important to highlight the fact that Freud added the first characteristic of infantile sexuality in 1915 is because it is the characteristic on which Laplanche will focus his entire reading of infantile sexuality in *Life and Death in Psychoanalysis*. This would be one insight lost if we were to follow his orders and prune away the post-1905 additions to the text.

9. Now for Laplanche, sexuality must come *entirely* from without, otherwise a regression into an instinctual model is inevitable; the *Trieb* cannot just magically appear from the infant as some endogenous or innate process issuing from itself. Something must come from the outside to pervert the vital instincts from which the autoerotic activity of infantile sexuality deviates. That something coming from without for Laplanche is nothing other than the (adult) other qua caregiver. In chapter 6, we will attempt to complicate this picture.

Chapter 5

1. It is curious to note that although the authors employ the term *deconstruction* many times to describe the stakes of Freud's *Three Essays*, Derrida is not

mentioned a single time. Instead, two of Derrida's contemporaries are frequently called on in relation to this term, namely, Deleuze and Foucault.

2. The editors do note that the "Oedipal fable" is mentioned, but they claim that "one can hardly consider this an acknowledgment of a psychological Oedipal complex" (Van Haute and Westerink 2016, viiin).

3. In perhaps an ironic act of confession, Foucault himself candidly admits in a roundtable interview with a group of psychoanalysts that he did not base his reading of Freud's theory of sexuality in *The History of Sexuality, Volume 1* on Freud's *Three Essays* (Foucault 1980, 213). There, he dismisses the entire text as putting forward nothing more than a mere theory of development, which makes sexuality the secret behind the neuroses (Foucault 1980, 213). Furthermore, it must be said that Foucault does not cite or quote Freud or the *Three Essays* at any point in *The History of Sexuality*, in which Freud is mentioned by name only twelve times (Foucault 1990). As such, many commentators have pointed out that the Freud who Foucault seeks to critique in the *History of Sexuality* is very much a caricature of Freudian psychoanalysis (Ali 2019, 18–19; Copjec 2010, 69). In fact, in responding to an auditor during a talk given in 1981, Foucault himself admits that the psychoanalysis he is looking at in *The History of Sexuality* is of a Reichian and Marcusian vein (Foucault 1994, 198). Admissions such as these ultimately lead Mladen Dolar to put it most harshly when he writes: "If *History of Sexuality* is an attempt at a genealogy of psychoanalysis, then this is a genealogy singularly devoid of any statements, *énoncés*. He blatantly imputed so many views to this opponent that neither Freud nor Lacan would ever dream of espousing" (Dolar 2019, 44–45). While not without its merit, Foucault ends up with a book that critiques something like the popular opinion of psychoanalysis, and not psychoanalysis itself.

4. Van Haute and Westerink base their reading of the objectlessness of infantile sexuality on something that Freud mentions in the conclusion to the *Three Essays*, where he writes: "in childhood the sexual drive is without an object [*objektlos*], that is, autoerotic" (RTE 82). But does this statement necessarily imply that infantile sexuality is completely objectless—that is, without an object *altogether*? Even the 1905 edition of the *Three Essays* remains ambiguous on this point. In the second essay, where Freud begins his discussion of infantile sexuality, he defines autoerotism as follows (quoting again from Kistner's revised translation): "We will raise the most striking feature of this sexual activity, namely that the drive is not directed toward other persons but obtains satisfaction from one's own body. It is autoerotic, to call it by a felicitous term introduced by Havelock Ellis" (RTE 42). In this way, autoerotism would not be without an object *überhaupt*. What Freud calls the "object" here refers to the way the "sexual object" is tentatively defined at the opening of the first essay, where it is construed as "the *person* from whom the attraction on the other sex emanates" (RTE 1). Of course, as we know, Freud comes to complicate this very understanding of the sexual object, showing that the object toward which one becomes attracted—or to which one becomes soldered—could be any number of animate, inanimate, fantasmatic, partial, and so on objects. In this

way, it is not so much that there is no object whatsoever, but rather that the *object is not another person*, because the object is to be found on the child's own body.

5. See Book VIII of the *Laws*. Plato argues that there should be laws against autoerotic activity, and all kinds of other "non-natural" pleasures, to bring them in conformity with nature (Plato 2004, 838A–39D).

6. Aquinas infamously claims that masturbation is a greater sin than rape because it is more unnatural than any form of intercourse, however consensual it may be. See, "Of Parts of Lust," and especially the section "Whether the unnatural vice is the greatest sin among the species of lust?" (Aquinas 2000).

7. See, for example, the section, "On Defiling Oneself by Lust" in the *Metaphysics of Morals* (Kant 1991, 220–22).

8. See, for example, his article "Sexual Perversion" (Nagel 1969).

9. Of course, it is worth pointing out Derrida's use of the term "speculate" here. In his treatment of Freud's *Beyond the Pleasure Principle* in "To Speculate on Freud" and the *Life Death Seminar*, Derrida will underscore Freud's curious use of the term *speculate*. Derrida seeks to use this term in order to draw out the relation between psychoanalysis and philosophy, which Freud seeks to establish. In "To Speculate," Derrida argues that speculation is meant to be "foreign to philosophy or to metaphysics; it is not, for example, the speculative in Hegel" (Derrida 1987, 295–96; 1980, 296). And he makes similar remarks in the *Life Death* Seminar (Derrida 2019, 283–86; 2020, 227–29). For an excellent Derridean account of Freud's speculation in *Beyond the Pleasure Principle* see chapter 5 of Elizabeth Rottenberg's *For the Love of Psychoanalysis* (Rottenberg 2019, 68–98). There, Rottenberg argues, among other things, that Freud plays a certain *fort/da* with his speculation and philosophy.

10. This is what Lacan might have called extimacy, *extimité*, which is meant to complicate the very opposition between inside and outside: what is other is always already there in the most intimate (self-)relation of the subject to itself. See Lacan's *The Seminar. Book VII: The Ethics of Psychoanalysis* (Lacan 1986, 139; 2007a, 167).

11. Lacan, however, does attribute this remark to Freud without any direct reference to Freud's work in his Eleventh Seminar (Lacan 1973, 179; 1981, 201)179; 1981, 201.

12. Van Haute and Westerink seek to answer this question with a supplement in their own chain of supplements: In order to stave off the Oedipus complex, and in order to save the purity of polymorphous infantile sexuality and the auto-affection of autoeroticism from the threat of normativity, they are forced to declare that puberty is the origin of the relation to the other, fantasy, and so on. If we follow Van Haute and Westerink's suggestion that puberty is the origin of this type of object-related sexuality, would this not fall into precisely the same functionalism that Freud dismantles in the first essay? Does this not reinscribe sexuality within a biologistic, functional framework?

13. This is precisely the problem that Freud is getting at in his infamous lectures on femininity in the *New Introductory Lectures on Psychoanalysis*, when he writes: "In conformity with its peculiar nature, psychoanalysis does not try to describe what a woman is—that would be a task it could scarcely perform—but sets about inquiring how she comes into being—how a woman develops out of a child with a bisexual disposition" (SE 22: 116/GW 15: 124). The question here for Freud is: how is that a polymorphously perverse child (note Freud's choice not to gender the child) with its bisexual disposition (i.e., nonteleological, nonfunctional, and polymorphous infantile sexuality) can come to develop predominantly feminine traits, or become what we call women? What is this process of socialization/normalization that takes place, in the case of a female child, which shapes a child with a bisexual predisposition into what we call a woman? What is the process of heteronormalization or even heterosexualization? As we know by now, it's certainly not natural, so we need some account of these processes.

14. See, for example, his text "'Civilized' Sexual Morality and Modern Nervous Illness." Freud claims that we must understand that human sexuality is not inherently or originally designed for the purpose of reproduction (SE 9: 188/GW 7: 151). Once we do so, we can: (1) see how our present heteronormative society creates psychical problems for a vast majority of people; and (2) begin imagining a more liberated society no longer organized around reproduction as the be-all-end-all of sexuality.

15. In "'Civilized' Sexual Morality" Freud will claim that women who find themselves (often coerced) into unfulfilling marriages should find sexually satisfying relationships outside of their marriages to prevent developing or worsening neurotic illnesses owed to these disappointing relationships (SE 9: 195/GW 7: 157–58).

16. See, for example, his letter to an American mother, which was written in 1935 (Freud 1951). There Freud claims that psychoanalysis is not in the business of curing patients of their homosexuality but working through their neurotic illnesses whatever this shall come to mean for that individual patient. Freud famously claims in this letter that homosexuality is not the indication of some innate mental defect or degeneracy of the sexual function and, moreover, that seeking to force someone through a process of normalization could only cause the person mental anguish and suffering.

Chapter 6

1. Again, we can see this in Lacan's graph of desire. There is no complete circuit in the diagram; in no iteration of the graph does the biological need ever return to itself in the process.

2. Lacan highlights this in the various stages of the notorious graphs of desire that he elaborates throughout "Subversion of the Subject and Dialectic in

the Freudian Unconscious." On the one hand, in passing from the first graph to the second graph, the mythical biological being (represented on the graph as delta, Δ) is immediately replaced by the barred subject (represented on the graph as $), which has passed through the march of the signifier. In this way, we see that the mythical biological being never existed because it always already had passed through the march of the signifier. On the other hand, we can see just by the very nature of the diagrams that Lacan draws, there is always a process of retroaction. The graphs do not simply flow chronologically from left to right, like the signifying chain through which the subject must pass, but the subject is always caught in a process of retroaction.

3. See, for example, "On the Grounds for Detaching a Particular Syndrome from Neurasthenia under the Description 'Anxiety Neurosis'" (SE 3: 109/GW 1: 335); *Jokes and their Relation to the Unconscious* (SE 8: 99/GW 6: 108); "The Sexual Enlightenment of Children" (SE 9: 131, 132, 133/GW 7:19, 20, 21); "Civilized Sexual Morality" (SE 9: 190/GW 7: 153); "On the Sexual Theories of Children" (SE 211:/GW 7: 173); "Leonardi da Vinci and a Memory of His Childhood" (SE 11: 132/GW 8: 205); *Beyond the Pleasure Principle* (SE 18: 57/GW 13: 62); "Group Psychology and Ego-Analysis" (SE 18: 119/GW 13: 132).

4. In "On the Grounds for Detaching a Particular Syndrome from Neurasthenia under the Description 'Anxiety Neurosis,'" the terms seem to be used in a distinction between a male and female *Triebe*, but it is not entirely evident why Freud deploys two different terms when referring to the male and female *Triebe* respectively (SE 3: 108–9; GW 1: 334–35).

5. See, for example, Derrida's *Geschlecht III*, in which he describes and traces the ways in which the term *Geschlecht* takes on manifold meanings in Heidegger's thought. It conjures up ideas of humanity, nations, race, species, genre, sex, and so on (Derrida 2018). Alexandre Abensour, in *Dictionary of Untranslatables*, for example, traces the various ways in which the term *Trieb* has been translated into English, not just in Freud but also in the history of philosophy (Abensour 2014).

6. As we have already seen, Freud problematizes the "chemical" understanding of heterosexuality (SE 7: 146n/GW 5: 44n). Furthermore, at the end of the first essay, Freud explains in great detail how infantile sexuality plays a deciding factor in later adult life (SE 7: 71–72/GW 5: 171–72).

7. In the second essay, "Infantile Sexuality," Freud claims that sexual object choice happens in two phases: the first during infantile sexuality and the second after puberty. There, he writes: "the second wave sets in with puberty and determines the final outcome of sexual life" (SE 7: 200/GW 5: 100). Yet, he continues: "The resultants of infantile object-choice are carried over into the later period. They either persist as such or are revived at the actual time of puberty. But as a consequence of the repression which has developed between the two phases, they prove unutilizeable" (SE 7: 200/GW 5: 100–1). Thus, although puberty establishes some

permanence over sexual life, it does so only with respect to the prior developments of infantile sexuality.

   8. In the section titled the "Finding of an Object," Freud is unequivocal that the pathways for sexual attraction are already formed and laid down in infancy. Puberty is not the only or the decisive factor in post-pubertal attraction (SE 7: 222–30/GW 5: 123–31). Finding a sexual object later in life is, Freud famously declares, after all, only the refinding of the object.

   9. Particularly important essays in this respect are the ones in which Freud explicitly discusses infantile sexuality. See, for example "The Sexual Enlightenment of Children" (SE 9: 132–33/GW 7: 21–22); "On the Sexual Theories of Children" (SE 9: 210/GW 7: 172); and the fourth lecture of *Five Lectures on Psychoanalysis* (SE 7: 40–48/GW 8: 41–51). Other important essays in this respect include ones where Freud discusses the development of sensual and affectionate currents. See, for example, "A Special Type of Choice of Object Made by Men" (SE 11: 165–75/GW 8: 66–77); and "On the Universal Tendency Towards Debasement in the Sphere of Love" (SE 11: 179–90/GW 8: 78–91).

   10. Even Freud himself talks about the diphasic nature of the object-choice in sexuality, by which Freud means that object-choice occurs in two phases: one during childhood and the other during puberty, which gives a final form to and cements the childhood object-choice (SE 7: 200/GW 5: 100–1).

   11. Freud also notes that many infantile theories of birth suppose that the newborn is either cut out of the mother, that it is passed through the bowels just like excrement, or children are told that babies are brought via the stork. See, for example, *Three Essays* (SE 7: 196/GW 5: 96); "The Sexual Enlightenment of Children" (SE 9: 136–38/GW 7: 24–35); and "On the Sexual Theories of Children" (SE 9: 218–26/GW 7: 181–88). In this way, the child is led to theorize that anyone has the capacity to have a child independent of their actual physiological ability to conceive and bear a child and everything else that goes along with it. This means that, according to these infantile theories, which still consciously and unconsciously structure our understanding of sexuality, anyone could have a child regardless of whether or not they have gone through puberty or whether they desire having heterosexual intercourse. We can think, for example, of religious doctrines that would have their followers believe that a virgin woman conceived and gave birth to a child without ever having sexual intercourse.

   12. This is why Laplanche seeks to revivify and universalize Freud's once abandoned theory of seduction, and it is why he later turns to the idea of the "enigmatic message" in his attempts to revivify Freud's theory of seduction: "Once Freud abandons the theory of seduction, the return to a purely endogenous conception of sexuality is inevitable" (FB 3/9). Only by universalizing the theory of seduction can Laplanche maintain the opposition between the sexual and the nonsexual domains. It is the only way, according to Laplanche, to preserve the revolutionary and polemical force,

the perversity, of Freud's theory of sexuality. The sexual realm of the adult, opposed to the pure vital, instinctual life of the infant, must come from without, must come into opposition with it in order to corrupt it, to pervert it. The nonsexual infant is corrupted by the (infantile) sexuality of the adult. The adult's (infantile) sexuality must come from without, must be something distinct, must be something opposed to the infant. It is the sexual opposed to the nonsexual that puts the whole thing in motion. It can never be innate. It can never be endogenous. Sexuality has to come from the other; it has to be entirely *other*, entirely other to the nonsexual realm. However, as we will see, Laplanche's emphasis on the other eventually becomes a little one-sided. As a perversion, sexuality cannot come purely from without unless that which it emerges from is itself structurally pervertible.

13. See, for example, what Elissa Marder calls the "Case of the Freezer," in which a woman gives birth to two children without telling her husband, strangles them, and stores them in the freezer (Marder 2012, 24–26).

Conclusion

1. See, for example, Lorenzo Chiesa's *The Not-Two: Logic and God in Lacan*. In this text, Chiesa seeks to use Lacan's claim that there is no sexual relation as a point of departure for making claims about logic and God in order to develop what he calls a para-ontology (Chiesa 2016, xi–xxvii).

2. For decades, Žižek has been calling for us to take seriously the denaturalizing of nature implied in psychoanalytic and German idealist discourses. As recent as his 2015 *Absolute Recoil*, Žižek claims that understanding some of psychoanalysis' greatest insights and founding a new dialectical materialism can only be done by "de-naturalizing nature itself" (Žižek 2015, 28). Here, it is less of a question of denaturalizing nature as a means of critique, but of a nature self-denaturalizing. For and excellent analysis of these debates, see Adrian Johnston's " 'Naturalism or Anti-naturalism? No, Thanks—Both Are Worse!': Science, Materialism, and Slavoj Žižek" (Johnston 2012) and, more recently, his book-length study *A New German Idealism: Hegel, Žižek, and Dialectical Materialism* (Johnston 2018a).

3. The *GW* is not cited here because, of course, this sentence was removed from the 1915 edition onward.

4. We might wonder why Freud chooses to take this passage out, when he does not do so with the numerous other charges of teleology and naturalism that, for example, Jean Laplanche points out. Perhaps Freud did not think that they were not so naturalistic or teleological as has been assumed, which becomes clearer after taking his problem of sexuality seriously, as we have hopefully achieved in this work.

5. Many contemporary critical theorists seek to damn Freud and the psychoanalytic tradition owed to him—condemning him to the very same popular opinion

(that is, heteronormative and biologistic ideology) that he tirelessly combated. For example, many a feminist and queer theorist have charged Freud with, among other things, being patriarchal, sexist, and even transphobic. (See, as paradigmatic, Preciado's *Can the Monster Speak?* In a single text, and without textual evidence, Freud and the psychoanalytic tradition owed to him are labeled as colonialist, patriarchal, sexist, heteronormative, and transphobic.) This is because, it is claimed, at the core of the theory and practice of psychoanalysis there is a mission to (hetero)normalize nonnormative sexualities and genders. Probably the most well-known formulation of this criticism of psychoanalysis was articulated by Michel Foucault in his *The History of Sexuality, Volume 1*. I have already made remarks elsewhere about how Foucault provides no textual evidence to propagate a series of misunderstandings about the practice of psychoanalysis (Ramos 2022). It is worth noting that during his own time Freud's theory of sexuality was demonized precisely for being so unabashedly opposed to the predominant heterosexual morality of his time. As if already anticipating this shifting point of attack against his psychoanalytic theory of sexuality, Freud himself writes later in his career: "the charge was brought against psycho-analysis of having made an unjustifiable extension of the concept of sexuality; yet, when it became convenient for controversial ends, this crime was forgotten and we were once more held down to the narrowest meaning of the word" (SE 20: 55/GW 14: 81). In more contemporary terms, what Freud noticed is that, when it comes to his theory of sexuality, his detractors often see it as either fundamentally at odds with heteronormativity *or* inescapably and irredeemably heteronormative—all that matters is from which side of the divide one decides to attack him. The fact that Freud is so vehemently condemned for both challenging heteronormativity and also being heteronormative seems to indicate that we still have not quite understood the core theses of Freud's theory of sexuality. Or, perhaps better said: while our vehement reactions show that we register on some level that Freud challenges our spontaneous conceptions of sexuality and our attachments to them, we have been unable to process and digest these revolutionary insights.

6. For years, many have called for such a denaturalization of gender. For example, from her earliest works, Judith Butler has suggested that the repetition and institutionalization of heteronormative conceptions of gender have led to them being "naturalized." That is, certain sociohistorical ways of enacting gender have become so established and so ingrained that they now appear to us to be natural, that is, the way it has always been and will always be (Butler 1988, 520–24). As such, gender is mistakenly understood as being governed, not by the sociohistorical forces that shape and maintain it, but by natural law. However, the key for Butler is to show that *all* gender is performative (even and especially what is typically considered to be "natural" and "normal") and is, therefore, nonnatural (Butler 1988, 529–31). In so doing, Butler seeks to denaturalize gender, that is, to demonstrate that it is not a natural category. Denaturalizing in this way is meant dissolve the naturalistic

justification that undergirds our predominantly heterosexist and heteronormative society. Under the banner of "queering nature" or "queer ecology" some have even argued for, similar to Zupančič and Žižek, projecting precisely this sort of denaturalizing gesture onto nature itself in order to further undermine traditional ways of understanding gender. See, for example: Donna Haraway's "A Game of Cat's Cradle: Science Studies, Feminist Theory, Cultural Studies" (Haraway 1994, 60); Jonathan Gray's "Heteronormativity without Nature: Toward a Queer Ecology" (Gray 2017); Helen Merrick's "Queering Nature: Close Encounters with the Alien in Ecofeminist Science Fiction" (Merrick 2008).

7. For an excellent diagnosis of this denaturalizing tendency in contemporary critical theory, see the introduction to Hasana Sharp's *The Politics of Renaturalization* (Sharp 2011, 6–10).

8. See, for example, the various ways in which the denaturalization of sexuality is called for or taken for granted in (Pearson 2004; Bell 2009; Wiegman & Wilson 2015; Blackmore 2011; Pérez 2020).

9. See foundational texts in queer theory, such as Eve Kosofsky Sedgwick's *Epistemology of the Closet*. As the title suggests, nonnormative sexualities having to pass through the experience of being in and coming out of the closet have access to a unique epistemology (Sedgwick 2008). Others have claimed that queer sexualities not only force us to reconceive traditional epistemologies, but break with them (Santos 2023, 89–91).

10. The idea that queer sexualities alter heteronormative conceptions of time, or even have access to altogether different forms of temporality, have become so popular that Duke University Press's *GLQ* dedicated an entire special issue to the topic ("Queer Temporalities" 2007). Also see Judith Halberstam's *In Queer Time and Place* (Halberstam 2005) and Elizabeth Freeman's *Time Binds: Queer Temporalities, Queer Histories* (Freeman 2010).

11. One of the most influential texts in this vein has to be Sara Ahmed's *Queer Phenomenology* (Ahmed 2006). Among other things, Ahmed claims that queer bodies move differently in the world and, as such, disrupt the normal run of things. As such, queer bodies become a privileged point at which not only the status quo is challenged, but also a place from which we should reconceive political practice and put old theories of politics into question.

12. Queer sexualities are sometimes said to have unique access to certain forms of pleasure not available to, and often repressed by, heterosexuals. Some argue that certain studies show that, from their exceptionality, queer women have better sex (Thorpe et al. 2022). It is also argued that queer pleasure provides one with unique experiences of not only sexuality but also, for example, the kitchen and cooking (Klassen 2016). In queer theory, uniquely queer pleasures and the practice of "queering" pleasure are often intimately bound up with politics (Sullivan 1999). In fact, queer pleasures can also provide us with a unique position from which to understand complicated social structures like prisons (Vasiliou 2020).

13. For an excellent account of this practice of endless critique in queer theory, see Oakes (1995).

Bibliography

Abensour, Alexandre. 2014. "Drive, Instinct, Impulse." In *Dictionary of Untranslatables: A Philosophical Lexicon*, edited by Barbara Cassin, 230–35. Princeton, NJ: Princeton University Press.

Ahmed, Sara. 2006. *Queer Phenomenology: Orientations, Objects, Others*. Durham, NC: Duke University Press.

Ali, Nadia Bou. 2019. "Measure against Measure: Why Lacan Contra Foucault." In *Lacan Contra Foucault*, edited by Nadia Bou Ali. London: Bloomsbury.

Althusser, Louis. 1991. "On Marx and Freud." Translated by Warren Montag. *Rethinking Marxism* 4 (1): 17–30.

———. 1993a. "Freud et Lacan." In *Écrits sur la psychanalyse: Freud et Lacan*, edited by Olivier Corpet and François Matheron, 7–54. Édition posthume d'oeuvres de Louis Althusser 3. Paris: Stock.

———. 1993b. "La découverte du Docteur Freud." In *Écrits sur la psychanalyse: Freud et Lacan*, edited by Olivier Corpet and François Matheron, 195–219. Édition posthume d'oeuvres de Louis Althusser 3. Paris: Éditions Stock/IMEC.

———. 1993c. "Sur Marx et Freud." In *Écrits sur la psychanalyse: Freud et Lacan*, edited by Olivier Corpet and François Matheron, 222–45. Édition posthume d'oeuvres de Louis Althusser 3. Paris: Stock.

———. 1993d. "Trois notes sur la théorie des discours." In *Écrits sur la psychanalyse: Freud et Lacan*, edited by Olivier Corpet and François Matheron, 111–70. Édition posthume d'oeuvres de Louis Althusser 3. Paris: Éditions Stock/IMEC.

———. 1994. "Correspondence: Lettres de Louis Althusser à Fernanda Navarro à Propos de l'édition de Philosophie et Marxisme, Précédées d'une Lettre à Mauricio Malamud (1984–87)." In *Sur La Reproduction*, edited by Olivier Corpet, 87–138. Paris: Gallimard.

———. 1996a. "Freud and Lacan." In *Writings on Psychoanalysis: Freud and Lacan*, edited by Olivier Corpet and François Matheron, translated by Jeffrey Mehlman, 7–32. New York: Columbia University Press.

———. 1996b. "On Marx and Freud." In *Writings on Psychoanalysis: Freud and Lacan*, edited by Olivier Corpet and François Matheron, translated by Jeffrey Mehlman, 105–24. New York: Columbia University Press.

———. 1996c. *Psychanalyse et sciences humaines: deux conferences (1963–1964)*. Edited by Olivier Corpet and François Matheron. Le livre de poche Biblio essais 4229. Paris: Librairie Générale Francaise.

———. 1996d. *Psychoanalysis and the Human Sciences*. Translated by Steven Rendall. New York: Columbia University Press.

———. 1996e. "The Discovery of Dr. Freud." In *Writings on Psychoanalysis: Freud and Lacan*, edited by Olivier Corpet and François Matheron, translated by Jeffrey Mehlman, 85–105. New York: Columbia University Press.

———. 2003. "Three Notes on the Theory of Discourse." In *The Humanist Controversy and Other Writings, 1966–67*, edited by François Matheron, translated by G. M. Goshgarian, 33–84. London; New York: Verso.

———. 2014. *Initiation à La Philosophie Pour Les Non-Philosophes*. Edited by G. M. Goshgarian. 1st ed. Perspectives Critiques. Paris: Presses universitaires de France.

———. 2015. *Être marxiste en philosophie*. Edited by G. M. Goshgarian. 1st ed. Perspectives critiques. Paris: Presses Universitaires de France.

Althusser, Louis, Étienne Balibar, Roger Establet, Pierre Macherey, and Jacques Rancière. 2014. *Lire Le capital*. Paris: Presses Universitaires de France.

Anderson, Ellie. 2017. "Auto-Erotism: Rethinking Self-Love with Derrida and Irigaray." *PhænEx* 12 (1): 53–70.

Aquinas, Thomas. 2000. *St. Thomas Aquinas Summa Theologica: Complete English Edition in Five Volumes*. Reprint. Notre Dame, IN: Christian Classics.

Aristotle. 2013. *Aristotle's Politics*. Translated by Carnes Lord. 2nd ed. Chicago, IL: University of Chicago Press.

Augustine, Aurelius. (1961) 1982. *Confessions*. Translated by R. S. Pine-Coffin. Penguin Classics. Reprint. Harmondsworth, Middlesex, UK: Penguin Books.

Bacon, Francis. 2000. *The New Organon*. Edited by Lisa Jardine and Michael Silverthorne. Cambridge Texts in the History of Philosophy. Cambridge, UK; New York: Cambridge University Press.

Bell, David. 2009. "Heteronormativity." In *International Encyclopedia of Human Geography*, 2nd ed., edited by Audrey Kobayashi, 387–91. Oxford, UK: Elsevier.

Benson, Hugh H. 1990. "Misunderstanding the 'What-Is-F-ness?' Question." *Archiv Für Geschichte Der Philosophie* 72 (2): 125–42.

Bettelheim, Bruno. 1984. *Freud and Man's Soul*. 1st Vintage Books ed. New York: Vintage Books.

Bianchi, Emanuela. 2014. *The Feminine Symptom: Aleatory Matter in the Aristotelian Cosmos*. New York: Fordham University Press.

Blackmore, Chelsea. 2011. "How to Queer the Past without Sex: Queer Theory, Feminisms and the Archaeology of Identity." *Archaeologies* 7 (1): 75–96.

Bompard-Porte, Michèle. 2019. "Homophobie: Peur de Soi? Peur Du Même?" In *L'homophobie: Et Les Expressions de l'ordre Hétérosexiste*, edited by Christèle Fraïssé, 19–26. Psychologies. Rennes: Presses universitaires de Rennes.

Bourguignon, André, ed. 1989. *Traduire Freud*. 1. ed. Paris: Presses Universitaires de France.

Brennan, Tad. 1996. "Epicurus on Sex, Marriage, and Children." *Classical Philology* 91 (4): 346–52.
Butler, Judith. 1988. "Performative Acts and Gender Constitution: An Essay in Phenomenology and Feminist Theory." *Theatre Journal* 40 (4): 519–31.
Caruth, Cathy, and Jean Laplanche. 2001. "An Interview with Jean Laplanche." *Postmodern Culture* 11 (2): 1–30.
Chiesa, Lorenzo. 2016. *The Not-Two: Logic and God in Lacan*. Short Circuits. Cambridge, MA: MIT Press.
Cixous, Hélène, and Jacques Derrida. 2019. "On Deconstruction and Childhood." Translated by Peggy Kamuf. *Oxford Literary Review* 41 (2): 149–59.
Clark, Randall Baldwin. 2017. "Platonic Love in a Colorado Courtroom: Martha Nussbaum, John Finnis, and Plato's Laws in Evans v. Romer." Edited by Richard O. Brooks. *Plato and Modern Law* 12 (1): 405–42. https://doi.org/10.4324/9781315089737-17.
Copjec, Joan. 2010. "The Fable of the Stork and Other False Sexual Theories." *Differences: A Journal of Feminist Cultural Studies* 21 (1): 63–73.
Davidson, Arnold. 1983. "On the Englishing of Freud." *London Review of Books*, November 3, 1983.
———. 1987. "How to Do the History of Psychoanalysis: A Reading of Freud's 'Three Essays on the Theory of Sexuality.'" *Critical Inquiry* 13 (2): 252–77.
Deleuze, Gilles. 1994. *Difference and Repetition*. New York: Columbia University Press.
Derrida, Jacques. 1967. *De La Grammatologie*. Collection "Critique." Paris: Éditions de Minuit.
———. 1972a. "Le Cercle Linguistique de Genève." In *Marges de La Philosophie*, 365–93. Paris: Ed. de Minuit.
———. 1972b. *Marges de la philosophie*. Collection "Critique." Paris: Ed. de Minuit.
———. 1972c. "Signature Événement Contexte." In *Marges de La Philosophie*, 365–93. Paris: Ed. de Minuit.
———. 1980. "Spéculer–Sur 'Freud.'" In *La Carte Postale: De Socrate à Freud et Au-Delà*, 275–438. La Philosophie En Effet. Paris: Flammarion.
———. 1982a. *Margins of Philosophy*. Chicago, IL: University of Chicago Press.
———. 1982b. "Signature, Event, Context." In *Margins of Philosophy*, 307–30. Chicago, IL: University of Chicago Press.
———. 1987. "To Speculate—On Freud." In *The Post Card: From Socrates to Freud and Beyond*, translated by Alan Bass, 257–409. Chicago, IL: Chicago University Press.
———. 1997. *Of Grammatology*. Translated by G. C. Spivak. Baltimore: Johns Hopkins University Press.
———. 2005. *On Touch—Jean Luc Nancy*. Translated by Christine Irizarry. Stanford, CA: Stanford University Press.
———. 2018. *Geschlecht III: Sexe, Race, Nation, Humanité*. Edited by Geoffrey Bennington, Katie Chenoweth, and Therezo. Paris: Éditions du Seuil.

———. 2019. *La Vie La Mort: Séminaire (1975–1976)*. Edited by Pascale-Anne Brault and Peggy Kamuf. Bibliothèque Derrida. Paris: Éditions du Seuil.

———. 2020. *Life Death*. Edited by Pascale-Anne Brault and Peggy Kamuf. Translated by Michael Naas. Seminars of Jacques Derrida. Chicago, IL: University of Chicago Press.

Descartes, René. 1989. *The Passions of the Soul*. Translated by Stephen Voss. Indianapolis, IN: Hackett.

Dolar, Mladen. 2019. "Cutting Off the King's Head." In *Lacan Contra Foucault*, edited by Nadia Bou Ali. London: Bloomsbury.

Evans, Dylan. 1996. *An Introductory Dictionary of Lacanian Psychoanalysis*. London: Routledge.

Foucault, Michel. 1980. "The Confession of the Flesh." In *Power/Knowledge: Selected Interviews and Other Writings, 1972–1977*, edited by Colin Gordon, translated by Colin Gordon, Leo Marshall, John Mepham, and Kate Soper, 194–228. New York: Pantheon.

———. 1990. *The History of Sexuality*. New York: Vintage Books.

———. 1994. "Les Mailles Du Pouvoir." In *Dits et Écrits IV*, IV: 182–201. Paris: Gallimard.

Freeman, Elizabeth. 2010. *Time Binds: Queer Temporalities, Queer Histories*. Durham, NC: Duke University Press.

Freud, Sigmund. (1923) 1940a. "Das Ich und das Es." In *Gesammelte Werke*, 13: 237–89. Frankfurt am Main: Fischer.

———. (1923) 1940b. "Das Ökonomische Problem des Masochismus." In *Gesammelte Werke*, 13: 371–83. Frankfurt am Main: Fischer.

———. (1905) 1940c. "Der Witz und seine Beziehung zum Unbewußten." In *Gesammelte Werke*. Vol. 6. Frankfurt am Main: Fischer.

———. (1923) 1940d. "Die Infantalen Genitalorganisation: Eine Einschaltung in die Sexualtheorie." In *Gesammelte Werke*, 13:291–98. Frankfurt am Main: Fischer.

———. (1920) 1940e. *Jenseits des Lustprinzips*. In *Gesammelte Werke*, 13:3–69. Frankfurt am Main: Fischer.

———. (1921) 1940f. "Massenpsychologie und Ich-Analyse." In *Gesammelte Werke*, 13: 71–161. Frankfurt am Main: Fischer.

———. (1933) 1940g. "Neue Folge der Vorlesungen zur Einführung in die Psychoanalyse." In *Gesammelte Werke*, 15: 1–207. Frankfurt am Main: Fischer.

———. (1914) 1940h. "Totem und Tabu." In *Gesammelte Werke*, 9: 1–205. Frankfurt am Main: Fischer.

———. (1922) 1940i. "Traum und Telepathie." In *Gesammelte Werke*, 13: 165–91. Frankfurt am Main: Fischer.

———. (1933) 1940j. "Über eine Weltanschauung." In *Gesammelte Werke*, 15: 170–207. Frankfurt am Main: Fischer.

———. (1909) 1941a. "Analyse der Phobie eines Fünfjährigen Knaben [1909]." In *Gesammelte Werke*, 7: 243–377. Frankfurt am Main: Fischer.

———. (1907) 1941b. "Der Wahn und die Träume in W. Jensens Gradiva." In *Gesammelte Werke*, 7: 31–125. Frankfurt am Main: Fischer.

———. (1908) 1941c. "Die 'Kulturelle' Sexualmoral und die Moderne Nervosität." In *Gesammelte Werke*, 7: 143–67. Frankfurt am Main: Fischer.

———. (1908) 1941d. "Über Infantile Sexualtheorien." In *Gesammelte Werke*, 7: 171–88. Frankfurt am Main: Fischer.

———. (1904) 1941e. "Zur Psychopathologie des Alltagsleben." In *Gesammelte Werke*. Vol. 4. Frankfurt am Main: Fischer.

———. (1908) 1941f. "Zur Sexuellen Aufklärung der Kinder: Offener Brief an Dr. M. Fürst." In *Gesammelte Werke*, 7: 19–27. Frankfurt am Main: Fischer.

———. (1900) 1942a. "Die Traumdeutung." In *Gesammelte Werke*. Vol. 2–3. Frankfurt am Main: Fischer.

———. (1905) 1942b. "Drei Abhandlungen zur Sexualtheorie." In *Gesammelte Werke*, 5:29–145. Frankfurt am Main: Fischer.

———. (1906) 1942c. "Meine Ansichten Über die Rolle der Sexualität in der Ätiologie der Neurosen." In *Gesammelte Werke*, 5: 149–59. Frankfurt am Main: Fischer.

———. (1910) 1943a. "Beiträge zur Psychologie des Liebeslebens I: Über einen Besonderen Typus der Objektwahl beim Manne." In *Gesammelte Werke*, 8:66–77. Frankfurt am Main: Fischer.

———. (1912) 1943b. "Beiträge zur Psychologie des Liebeslebens II: Über die Allgemeinste Erniedrigung des Liebeslebens." In *Gesammelte Werke*, 8:78–91. Frankfurt am Main: Fischer.

———. (1913) 1943c. "Das Interesse an der Psychoanalyse." In *Gesammelte Werke*, 8:390–420. Frankfurt am Main: Fischer.

———. (1910) 1943d. "Eine Kindheitserinnerung des Leonardo da Vinci." In *Gesammelte Werke*, 8: 128–211. Frankfurt am Main: Fischer.

———. (1910) 1943e. "Über Psychoanalyse." In *Gesammelte Werke*, 8: 3–60. Frankfurt am Main: Fischer.

———. (1915–17) 1943f. "Vorlesungen zur Einführung in die Psychoanalyse." In *Gesammelte Werke*. Vol. 11. Frankfurt am Main: Fischer.

———. (1912) 1943g. "Zur Onanie-Diskussion." In *Gesammelte Werke*, 8: 332–45. Frankfurt am Main: Fischer.

———. (1915) 1946a. "Das Unbewußte." In *Gesammelte Werke*, 10: 264–303. Frankfurt am Main: Fischer.

———. (1915) 1946b. "Einige Charaktertypen aus der Psychoanalytischen Arbeit." In *Gesammelte Werke*, 10: 364–91. Frankfurt am Main: Fischer.

———. (1915) 1946c. "Triebe und Triebschicksale." In *Gesammelte Werke*, 10: 210–32. Frankfurt am Main: Fischer.

———. (1915) 1946d. "Vergänglichkeit." In *Gesammelte Werke*, 10: 358–61. Frankfurt am Main: Fischer.

———. (1915) 1946e. "Zeitgemässes Über Krieg und Tod." In *Gesammelte Werke*, 10: 324–55. Frankfurt am Main: Fischer.

———. (1914) 1946f. "Zur Einführung des Narzissmus." In *Gesammelte Werke*, 10: 138–70. Frankfurt am Main: Fischer.

———. (1914) 1946g. "Zur Geschichte der Psychoanalytischen Bewegung." In *Gesammelte Werke*, 10: 44–113. Frankfurt am Main: Fischer.

———. (1918) 1947a. "Aus der Geschichte einer Infantilen Neurose." In *Gesammelte Werke*, 12: 29–157. Frankfurt am Main: Fischer.

———. (1917) 1947b. "Eine Schwiergkeit der Psychoanalyse." In *Gesammelte Werke*, 12: 3–12. Frankfurt am Main: Fischer.

———. (1920) 1947c. "Über die Psychogenese eines Falles von Weiblicher Homosexualität." In *Gesammelte Werke*, 12: 271–302. Frankfurt am Main: Fischer.

———. (1930) 1948a. "Das Unbehagen in der Kultur." In *Gesammelte Werke*, 14: 421–506. Frankfurt am Main: Fischer.

———. (1925) 1948b. "Die Verneinung." In *Gesammelte Werke*, 14: 11–15. Frankfurt am Main: Fischer.

———. (1928) 1948c. "Dostojewski und die Vatertötung." In *Gesammelte Werke*, 14: 399–418. Frankfurt am Main: Fischer.

———. (1926) 1948d. "Hemmung, Symptom, und Angst." In *Gesammelte Werke*, 14: 113–205. Frankfurt am Main: Fischer.

———. (1925) 1948e. "Selbstdarstellung." In *Gesammelte Werke*, 14: 33–96. Frankfurt am Main: Fischer.

———. (!939) 1950a. "Der Mann Moses und die Monotheistische Religion: Drei Abhandlungen." In *Gesammelte Werke*, 16101–246. Frankfurt am Main: Fischer.

———. (1937) 1950b. "Die Endliche und die Unendliche Analyse." In *Gesammelte Werke*, 16: 59–99. Frankfurt am Main: Fischer.

———. 1951. "A Letter from Freud." *The American Journal of Psychiatry* 107: 786–87.

———. (1898) 1952a. "Die Sexualität in der Ätiologie der Neurosen." In *Gesammelte Werke*, 1: 491–516. Frankfurt am Main: Fischer.

———. (1894) 1952b. "Über die Berechtigung von der Neurasthenie einen Bestimmen Symptomenkomplex als 'Angstneurose' Abzutrennen." In *Gesammelte Werke*, 1: 315–42. Frankfurt am Main: Fischer.

———. 1953a. "My Views on the Part Played by Sexuality in the Aetiology of the Neuroses." In *The Standard Edition of the Complete Psychological Works of Sigmund Freud*, edited by Anna Freud, Alix Strachey, and Alan Tyson, translated by James Strachey, 7: 271–79. London: Hogarth.

———. 1953b. "The Interpretation of Dreams." In *The Standard Edition of the Complete Psychological Works of Sigmund Freud*, edited by Anna Freud, Alix Strachey, and Alan Tyson, translated by James Strachey. Vol. 4–5. London: Hogarth.

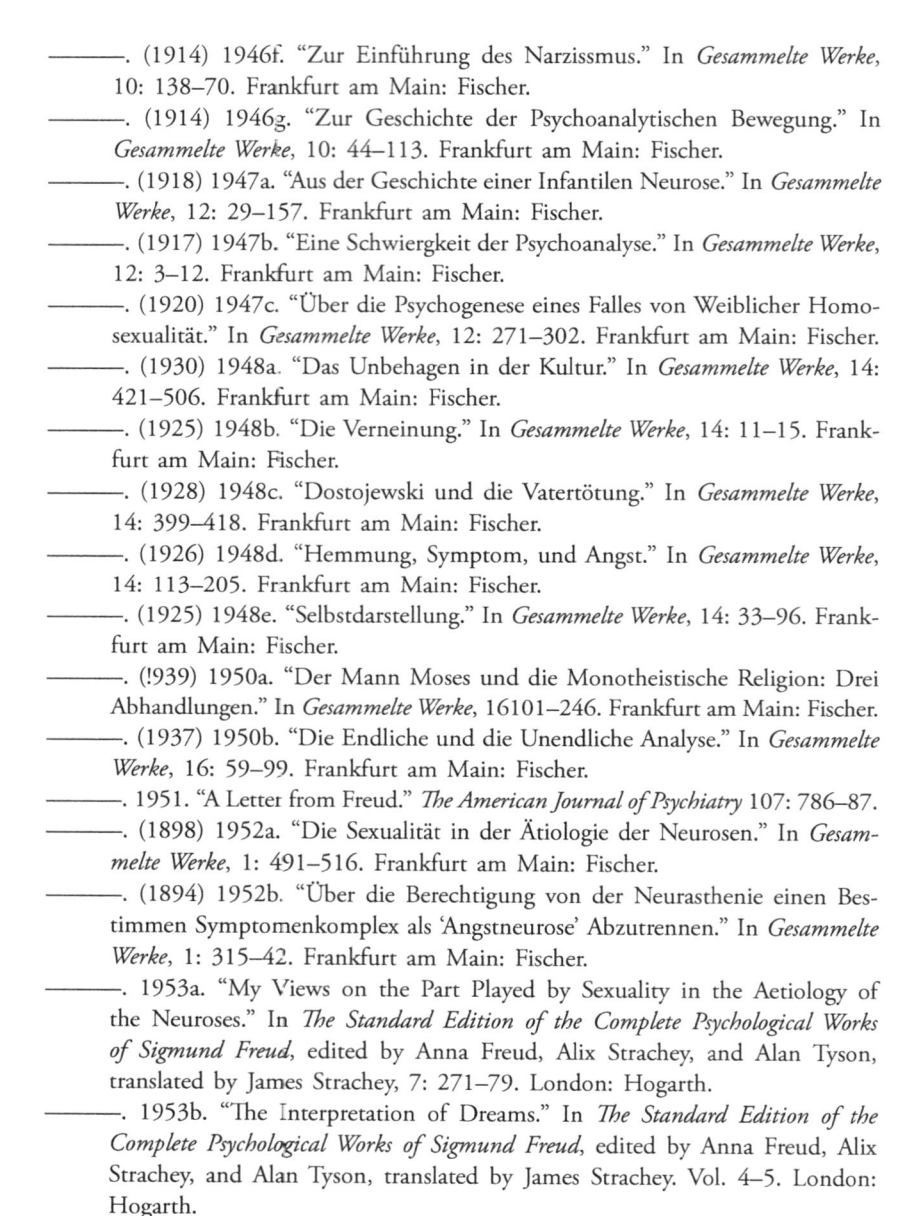

———. 1953c. "Three Essays On The Theory of Sexuality." In *The Standard Edition of the Complete Psychological Works of Sigmund Freud*, edited by Anna Freud, Alix Strachey, and Alan Tyson, translated by James Strachey, 7: 135–243. London: Hogarth.

———. 1955a. "Analysis of a Phobia in a Five-Year-Old Boy." In *The Standard Edition of the Complete Psychological Works of Sigmund Freud*, edited by Anna Freud, Alix Strachey, and Alan Tyson, translated by James Strachey, 10: 5–149. London: Hogarth.

———. 1955b. *Beyond the Pleasure Principle*. In *The Standard Edition of the Complete Psychological Works of Sigmund Freud*, edited by Anna Freud, Alix Strachey, and Alan Tyson, translated by James Strachey, 18: 7–64. London: Hogarth.

———. 1955c. "Dreams and Telepathy." In *The Standard Edition of the Complete Psychological Works of Sigmund Freud*, edited by Anna Freud, Alix Strachey, and Alan Tyson, translated by James Strachey, 18: 197–220. London: Hogarth.

———. 1955d. "Group Psychology and the Analysis of the Ego." In *The Standard Edition of the Complete Psychological Works of Sigmund Freud*, edited by Anna Freud, Alix Strachey, and Alan Tyson, translated by James Strachey, 18: 69–143. London: Hogarth.

———. 1955e. "The Psychogenesis of a Case of Homosexuality in a Woman." In *The Standard Edition of the Complete Psychological Works of Sigmund Freud*, edited by Anna Freud, Alix Strachey, and Alan Tyson, translated by James Strachey, 18: 147–72. London: Hogarth.

———. 1957a. "A Special Type of Choice of Object Made by Men." In *The Standard Edition of the Complete Psychological Works of Sigmund Freud*, edited by Anna Freud, Alix Strachey, and Alan Tyson, translated by James Strachey, 11: 165–75. London: Hogarth.

———. 1957b. "Five Lectures on Psychoanalysis." In *The Standard Edition of the Complete Psychological Works of Sigmund Freud*, edited by Anna Freud, Alix Strachey, and Alan Tyson, translated by James Strachey, 11: 9–55. London: Hogarth.

———. 1957c. "Instincts and Their Vicissitudes." In *The Standard Edition of the Complete Psychological Works of Sigmund Freud*, edited by Anna Freud, Alix Strachey, and Alan Tyson, translated by James Strachey, 14: 117–40. London: Hogarth.

———. 1957d. "Leonardo Da Vinci and a Memory of His Childhood." In *The Standard Edition of the Complete Psychological Works of Sigmund Freud*, edited by Anna Freud, Alix Strachey, and Alan Tyson, translated by James Strachey, 11: 63–137. London: Hogarth.

———. 1957e. "On Narcissism: An Introduction." In *The Standard Edition of the Complete Psychological Works of Sigmund Freud*, edited by Anna Freud, Alix Strachey, and Alan Tyson, translated by James Strachey, 14: 73–102. London: Hogarth.

———. 1957f. "On the History of the Psychoanalytic Movement." In *The Standard Edition of the Complete Psychological Works of Sigmund Freud*, edited by Anna Freud, Alix Strachey, and Alan Tyson, translated by James Strachey, 14: 7–66. London: Hogarth.

———. 1957g. "On the Universal Tendency to Debasement in the Sphere of Love." In *The Standard Edition of the Complete Psychological Works of Sigmund Freud*, edited by Anna Freud, Alix Strachey, and Alan Tyson, translated by James Strachey, 11: 179–90. London: Hogarth.

———. 1957h. "On Transience." In *The Standard Edition of the Complete Psychological Works of Sigmund Freud*, edited by Anna Freud, Alix Strachey, and Alan Tyson, translated by James Strachey, 14: 305–7. London: Hogarth.

———. 1957i. "Some Character-Types Met with in Psycho-Analytic Work." In *The Standard Edition of the Complete Psychological Works of Sigmund Freud*, edited by Anna Freud, Alix Strachey, and Alan Tyson, translated by James Strachey, 14: 311–33. London: Hogarth.

———. 1957j. "The Unconscious." In *The Standard Edition of the Complete Psychological Works of Sigmund Freud*, edited by Anna Freud, Alix Strachey, and Alan Tyson, translated by James Strachey, 14: 166–215. London: Hogarth.

———. 1957k. "Thoughts for the Times on War and Death." In *The Standard Edition of the Complete Psychological Works of Sigmund Freud*, edited by Anna Freud, Alix Strachey, and Alan Tyson, translated by James Strachey, 14: 275–302. London: Hogarth.

———. 1958a. "A Difficulty on the Path of Psycho-Analysis." In *The Standard Edition of the Complete Psychological Works of Sigmund Freud*, edited by Anna Freud, Alix Strachey, and Alan Tyson, translated by James Strachey, 17: 137–44. London: Hogarth.

———. 1958b. "Contributions to a Discussion on Masturbation." In *The Standard Edition of the Complete Psychological Works of Sigmund Freud*, edited by Anna Freud, Alix Strachey, and Alan Tyson, translated by James Strachey, 12: 243–54. London: Hogarth.

———. 1958c. "From the History of an Infantile Neurosis." In *The Standard Edition of the Complete Psychological Works of Sigmund Freud*, edited by Anna Freud, Alix Strachey, and Alan Tyson, translated by James Strachey, 17: 7–123. London: Hogarth.

———. 1958d. "The Claims of Psychoanalysis to Scientific Interest." In *The Standard Edition of the Complete Psychological Works of Sigmund Freud*, edited by Anna Freud, Alix Strachey, and Alan Tyson, translated by James Strachey, 13: 165–90. London: Hogarth.

———. 1958e. "Totem and Taboo." In *The Standard Edition of the Complete Psychological Works of Sigmund Freud*, edited by Anna Freud, Alix Strachey, and Alan Tyson, translated by James Strachey, 13: 1–161. London: Hogarth.

———. 1959a. " 'Civilized' Sexual Morality and Modern Nervous Illness." In *The Standard Edition of the Complete Psychological Works of Sigmund Freud*, edited by Anna Freud, Alix Strachey, and Alan Tyson, translated by James Strachey, 9: 181–204. London: Hogarth.

———. 1959b. "Delusions and Dreams in Jensen's Gradiva." In *The Standard Edition of the Complete Psychological Works of Sigmund Freud*, edited by Anna

Freud, Alix Strachey, and Alan Tyson, translated by James Strachey, 9: 7–95. London: Hogarth.

———. 1959c. "Inhibitions, Symptoms, and Anxiety." In *The Standard Edition of the Complete Psychological Works of Sigmund Freud*, edited by Anna Freud, Alix Strachey, and Alan Tyson, translated by James Strachey, 20: 87–174. London: Hogarth.

———. 1959d. "On the Sexual Theories of Children." In *The Standard Edition of the Complete Psychological Works of Sigmund Freud*, edited by Anna Freud, Alix Strachey, and Alan Tyson, translated by James Strachey, 9: 209–26. London: Hogarth.

———. 1959e. "The Sexual Enlightenment of Children: An Open Letter to Mr. Furst." In *The Standard Edition of the Complete Psychological Works of Sigmund Freud*, edited by Anna Freud, Alix Strachey, and Alan Tyson, translated by James Strachey, 9: 131–39. London: Hogarth.

———. 1960a. "Jokes and Their Relation to the Unconscious." In *The Standard Edition of the Complete Psychological Works of Sigmund Freud*, edited by Anna Freud, Alix Strachey, and Alan Tyson, translated by James Strachey. Vol. 8. London: Hogarth.

———. 1960b. "The Psychopathology of Everyday Life." In *The Standard Edition of the Complete Psychological Works of Sigmund Freud*, edited by Anna Freud, Alix Strachey, and Alan Tyson, translated by James Strachey. Vol. 6. London: Hogarth.

———. 1961a. "Civilization and Its Discontents." In *The Standard Edition of the Complete Psychological Works of Sigmund Freud*, edited by Anna Freud, Alix Strachey, and Alan Tyson, translated by James Strachey, 21: 64–145. London: Hogarth.

———. 1961b. "Dotstoevski and Parricide." In *The Standard Edition of the Complete Psychological Works of Sigmund Freud*, edited by Anna Freud, Alix Strachey, and Alan Tyson, translated by James Strachey, 21: 177–96. London: Hogarth.

———. 1961c. "Negation." In *The Standard Edition of the Complete Psychological Works of Sigmund Freud*, edited by Anna Freud, Alix Strachey, and Alan Tyson, translated by James Strachey, 19: 235–39. London: Hogarth.

———. 1961d. "New Introductory Lectures to Psychoanalysis." In *The Standard Edition of the Complete Psychological Works of Sigmund Freud*, edited by Anna Freud, Alix Strachey, and Alan Tyson, translated by James Strachey, 22: 7–182. London: Hogarth.

———. 1961e. "The Economic Problem of Masochism." In *The Standard Edition of the Complete Psychological Works of Sigmund Freud*, edited by Anna Freud, Alix Strachey, and Alan Tyson, translated by James Strachey, 19: 159–70. London: Hogarth.

———. 1961f. "The Ego and the Id." In *The Standard Edition of the Complete Psychological Works of Sigmund Freud*, edited by Anna Freud, Alix Strachey, and Alan Tyson, translated by James Strachey, 19: 12–68. London: Hogarth.

———. 1961g. "The Infantile Genital Organization: An Interpolation into the Theory of Sexuality." In *The Standard Edition of the Complete Psychological Works of Sigmund Freud*, edited by Anna Freud, Alix Strachey, and Alan Tyson, translated by James Strachey, 19: 141–45. London: Hogarth.

———. 1961h. "The Question of a Weltanschauung." In *The Standard Edition of the Complete Psychological Works of Sigmund Freud*, edited by Anna Freud, Alix Strachey, and Alan Tyson, translated by James Strachey, 22: 158–82. London: Hogarth.

———. 1962a. "On the Grounds for Detaching a Particular Syndrome from Neurasthenia under the Description 'Anxiety Neurosis.'" In *The Standard Edition of the Complete Psychological Works of Sigmund Freud*, edited by Anna Freud, Alix Strachey, and Alan Tyson, translated by James Strachey, 3: 90–117. London: Hogarth.

———. 1962b. "Sexuality in the Aetiology of Neuroses." In *The Standard Edition of the Complete Psychological Works of Sigmund Freud*, edited by Anna Freud, Alix Strachey, and Alan Tyson, translated by James Strachey, 3: 263–85. London: Hogarth.

———. 1963. "Introductory Lectures on Psychoanalysis." In *The Standard Edition of the Complete Psychological Works of Sigmund Freud*, edited by Anna Freud, Alix Strachey, and Alan Tyson, translated by James Strachey. Vol. 15–16. London: Hogarth.

———. 1964a. "An Autobiographical Study." In *The Standard Edition of the Complete Psychological Works of Sigmund Freud*, edited by Anna Freud, Alix Strachey, and Alan Tyson, translated by James Strachey, 20: 7–76. London: Hogarth.

———. 1964b. "Analysis Terminable and Interminable." In *The Standard Edition of the Complete Psychological Works of Sigmund Freud*, edited by Anna Freud, Alix Strachey, and Alan Tyson, translated by James Strachey, 23: 216–53. London: Hogarth.

———. 1964c. "Moses and Monotheism." In *The Standard Edition of the Complete Psychological Works of Sigmund Freud*, edited by Anna Freud, Alix Strachey, and Alan Tyson, translated by James Strachey, 23: 7–137. London: Hogarth.

———. 1966. "Project for a Scientific Psychology." In *The Standard Edition of the Complete Psychological Works of Sigmund Freud*, edited by Anna Freud, Alix Strachey, and Alan Tyson, translated by James Strachey, 1: 283–397. London: Hogarth.

———. 1987. "Entwurf Einer Psychologie." In *Gesammelte Werke, Nachtragsband, Texte Aus Den Jahren 1885 Bis 1938*, edited by Angela Richards, 387–486. Frankfurt am Main: Fischer.

———. 2016. *Three Essays on the Theory of Sexuality: The 1905 Edition*. Edited by Philippe Van Haute and Herman Westerink. Translated by Ulrike Kistner. London; New York: Verso.

Freud, Sigmund, and Josef Breuer. (1895) 1952. "Studien Über Hysterie." In *Gesammelte Werke*, 1: 77–312. Frankfurt am Main: Fischer.

———. 1955. "Studies on Hysteria." In *The Standard Edition of the Complete Psychological Works of Sigmund Freud*, edited by Anna Freud, Alix Strachey, and Alan Tyson, translated by James Strachey. Vol. 2. London: Hogarth.

Gray, Jonathan M. 2017. "Heteronormativity without Nature: Toward a Queer Ecology." *QED: A Journal in GLBTQ Worldmaking* 4 (2): 137–42.

Hägglund, Martin. 2008. *Radical Atheism: Derrida and the Time of Life*. Meridian, Crossing Aesthetics. Stanford, CA: Stanford University Press.

Halberstam, Judith. 2005. *Queer Temporality and Postmodern Geographies*. New York: New York University Press.

Haraway, Donna Jeanne. 1994. "A Game of Cat's Cradle: Science Studies, Feminist Theory, Cultural Studies." *Configurations* 2 (1): 59–71.

Haute, Philippe Van. 2002. *Against Adaptation: Lacan's "Subversion of the Subject."* The Lacanian Clinical Field. New York: Other Press.

Haute, Phillipe Van, and Herman Westerink. 2016. "'Introduction: Hysteria, Sexuality, and the Deconstruction of Normativity: Rereading Freud's 1905 Edition of Three Essays on the Theory of Sexuality.'" In *Three Essays on the Theory of Sexuality: The 1905 Edition*. London; New York: Verso.

———. 2017. "Excavating a Theory of Sexuality." In *Deconstructing Normativity?: Re-Reading Freud's 1905 Three Essays*, edited by Philippe Van Haute and Herman Westerink, 1–5. London; New York: Routledge.

———. 2021. *Reading Freud's Three Essays on the Theory of Sexuality: From Pleasure to the Object*. New York: Routledge.

Hegel, Georg Wilhelm Friedrich. 2012. *Elements of the Philosophy of Right*. Edited by Allen W. Wood. Translated by Hugh Barr Nisbet. Cambridge Texts in the History of Political Thought. Cambridge: Cambridge University Press.

Hock, Udo. 2007. "Laplanche's Trieb." *Libres Cahiers Pour La Psychanalyse* 1 (15): 73–84.

Holder, Alex. 1970. "Instinct and Drive." In *Basic Psychoanalytic Concepts on the Theory of Instincts*, edited by Humberto Nagera, 19–22. London; New York: Routledge.

Husserl, Edmund. (1936) 1976. "Beilage III." In *Die Krisis der europäischen Wissenschaften und die transzendentale Phänomenologie: eine Einleitung in die phänomenologische Philosophie*, edited by Walter Biemel, 2. Aufl., photomechan, 365–86. Gesammelte Werke 6. Reprint. Dordrecht: Kluwer.

———. 1984. "The Origin of Geometry." In *The Crisis of European Sciences and Transcendental Phenomenology: An Introduction to Phenomenological Philosophy*, 6th ed., translated by David Carr, 353–79. Studies in Phenomenology & Existential Philosophy. Evanston, IL: Northwestern University Press.

Irigaray, Luce. 1980. "When Our Lips Speak Together." Translated by Carolyn Burke. *Signs* 6 (1): 69–79.

———. 1993. "Sorcerer Love: A Reading of Plato, Symposium, Diotima's Speech." In *An Ethics of Sexual Difference*, translated by Carolyn Burke and C. Gillian, 20–33. Ithaca, NY: Cornell University Press.

Johnston, Adrian. 2005. *Time Driven: Metapsychology and the Splitting of the Drive*. Northwestern University Studies in Phenomenology and Existential Philosophy. Evanston, IL: Northwestern University Press.

———. 2012. "'Naturalism or Anti-Naturalism? No, Thanks—Both Are Worse!': Science, Materialism, and Slavoj Žižek." *Revue Internationale de Philosophie* 261 (3): 321–46.

———. 2018a. *A New German Idealism: Hegel, Žižek, and Dialectical Materialism*. New York: Columbia University Press.

———. 2018b. "The Late Innate: Jean Laplanche, Jaak Panksepp, and the Distinction between Sexual Drives and Instincts." In *Inheritance in Psychoanalysis*, 57–84. Albany, NY: SUNY Press.

Kant, Immanuel. 1991. *The Metaphysics of Morals*. Texts in German Philosophy. Cambridge, UK; New York: Cambridge University Press.

Kirkland, Sean D. 2013. *The Ontology of Socratic Questioning in Plato's Early Dialogues*. Albany, NY: SUNY Press.

Kistner, Ulrike. 2016. "Translating the First Edition of Freud's Drei Abhandlungen Zur Sexualtheorie." In *Three Essays on the Theory of Sexuality: The 1905 Edition*, lxxvii–xc. London; New York: Verso.

Klassen, Stephanie Rosenbaum. 2016. "In The Queer Kitchen: 'Food That Takes Pleasure Seriously.'" *NPR*, July 5, 2016, sec. The Salt. https://www.npr.org/sections/thesalt/2016/07/05/484354089/in-the-queer-kitchen-food-that-takes-pleasure-seriously.

Koyré, Alexandre. 1968. "Galileo and the Scientific Revolution of the Seventeenth Century." In *Metaphysics and Measurement: Essays in Scientific Revolution*, 1–15. Cambridge, MA: Harvard University Press.

Lacan, Jacques. 1966a. "'La Signification Du Phallus.'" In *Écrits*, 685–97. Paris: Éditions du Seuil.

———. 1966b. "'Le Stade Du Miroir Comme Fondateur de La Fonction Du Je.'" In *Écrits*, 93–100. Paris: Éditions du Seuil.

———. 1966c. "Position de l'inconscient." In *Écrits*, 829–50. Paris: Éditions du Seuil.

———. 1966d. "Subversion Du Sujet et Dialectique Du Desir Dans l'inconscient Freudien." In *Écrits*, 793–827. Paris: Éditions du Seuil.

———. 1973. *Le séminaire de Jacques Lacan, Livre XI: Les quatre concepts fondamentaux de la psychoanalyse, 1963–1964*. Le séminaire de Jacques Lacan, VII. Paris: Éditions du Seuil.

———. 1981. *The Seminar of Jacques Lacan, Book XI: The Four Fundamental Concepts of Psychoanalysis, 1963–1964*. Translated by Russell Grigg. New York & London: W. W. Norton.

———. 1983. "Interview Donnée Par Jacques Lacan à François Wahl à Propos de La Parution Des Écrits." *Le Bulletin de l'Association Freudienne* 3 (May): 6–7.

———. 1986. *Le séminaire de Jacques Lacan, Livre VII: L'éthique de la psychoanalyse, 1959–1960*. Le séminaire de Jacques Lacan, VII. Paris: Éditions du Seuil.

———. 1991. *Le séminaire de Jacques Lacan, Livre XVII: L' envers de la psychoanalyse, 1969–1970*. Le séminaire de Jacques Lacan, XVII. Paris: Éditions du Seuil.

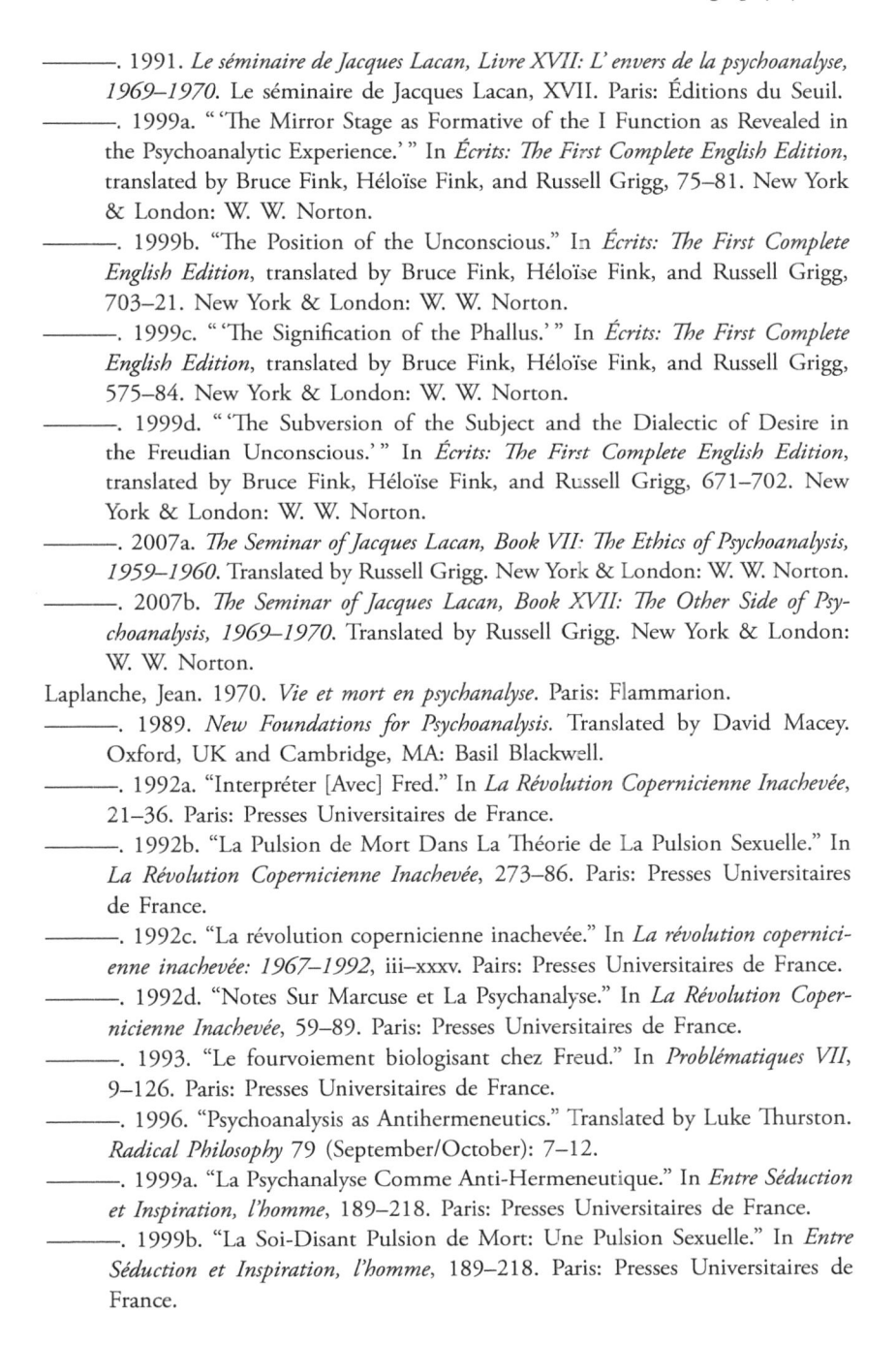

———. 1999a. "'The Mirror Stage as Formative of the I Function as Revealed in the Psychoanalytic Experience.'" In *Écrits: The First Complete English Edition*, translated by Bruce Fink, Héloïse Fink, and Russell Grigg, 75–81. New York & London: W. W. Norton.

———. 1999b. "The Position of the Unconscious." In *Écrits: The First Complete English Edition*, translated by Bruce Fink, Héloïse Fink, and Russell Grigg, 703–21. New York & London: W. W. Norton.

———. 1999c. "'The Signification of the Phallus.'" In *Écrits: The First Complete English Edition*, translated by Bruce Fink, Héloïse Fink, and Russell Grigg, 575–84. New York & London: W. W. Norton.

———. 1999d. "'The Subversion of the Subject and the Dialectic of Desire in the Freudian Unconscious.'" In *Écrits: The First Complete English Edition*, translated by Bruce Fink, Héloïse Fink, and Russell Grigg, 671–702. New York & London: W. W. Norton.

———. 2007a. *The Seminar of Jacques Lacan, Book VII: The Ethics of Psychoanalysis, 1959–1960*. Translated by Russell Grigg. New York & London: W. W. Norton.

———. 2007b. *The Seminar of Jacques Lacan, Book XVII: The Other Side of Psychoanalysis, 1969–1970*. Translated by Russell Grigg. New York & London: W. W. Norton.

Laplanche, Jean. 1970. *Vie et mort en psychanalyse*. Paris: Flammarion.

———. 1989. *New Foundations for Psychoanalysis*. Translated by David Macey. Oxford, UK and Cambridge, MA: Basil Blackwell.

———. 1992a. "Interpréter [Avec] Fred." In *La Révolution Copernicienne Inachevée*, 21–36. Paris: Presses Universitaires de France.

———. 1992b. "La Pulsion de Mort Dans La Théorie de La Pulsion Sexuelle." In *La Révolution Copernicienne Inachevée*, 273–86. Paris: Presses Universitaires de France.

———. 1992c. "La révolution copernicienne inachevée." In *La révolution copernicienne inachevée: 1967–1992*, iii–xxxv. Pairs: Presses Universitaires de France.

———. 1992d. "Notes Sur Marcuse et La Psychanalyse." In *La Révolution Copernicienne Inachevée*, 59–89. Paris: Presses Universitaires de France.

———. 1993. "Le fourvoiement biologisant chez Freud." In *Problématiques VII*, 9–126. Paris: Presses Universitaires de France.

———. 1996. "Psychoanalysis as Antihermeneutics." Translated by Luke Thurston. *Radical Philosophy* 79 (September/October): 7–12.

———. 1999a. "La Psychanalyse Comme Anti-Hermeneutique." In *Entre Séduction et Inspiration, l'homme*, 189–218. Paris: Presses Universitaires de France.

———. 1999b. "La Soi-Disant Pulsion de Mort: Une Pulsion Sexuelle." In *Entre Séduction et Inspiration, l'homme*, 189–218. Paris: Presses Universitaires de France.

———. 1999c. "Responsabilité et Réponse." In *Entre Séduction et Inspiration, l'homme*, 147–72. Paris: Presses Universitaires de France.

———. 1999d. "The Unfinished Copernican Revolution." In *Essays on Otherness*, translated by John Fletcher, 53–85. Warwick Studies in European Philosophy. London; New York: Routledge.

———. 2008a. "À Partir de La Situation Anthropologique Fondamentale." In *La Sexualité Élargie au Sens Freudien*, 95–108. Paris: Presses Universitaires de France.

———. 2008b. "Les Trois Essai et la théorie de la séduction." In *La sexualité élargie au sens freudien*, 241–56. Paris: Presses Universitaires de France.

———. 2008c. "Pulsion et Instinct." In *La Sexualité Élargie au Sens Freudien*, 7–25. Paris: Presses Universitaires de France.

———. 2008d. "'Trois Acceptations Du Mot "Inconscient" Dans le Cadre de la Théorie de la Séduction Généralisée.'" In *La Sexualité Élargie au Sens Freudien*, 195–213. Paris: Presses Universitaires de France.

———. 2011a. "Drive and Instinct: Distinctions, Oppositions, Supports, and Intertwinings." In *Freud and the Sexual*, 5–26. New York: Unconscious in Translation.

———. 2011b. "Starting from the Fundamental Anthropological Situation." In *Freud and the Sexual*, 99–114. New York: Unconscious in Translation.

———. 2011c. "The Three Essays and the Theory of Seduction." In *Freud and the Sexual*, 249–66. New York: Unconscious in Translation.

———. 2011d. "Three Meanings of the Term 'Unconscious' in the Framework of the General Theory of Seduction." In *Freud and the Sexual*, 203–22. New York: Unconscious in Translation.

———. 2013. *Life and Death in Psychoanalysis*. Translated by Jeffrey Mehlman. Baltimore: Johns Hopkins University Press.

———. 2015a. "Responsibility and Response (1994)." In *Between Seduction and Inspiration: Man*, translated by Jeffrey Mehlman, 123–44. New York: Unconscious in Translation.

———. 2015b. "The So-Called Death Drive: A Sexual Drive (1997)." In *Between Seduction and Inspiration: Man*, translated by Jeffrey Mehlman, 159–82. New York: Unconscious in Translation.

———. 2015c. *The Temptation of Biology: Freud's Theories of Sexuality; Followed by, Biologism and Biology*. Translated by Donald Nicholson-Smith. 1st ed. New York: Unconscious in Translation.

———. 2020a. "Interpreting (with) Freud (1968)." In *The Unfinished Copernican Revolution*, translated by Luke Thurston, 57–74. New York: Unconscious in Translation.

———. 2020b. "Notes on Marcuse and Psychoanalysis (1969)." In *The Unfinished Copernican Revolution*, translated by Luke Thurston, 101–34. New York: Unconscious in Translation.

———. 2020c. "The Death Drive in the Theory of Sexual Drives (1986)." In *The Unfinished Copernican Revolution*, translated by Luke Thurston, 351–66. New York: Unconscious in Translation.

Laplanche, Jean, and Serge Leclaire. 1981. "L'inconscient une étude psychanalytique." In *L'inconscient et le ça: suivi de l'inconscient une étude psychanalytique*, 261–321. Paris: Presses universitaires de France.

Laplanche, Jean, and Jean-Bertrand Pontalis. 2009. *Vocabulaire de la psychanalyse*. 5th ed. Bibliothéque de psychoanalyse. Paris: Pr. Univ. de France.

Laurentis, Teresa de. 1998. "The Stubborn Drive." *Critical Inquiry* 24 (4): 851–77.

Lear, Jonathan. 2005. *Freud*. Routledge Philosophers. Reprint. New York: Routledge.

Marder, Elissa. 2012. *The Mother in the Mechanical Age of Reproduction: Psychoanalysis, Photography, Deconstruction*. New York: Fordham University Press.

Maruzzella, David. 2019. "The Two Bachelards of Louis Althusser." *Parrhesia* 31.

Matheron, Alexandre. 2020. "Spinoza and Sexuality." In *Politics, Ontology and Knowledge in Spinoza*, edited by Filippo Del Lucchese, translated by Gil Morejon and David Maruzzella, 239–59. Edinburgh: Edinburgh University Press.

Merleau-Ponty, Maurice. 1982. "Phenomenology and Psychoanalysis: Preface to Hesnard's L'Oeuvre de Freud." *Review of Existential Psychology & Psychiatry* 18 (1–3): 67–72.

———. 2002. *Phenomenology of Perception*. Translated by Colin Smith. London; New York: Routledge.

Merrick, Helen. 2008. "Queering Nature: Close Encounters with the Alien in Ecofeminist Science Fiction." In *Queer Universes: Sexualities in Science Fiction*, edited by Joan Gordon, Veronica Hollinger, and Wendy Gay Pearson, 216–32. Liverpool, UK: Liverpool University Press.

Mitchell, Juliet. 1990. "Psychoanalysis and Women." In *Essential Papers on the Psychology of Women*, 331–43. New York & London: New York University Press.

Murray, Martin. 2016. *Jacques Lacan: A Critical Introduction*. London: Pluto Press.

Naas, Michael. 2008. *Derrida from Now On*. New York: Fordham University Press.

Nagel, Thomas. 1969. "Sexual Perversion." *e Journal of Philosophy* 66 (1): 5–17.

Oakes, Guy. 1995. "Straight Thinking about Queer Theory." *International Journal of Politics, Culture, and Society* 8 (3): 379–88.

Oosterhuis, Harry. 2020. "Freud and Albert Moll: How Kindred Spirits Became Bitter Foes." *History of Psychiatry* 31 (3): 294–310.

Pearson, Wendy Gay. 2004. "The Queer as Traitor, the Traitor as Queer: Denaturalizing Concepts of Nationhood, Species and Sexuality." In *Flashes and Fantastic*, edited by David Ketterer, 77–91. Westport, CT: Praeger.

Pérez, Beatriz Febus. 2020. "The Sexual Subject in Queer Theologies: Implications for a Queer Latin American Liberation Theology?" In *The Indecent Theologies of Marcella Althaus-Reid*. London; New York: Routledge.

Plato. (1926) 2001. *Plato: In Twelve Volumes. 10: Laws: Books I–VI*. Translated by Robert Gregg Bury. Reprint. Cambridge, MA: Harvard University Press.

———. (1926) 2004. *Plato: In Twelve Volumes. 11: Laws: Books VII–XII.* Translated by Robert Gregg Bury. Reprint. Cambridge, MA: Harvard University Press.

Preciado, Paul B. 2021. *Can the Monster Speak? A Report to an Academy of Psychoanalysts.* Translated by Frank Wynne. South Pasadena, CA: Semiotext(e).

Priest, Ann-Marie. 2003. "Woman as God, God as Woman: Mysticism, Negative Theology, and Luce Irigaray." *Journal of Religion* 83 (1): 1–23.

"Queer Temporalities." 2007. *GLQ* 13 (2–3). https://www.dukeupress.edu/queer-temporalities.

Quinodoz, Jean-Michel. 2005. *Reading Freud: A Chronological Exploration of Freud's Writings.* Hove, UK; New York: Routledge.

———. 2011. "L'influence des traductions de Freud sur la pensée psychanalytique française." *L'Année psychanalytique internationale* 2011 (1): 29–53.

Ramos, Bradley. 2022. "There's Nothing Suspicious about Freud." *European Journal of Psychoanalysis* 9 (2).

Rottenberg, Elizabeth. 2019. *For the Love of Psychoanalysis: The Play of Chance in Freud and Derrida.* New York: Fordham University Press.

Salamon, Gayle. 2010. *Assuming a Body: Transgender and Rhetorics of Materiality.* New York: Columbia University Press.

Santos, Ana Cristina. 2023. "Embodied Queer Epistemologies: A New Approach to (a Monstrous) Citizenship." In *LGBTQ+ Intimacies in Southern Europe: Citizenship, Care and Choice,* edited by Ana Cristina Santos, 77–98. London: Palgrave Macmillan. https://doi.org/10.1007/978-3-031-13508-8_5.

Sartre, Jean-Paul. 1943. *L'être et Le Néant: Essai d'ontologie Phénoménologique.* Paris: Éditions Gallimard.

———. 2021. *Being and Nothingness: An Essay on Phenomenological Ontology.* Translated by Sarah Richmond. New York: Washington Square Press/Atria, an imprint of Simon & Schuster.

Sedgwick, Eve Kosofsky. 2008. *Epistemology of the Closet.* Updated with a new preface. Berkeley; London: University of California Press.

Senatore, Mauro. 2013. "Leaving a Trace in the World: Sexuality and Auto-Affection in Of Grammatology." *Derrida Today* 6 (2): 240–54. https://doi.org/10.3366/drt.2013.0066.

Sharp, Hasana. 2011. *Spinoza and the Politics of Renaturalization.* Chicago, IL: University of Chicago Press.

Soble, Alan. 2003. "Kant and Sexual Perversion." *Monist* 86 (1): 55–89.

Söderbäck, Fanny. 2017. "Liminal Spaces: Reflections on the In-Between." *Architecture and Culture* 5 (September): 383–93. https://doi.org/10.1080/20507828.2017.1362886.

Solms, Mark. 2013. "Notes on the Revised Standard Edition." *Psychoanalytic Review* 100 (1): 201–10.

Spinoza, Benedictus de. 1985. "Ethics." In *The Collected Works of Spinoza,* edited by E. M. Curley, 408–617. Princeton, NJ: Princeton University Press.

Strachey, James. 1953. "Notes on Some Technical Terms Whose Translation Calls for Comment." In *The Standard Edition of the Complete Psychological Works of Sigmund Freud: Pre-Psychoanalytic Publications and Unpublished Drafts*, 1: xxiii–xxvi. London: Hogarth.

Sullivan, Nikki. 1999. "Queer Pleasures: Some Thoughts." *Social Semiotics* 9 (2): 251–55.

Thorpe, Shemeka, Natalie Malone, Jardin N. Dogan, Marla R. Cineas, Kasey Vigil, and Candice N. Hargons. 2022. "Exploring Differences in Black Heterosexual and Queer Women's Sexual Experiences through a Black Queer Feminist Lens." *Sexual and Relationship Therapy*.

Vasiliou, Elena. 2020. "Penitentiary Pleasures: Queer Understandings of Prison Paradoxes." *Criminology & Criminal Justice* 20 (5): 577–89.

Whiteside, Shaun. 2006. "Translator's Preface." In *The Psychology of Love*, edited by A. Phillips and Shaun Whiteside, xxvii–xxxii. London: Penguin.

Wiegman, Robyn, and Elizabeth A. Wilson. 2015. "Introduction: Antinormativity's Queer Conventions." *Differences* 26 (1): 1–25.

Winnicott, D. W. 1965. "The Theory of the Parent-Infant Relationship." In *The Maturational Process and the Facilitating Environment: Studies in the Theory of Emotional Development*, 37–55. New York: International Universities Press.

Wollheim, Richard. 1981. *Sigmund Freud*. Cambridge, UK; New York: Cambridge University Press.

Žižek, Slavoj. 2012. "Hegel on Marriage." *E-Flux* 34 (April). https://www.e-flux.com/journal/34/68365/hegel-on-marriage/.

———. 2015. *Absolute Recoil: Towards a New Foundation of Dialectical Materialism*. London; New York: Verso.

Zupančič, Alenka. 2017. *What Is Sex?* Short Circuits. Cambridge, MA: MIT Press.

Index

Abraham, Karl, 41, 54, 55
adaptation, 40
Adler, Alfred, 53–54, 145n4
alterity, 91, 93, 94
Althusser, Louis, 10; biology and, 67, 68; "The Discovery of Doctor Freud," 60, 66–67, 68, 153n1; *étayage*, 68; ideology, 153–54n2; impossible difference, 66–67, 69, 75, 127, 139; limit concept, 10, 66, 68, 69; metapsychology and, 60, 64, 66; novelty of psychoanalysis and, 60, 153n1; "On Marx and Freud," 68; *Psychoanalysis and the Human Sciences*, 153–54n2; science and, 153n1, 153–54n2; "Three Notes on the Theory of Discourse," 67; *Trieb* and, 60, 61, 64, 66, 68, 78, 111, 153n1
Anderson, Ellie, 99
animal(s), 4, 18, 29, 149n4; instincts in, 147–48n4
Aquinas, Thomas, 4, 93, 158n6
Aristophanes, speech in *Symposium*. See Freud, terms/concepts: poetic fable
Aristotle, 3–4, 142n6, 145n1, 146n8
asexuality, 132
attachment (*Anlehnung*), 33, 81, 109. See also Laplanche: *étayage*
attraction, sexual, 144n11; to opposite sex, 3, 4, 18, 25, 26, 30, 33, 40, 93, 104, 122; to sexual object, 25, 28, 29, 30, 31–33, 89, 158n4, 161n8; soldering and, 34, 121–22
Augustine, 4
auto-affection, 11, 94, 95, 96, 101; as autoerotism, 92, 93, 98, 101, 103; as auto-hetero-affection, 97; deconstruction of, 96–97, 98; as hetero-affection, 97, 99; philosophers and, 93, 94, 96, 98. See also autoerotism
autoerotism, 11, 16, 88, 97, 101, 102; as auto-affection, 92, 93, 98, 101, 103; as auto-hetero-erotism, 99, 101, 102; Freud's definition of, 81; as nonfantasmatic (Van Haute and Westerink), 91, 92; as nonfunctional (Van Haute and Westerink), 89, 90, 91, 92, 104, 159n13; as nonintersubjective (Van Haute and Westerink), 91, 92; as objectless (Van Haute and Westerink), 90, 91, 92, 157n4; Oedipus complex and, 92, 102, 158n12; as perversion, 97. See also auto-affection; sexuality, infantile

Bacon, Francis, 142n6
Bianchi, Emanuela, 3–4

binary, 6, 33, 35, 75, 86, 92, 106, 126, 136, 137, 138
biologism, 40, 159n12; as criticism of Freud, xiv, 59; as ideology, 37, 38, 39
biology, 18. *See also* instinct; vital function; vital order
body, the, 77–78, 82, 90, 91–92, 101, 116; as autoerotic object, 100, 102, 158n4
Bonaparte, Marie, 45
breast, 80, 82, 91, 111; fantasmatic, 112. *See also* caregiver: breast/bottle feeding
Brill, Abraham, 45
Butler Judith, 163n6

care relation, 11, 16, 92, 102, 115–17, 127–28, 131, 132; breast/bottle feeding, 80, 82, 91, 111–12, 127; genesis of sexuality and, 79, 80–82, 85, 109, 112; as a sexual relation, 127–28, 129. *See also* caregiver; helplessness; sexuality, infantile
caregiver, 11, 16, 80–82, 91, 92, 111, 115–16, 156n6; sexuality of, 127, 128. *See also* care relation
childhood: Derrida and, 138, 140. *See also* sexuality, infantile
Cicero, 4
communication, 116, 117
contingency, 35, 89, 90, 106
conversion therapy, 106
critical theory, 136, 162n5, 164n7. *See also* queer theory
Crystal Principle, 114, 128
cure: homosexuality and, 26–27, 147n9, 159n16. *See also* normalization; pathologization

Darwin, Charles, xiii, 66
Davidson, Arnold, 18, 49, 150n12

deconstruction, 106, 149n6; Derrida and, 93–99, 103, 106, 138; Van Haute and Westerink and, 82, 87, 88, 92, 93, 98. *See also* auto-affection; Derrida
dehiscence, 114, 115, 118, 130
denaturalization, 133, 135, 136, 137, 138, 140, 162n2, 163n6, 164n7, 164n8; of the instinct, 129–30
Derrida, Jacques, 11, 103, 106, 138–40, 155n3, 160n5; condition of possibility/impossibility, 129; deconstruction of presence, 94–98; *différance*, 93, 96, 98, 99, 101; logic of the supplement, 95–96, 97, 99, 102, 118, 128; metaphysics of presence, 94; *Of Grammatology*, 93–99; *On Touching*, 97; *s'entendre parler*, 94; spacing (*espacement*), 95, 97; speculation, 158n9; trace, 94–95, 96, 101; voice (*la voix*), 94, 95; writing, 93–96, 99. *See also* auto-affection; autoerotism; deconstruction
Descartes, René, 4–5, 65
desexualization, 43, 150n8
desire, 3, 104, 105, 124–28, 132, 161n11. *See also* Lacan, need-demand-desire
deviation, 118; as defining of sexuality, 22, 35, 36, 80; *dérivation* and, 110, 112, 113, 128, 129, 131, 138; as *fourvoiement*, 67, 68, 78; from *Geschlechtstrieb*, 19, 22, 23, 33; infantile sexuality and, 81, 85, 90, 110–11, 124, 131, 137, 156n9; from instinct, 4, 11, 23, 78, 81, 85, 93, 110–11, 128, 129, 131, 138, 156n9; from heterosexuality, 23, 25, 26, 27, 28, 33, 137; norms and, 137; as perversion, 11, 22, 23, 35,

36, 93, 112, 113, 124, 129, 131, 138, 156n9, 156; sexual aberrations and, 19, 24–25, 26, 27. *See also* Laplanche: *dérivation*; Laplanche: *fourvoiement*; perversion; sexuality, infantile; *Trieb*
directionality, 34, 131, 135
Dolar, Mladen, 157n3
drive. See *Trieb*
drive theory. See *Trieblehre*

edging, 24
Epicurus, 4
epistemology, xiv, 136, 137; foundationalism, 64
erotogenic/erogenous zone, 56, 81–82, 91–92, 100–101, 111, 133
essentialism, 6, 40
exceptionality, xiv, 11, 20, 132, 133, 136, 137–39, 140, 164n12

fantasy, xiv, 31, 91, 92, 98, 127, 150n9, 158n4
femininity, 6, 159n13
feminism, 106, 154n7, 163n5
fetishism, 29, 89
final causality, 34, 142n6. *See also* teleology
fluidity, 7, 110, 137, 154n7
food, 31, 40, 76, 80, 129
Foucault, Michel, xiii, 86–88, 103, 106, 156–57n1, 157n3, 163n5
Freud, Sigmund: as clinician, 26, 106, 146n5, 147n9, 159n16; philosophy and, 1–2, 6, 7, 9, 54, 86, 93, 141–42n1, 143n2, 143n3m 143n4, 145n1, 147n8, 158n9; queer theory and, xiii, 85, 86, 93, 103, 137, 141n1, 141n3, 162–63n5; science and, xiii, 64–66, 133, 134, 142n5
Freud, Sigmund, terms/concepts: basic concept (*Grundbegriff*), 61, 64, 65; bisexual disposition, 159; border/limit concept (*Grenzbegriff*), 10, 68, 69; cathexis, 62; diphasic object choice, 102, 160n7, 161n10; disavowal, 24, 26; dream-work, 31; Eros, 54, 56, 155n4; fort/da, 68, 158n9; free association, xiv; indefiniteness (*Unbestimmtheit*), 48, 64, 65, 66, 67; kettle logic, 29–31; libidinal development, 6, 41, 54, 55, 56, 63; libido, 41, 54, 62, 119; metapsychology, 60, 64, 66, 113, 142n5; narcissism, 56, 62, 63, 86; parapraxis, 51, 146n6; phallic stage, 54, 56; pleasure principle, 63, 101, 156n4; poetic fable, 9, 41, 144n11, 147n8, 156n4; polymorphous perversity, 16, 56, 57, 104, 106, 149n6, 158n12, 159n13; second topography, 142n5, 153n29; sexual morality, xiv, 105, 146n7, 159n14, 159n15, 163n5; side effect (*Nebenwirkung*), 23, 81, 129; speculative superstructure, 66; sublimation, 35, 99, 131; substitute object, 80, 82, 102, 111, 112, 131; vicissitude, 8, 63, 124, 126, 127, 131, 132; weak spot, 113, 114, 115, 140. *See also* attachment; autoerotism; care relation; fantasy; *Geschlechtstrieb*; helplessness; homosexuality; hunger; instinct; *Instinkt*; liberation, sexual; neuroses; normalization; Oedipus complex; pathologization; perversion; popular opinion; puberty; sexual aberrations; sexual aim; sexual object; sexuality; sexuality, adult; sexuality, infantile; *Sexualtrieb*; soldering; speculation; temptation; *Trieb*; *Trieblehre*; unconscious; vicissitude

Freud, Sigmund, works by: "An Autobiographical Study," 66, 101, 142n5, 152n27; *Beyond the Pleasure Principle*, 62, 63, 153n28, 155n3, 155n4, 156n4, 158n9, 160n3; *Civilization and its Discontents*, 61, 62, 63, 64, 156n5; "'Civilized Sexual Morality and Modern Nervous Illness," 146n7, 146n8, 159n15, 159n16; "The Claims of Psycho-Analysis to Scientific Interest," 124–25; "On the Grounds for Detaching a Particular Syndrome from Neurasthenia under the Description 'Anxiety Neurosis'," 160n3, 160n4; "The History of An Infantile Neurosis" (Wolf Man case study), 53; "On the History of the Psychoanalytic Movement," 145n4; "The Infantile Genital Organization," 54; *Interpretation of Dreams*, 15, 29, 30, 31, 146n6, 148n4, 149n4; *Introductory Lectures on Psychoanalysis*, 148n4; *Jokes and their Relation to the Unconscious*, 30, 31, 47, 146n6, 160n3; "On Narcissism," 62; *New Introductory Lectures on Psychoanalysis*, 64, 113, 148n4, 159n13; "The Psychogenesis of a Case of Homosexuality in a Woman," 25, 45; *Psychopathology of Everyday Life*, 15, 146n6; "The Question of a *Weltanschauung*," 133, 142n5; "The Sexual Aetiology of the Neuroses," 146n6, 148n4; "The Sexual Enlightenment of Children," 160n3, 160n9, 160n11; "On the Sexual Theories of Children," 147n8, 160n3, 160n11; "A Special Type of Object Choice Made by Men," 161n9; "Triebe und Triebschicksale," 61, 63, 64, 68, 75, 77, 78, 152n26; *Totem and Taboo*, 147n2, 148n4, 149n4; "On the Universal Tendency Towards Debasement in the Sphere of Love," 161n9. See also *Gesammelte Werke*; *Les œuvres complètes de Freud*; *Standard Edition*; *Three Essays on the Theory of Sexuality*

gender, 29, 122, 159n13, 163n5, 163–64n6
gender studies, xiii, 85, 103, 141n1, 163n6
genitals, 6, 18, 23, 24, 25, 41, 82, 102, 123, 133, 134, 143n4; genital drive (Kistner), 120, 121, 122
Gesammelte Werke, 52, 53, 152n23
Geschlecht, 29, 121, 122; translation of, 160n5
Geschlechtstrieb, 29, 31; as analogous to hunger, 18, 75; etymology of, 122; Freud's contemporaries and, 18; infantile sexuality and, 125–26; Kistner's translation of, 120–21; as opposed to *Sexualtrieb*, 121, 123; popular opinion and, 18, 19, 23, 31, 32, 33, 37, 75, 126; relation to sexual aberrations, 19, 22, 23, 136; as reproductive instinct, 18, 23, 37, 119, 122, 123, 125, 131, 132, 134, 136; soldering and, 33, 120, 121–22, 125, 131; Strachey's translation of, 120–21, 123, 126; as vicissitude of infantile sexuality, 124, 125, 127, 132. See also heterosexuality; heteronormativity; instinct; sexuality, adult; *Trieb*

Hegel, G. W. F., 5, 57, 147n1, 155n2, 158n9
Heidegger, Martin, 147n1, 155n2, 160n5

helplessness (*Hilflosigkeit*), 16, 79, 80, 85, 114, 115, 132, 140
heredity, 40. *See also* phylogeny
heteronormativity, 40, 89, 136, 137, 139, 163, 164n6, 164n10; as criticism of Freud, xiv, 11, 56, 86, 87, 88, 92, 103, 104, 162–63n5; Freud against, xiv, 25, 104–106, 159n13; 159n14, 163n5. See also *Geschlechtstrieb*; heterosexuality; popular opinion; queer theory
heterosexuality: as instinct, 9, 16, 19, 28, 33, 37, 40, 49, 79, 89, 93, 111, 119, 124, 126, 132; as natural/normal, 2, 4, 16, 19, 31, 33, 34, 89, 93, 97, 105, 136, 137, 139, 163n5; popular opinion and, 9, 16, 19, 28, 33, 34, 37, 49, 79, 89, 119, 132, 136–37; problem of sexuality and, 6, 19, 31, 97, 104–106, 124–26, 132, 139, 149n6, 159n13, 160n6, 161n11; queer theory and, 93, 106, 136–37; 163n5, 164n6, 164n12; relation to infantile sexuality and, 16, 111, 119, 124–26, 132, 149n6; as teleology, 4, 37, 40; as vicissitude of infantile sexuality, 124–26, 132. See also *Geschlechtstrieb*; heteronormativity; instinct; puberty; reproduction; sexuality, adult
historicism, 88, 93
homosexuality, 4, 24–28, 41, 45, 144n11, 146n5, 147n9, 156n16. *See also* perversion; sexual aberrations; sexual object
hunger, 18, 23, 31, 40, 62, 63, 75, 76, 77, 81, 88, 111, 112, 129. See *also* food; nourishment; vital activity
Husserl, Edmund, 65, 154n6

in-between, 69, 154–55n7

ineffable, 69, 154–55n7
infans, 115, 140
instinct: complex relation with *Trieb*, 10–11, 44, 74, 80, 111; differential relation with *Trieb*, 11, 67, 128, 130, 131; for heterosexuality, 9, 16, 19, 28, 33, 37, 40, 49, 79, 89, 93, 111, 119, 124, 126, 132; for hunger, 18, 23, 31, 40, 62, 63, 75, 76, 77, 81, 88, 111, 112, 129; as internally self-differentiating, 11, 130, 131; maternal, 127–28, 156n6; perversion of, 9, 11, 23, 89, 110–15, 129, 130, 131, 132, 138; for reproduction, 4, 9, 18, 28, 37, 40, 41, 56, 63, 89, 111; self-denaturalization of, 129–30, 133; weakness of, 112–16, 118, 119, 129, 131. *See also* heterosexuality; *Instinkt*; popular opinion; *Trieb*; vital function
Instinkt, 26, 49; Freud's different usages of, 39, 121, 147n2, 147–49n4; translation of, 45, 46, 47
interpretation, 54, 107, 117, 152n21, 153n1; anti-instinctual, 39, 41–44, 59, 74, 120; biologizing-instinctual, 38, 39–41, 42, 43, 44, 47, 51
Irigaray, Luce, 154n7

Johnston, Adrian, 119, 151n14, 162n2
Jones, Ernst, 45
Jung, C. G., 53–54, 154n4, 155n3

Kant, Immanuel, 5, 50, 93
kinship, 105, 117
Kirkland, Sean, 21
kissing, 23, 92, 100–101
Kistner, Ulrike, 47, 86, 100, 121, 122, 123, 125, 141n2, 151n14
Klein, Melanie, 38, 105n9
Koyré, Alexandre, 65, 142n6

Lacan, Jacques, 42, 50–51, 149n5, 151n14, 157n3; Althusser and, 60, 153n1; extimacy, 158n10; graph of desire, 159n1, 159–60n2; Lacanianism, 38, 132, 141n1, 162n1; Laplanche's critique of, 38, 43; march of the signifier (*les défilés du signifiant*), 116, 117, 159–60n2; "The Mirror Stage," 115; need-demand-desire, 115, 116, 117, 118; "The Signification of the Phallus," 118; "The Subversion of the Subject," 115, 116, 159–60n2. *See also* dehiscence; signifier; symbolic order

Laplanche, Jean: *après-coup* (*Nachtraglichkeit*), 113, 156n7; complex relation between *Trieb* and instinct, 10–11, 44, 74, 80, 111; critique of hermeneutics, 38, 151n20; *dérivation* (derivation-deviation-drifting), 74, 110, 112, 113, 128, 129, 131, 138; *étayage* (*Anlehnung*), 109–10; *fourvoiement* (going astray), 47, 52, 55, 56, 67, 68, 78, 149n6, 150n7; *Le fourvoiement biologisant chez Freud*, 37, 38, 41, 42, 51, 52, 56, 67, 109, 142n4, 150m9, 150n10, 151n21, 152n21, 156n4, 161n12; Freud's dualism and, 42, 63, 74–75, 155n4, 155n4; "Interpreting (With) Freud," 152n21; *Life and Death in Psychoanalysis*, 10, 40, 41, 42, 46, 49, 50, 56, 73, 74, 76, 78, 80, 109, 110, 111, 112, 114, 129, 150n8, 156n8; locatability, 78, 79, 83, 156n7; "Pulsion et instinct," 38, 39, 40, 41, 43, 44, 46, 47, 51, 119, 149n6, 156n4; *rabattement*, 44, 51, 68, 149n6; seduction, 127, 129, 161n12; "The *Three Essays* and the Theory of Seduction," 37, 55, 56, 59, 86; "The Unfinished Copernican Revolution," 51, 67. *See also* attachment; care relation; caregiver; dehiscence; helplessness; hermeneutics; instinct; interpretation; *Les œuvres complètes de Freud*; perversion; philosophy; popular opinion; problem of sexuality; sexuality, adult; sexuality, infantile; teleology; temporality; temptation; translation; *Trieb*

law: institutional, 2, 3, 93; natural, 2, 3, 136, 137, 163n6

Lear, Jonathan, 20, 21, 22, 143n3, 145n1

Les œuvres complètes de Freud, 47, 52

liberation: sexual, 105, 159n14

love, 3, 4, 26, 62, 63, 81, 92; motherly love, 117, 127

Marcuse, Herbert, 38, 157n3
marginalization, 4, 5, 19
margins, 1, 3, 4, 55
marriage, 4, 5, 26, 139, 159n15
Marx, Karl, 57
masculinity, 6
masochism, 23, 76
mastery, 138–39
masturbation, 90, 132, 133, 134, 135, 158n6. *See also* autoerotism
Mitchell, Juliet, 105
mother, 18, 80, 127, 128, 156n6, 161n11. *See also* caregiver; care relation; instinct: maternal

Naas, Michael, 106
naturalism, 7, 135, 162n3
naturalistic (as ideology), 3, 5, 136, 138, 163n6; as criticism of Freud, 6, 7, 88, 135, 162n3; popular opinion and, 9, 10, 16, 19, 31, 35

naturalization, 34, 138
nature: denaturalization of, 133, 162n2, 164n6; as opposed to social constructions, 136, 137, 138; as nonteleological, xiii, 133–35, 142n6, 143n4; sexuality as an exception to, 132–33
neuroses, 54, 87, 104, 152–53n27, 157n3, 159n15, 159n16; homosexuality and, 147n9; importance for psychoanalysis, 106–107; obsessional, 107; suffering and, 106, 159n16. *See also* normalization; pathologization
normalization, 38, 86, 159n13; as criticism of Freud, 86, 87, 88, 92, 163n5; Freud against, xiv, 11, 103, 105, 106, 107; norm, xiv, 89, 105, 110, 133, 136, 137; normativity, 136, 156n12; popular opinion and, 3, 6, 9, 10, 16, 18, 19, 31, 35. *See also* heteronormativity; Oedipus complex; pathologization
nourishment, 18, 79, 80, 81, 82, 90, 110, 111, 112, 129
nuclear family, 86, 105, 106

Oedipus complex, xiv, 11, 54, 56, 102; criticisms of, 86–88, 92; defense of, 103, 104–107, 159–60n12
ontology, 132, 133, 135, 162n1
orgasm, 23, 24, 122
originality, 49, 143n2, 152n21

pansexualism, 43, 150n8
pathologization, 56, 87, 103. *See also* normalization
patriarchy, 3, 105, 106
perversion, 5, 98, 105, 124, 139; etymology of, 110; heterosexuality as, 125, 131; of instinct, 9, 23, 89, 93, 97, 111, 112, 113, 129–30; 131–32, 138; as nature of sexuality, 22, 24, 35–36, 124–25, 138; as origin of sexuality, 112, 114, 124, 125; popular opinion and, 23, 24; as preceding instinct, 17, 119. *See also* Laplanche: *dérivation*; deviation; instinct; pervertibility; sexuality, infantile
pervertibility, 114, 129, 130, 131, 138, 162n12
phenomenology, 65, 98, 154n6
philosophy, xiii, 2, 6, 8, 20, 86; Freud's critique of, 1, 142–43n1, 143n2; Freud siding with, 7, 54; Laplanche's critique of, 38, 74, 147n1, 155n2; sexuality and, 3–5, 93–94, 97, 132; similarities to popular opinion, 9, 18, 19; as speculation, 158n9. *See also* Freud, terms/concepts: poetic fable
phylogeny, 6, 40, 41. *See also* heredity
physiology, 5, 79, 80, 82, 124, 161n11
Plato: Eros, 3, 153n28; Freud and, 7, 8, 54, 143n1; *Laws*, 2, 9, 144n6, 158n5; sexuality and, 2–3, 93; *Symposium*, 3, 9, 41. *See also* Freud, terms/concepts: poetic fable
pleasure, 2, 4, 98, 102, 132, 135, 136, 137, 164n12; infantile sexuality and, 80, 81, 82–83, 85, 89, 90–92, 110, 111, 112, 127, 128, 130; possibility of, 77, 101. *See also* Freud, terms/ concepts, pleasure principle; satisfaction
politics, xiv, 88, 115, 136, 137, 164n11m 164m12
Politzer, Georges: critique of, 153n1
popular opinion (*die populäre Meinung*): as criticism of Freud, 88, 103, 163–64n6; definition of, 8, 18, 146n8; as *doxa*, 20–21; Freud's

192 | Index

popular opinion *(continued)*
challenging of, 9, 16, 17–20, 23–24, 25, 34–35, 104, 106, 107, 122; as heteronormative/naturalistic, 9, 16, 18–20, 24–25, 31, 35, 87, 132; as knowing more than it knows about sexuality, 9, 22, 35, 104; problem of sexuality and, 8, 9, 19, 25–28, 104, 125, 140, 149n6; queer theory as, 137, 138; as undermining itself, 19, 20, 24, 29, 30–31, 35, 104, 136. See also *Geschlechtstrieb*; Freud, terms/concepts: poetic fable
postpartum depression, 127–28
Preciado, Paul, 141n1, 162–63n5
problem: etymology of, 6, 138
problem of sexuality, 5–7, 9, 73, 75, 97, 103–107, 125, 126–27, 139–40, 144n10, 149n6; in the genesis of sexuality, 128–29; translation and, 17, 59
problematization: Derrida's critique of, 138–39
psychology (as ideology): critique of, 153n1
puberty, 16, 40, 79, 92, 102, 111, 118–19, 123–26, 131–32, 158–59n12, 160–61n7

queer theory, xiii, 85, 86, 93, 103, 106, 164n6; criticisms of Freud, 6, 86, 162–63n5; critique of, 136, 137, 139, 141n1, 163n5; exceptionality and, 164n9, 164n10, 164n11, 164n12; as new popular opinion, xiii, 103, 137, 139

relative autonomy, 112, 138
reproduction/procreation, 2–3, 4, 5, 139, 143n5; as instinct, 4, 9, 18, 28, 37, 40, 41, 56, 63, 89, 111; problem of sexuality and, 17, 79, 104, 119, 149n6, 159n15; as vicissitude of infantile sexuality, 123–26, 129, 132. See also *Geschlechtstrieb*; heterosexuality; instinct
Rottenberg, Elizabeth, 33, 34, 143n1, 143n2, 147n1, 151n19, 155n1, 156n7, 158n9
Rousseau, Jean-Jacques, 4, 93–99

sadism, 23, 76
satisfaction: as definition of sexual aim, 76–77; instinct and, 40, 82, 85, 89; sexuality and, 23, 37, 82, 89, 90, 92, 102, 111–12, 114–18, 127, 135, 157n4, 159n15
science, xiii, 64–66, 133, 134, 142n5, 142n6, 153–54n2, 154n6
self-preservation, 150n10; as instinctual, 40, 89; as opposed to sexuality, 62, 80–81, 85, 90, 111–12, 129, 132
sensual sucking, 80–81, 82–83, 90–91, 100–101, 110, 112, 128
sexual aberrations: as degeneracy, 26, 27, 28, 147n9, 159n16; as part of Freud's critique of popular opinion, 16, 19–20, 24, 35; 89, 122, 125, 136. *See also* fetishism; homosexuality; masochism; perversion; sadism; voyeurism
sexual aim, 23–24, 35, 76, 81, 82, 89
sexual difference, 3, 4, 6. *See also* attraction, sexual: to opposite sex; heteronormativity; heterosexuality
sexual object: Freud's usage of, 25, 28, 29, 31–35, 100, 120, 122; infantile sexuality and, 82, 89, 102; Oedipus complex and, 87; popular opinion's definition of, 18, 24–25, 30, 89; refinding of, 102, 111, 161n8

sexuality: genesis/origin of, 56, 78, 79–81, 82, 90, 110, 112, 114, 124, 125, 128, 131, 133, 156n7; as an inherent deviation/perversion, 22, 24, 35–36, 80, 124–25, 138; as nonteleological, xiii, 34, 133, 135, 142n4, 143n4, 159n13; as perversion of/deviation from instinct, 9, 11, 23, 89, 110–15, 129, 130, 131, 132, 138. *See also* heterosexuality; homosexuality; problem of sexuality; sexual aberrations; sexuality, adult; sexuality, infantile; *Trieb*

sexuality, adult: as synonymous with *Geschlechtstrieb*, 119, 120, 123, 131; as opposite of infantile sexuality, 119, 120, 123, 126, 149n6, 161–62n12; as vicissitude of infantile sexuality, 124, 125, 127, 132. See also *Geschlechtstrieb*; heterosexuality; puberty; reproduction

sexuality, infantile: characteristics of, 81–83, 109–10; as perversion of vital instinct, 9, 11, 23, 89, 110–15, 129, 130, 131, 132, 138. *See also* attachment; autoerotism; care relation; Laplanche: *dérivation*; deviation; erotogenic zone; helplessness; instinct; sexuality: genesis/origin of; perversion; *Sexualtrieb*; *Trieb*

Sexualtrieb, 23, 27, 33, 36, 62, 90, 155n4; Freud's usage of, 121, 122; as opposed to *Geschlechtstrieb*, 120, 123, 125; as synonymous with infantile sexuality, 120, 123; translation of, 46, 126. *See also* sexuality, infantile; *Trieb*

signifier, 94, 95, 116, 117, 159–60n2
sin, 4, 93, 139, 158n6
social construction, 136, 137

Socrates, 7, 8, 144n8, 144n9
soldering, 33–35, 77, 89, 100, 102, 120–22, 125, 131, 135, 158n4
Solms, Mark, 46, 47
sophistry, 30, 31
speculation, 63, 66, 90, 96, 97, 142n1, 153n28, 158n9
Spinoza, Baruch de, 142n6, 143n4
The Standard Edition, 44, 46, 47, 52, 53
stimulation, 77, 80, 82, 83, 91, 127–28. *See also* erotogenic zone; pleasure; satisfaction
Strachey, James, 10, 44–45, 53, 59, 81, 151n15, 15n19; critique of, 45–47, 109, 120–22; defense of, 48–49, 50, 51–52, 123, 126, 155n4
surplus, 80, 81, 95
symbolic order, 116, 117

teleology, xiii, xiv, 4, 6, 34, 37, 40, 41, 56, 80, 111, 122, 131, 133, 142n4, 155n4, 159n4; nonteleological, xiii–xiv, 34, 133, 135; 142n4, 143n4, 159n13
temporality, 98; lateness, 119; origin of sexuality and, 128; queer theory and, xiv, 136, 164n10. *See also* Derrida, spacing, différance; Laplanche: *après-coup*
temptation, 150n7; Freud and, 53; Laplanche's critique of Freud's temptation for biology, 51, 59, 67–68, 74, 142n4; Laplanche and, 119
Three Essays on the Theory of Sexuality: 1905 Edition of, 53, 55–57, 73, 86–87, 102, 103–104, 120; editorial history of, 15, 53–55; as event, 37, 55–56; problem of sexuality and, 6, 8, 9, 27; summary of, 15–17
touching, 23, 92, 93, 98, 99–100, 101

translation, 122, 150n7, 151n15, 160n5; Freud and, 54; Kistner and, 86, 100, 120, 121–23; Lacan and, 50–51, 116–17; Laplanche and, 44, 46, 49–50, 51–52, 59, 109, 151n20; problem of sexuality and, 17, 59; Strachey and, 45, 47–49, 62, 81, 109, 123, 126, 151n19, 155–56n4. See also *Geschlechtstrieb*: translation of; *Sexualtrieb*: translation of; *Trieb*: translation of
trauma, 55, 62
Trieb: as between border concept, 66, 68, 69; complex relation with instinct, 10–11, 44, 74, 80, 111; components of, 75–78; as denaturalization of instinct, 129–30; etymology of, 42, 46, 47, 48, 49, 50, 76, 150n12; difficulties in translating, 48–49, 150n11, 151n19, 160n5; *Ichtriebe*, 62, 63, 73; *Lebenstrieb*, 62, 63, 73, 153n28, 155n3, 155n4; as nonteleological, 34, 135; as perversion, 36, 110, 111, 129–30, 131; as self-differentiating, 11, 130, 131; as split, 75, 118, 130; *Todestrieb*, 62, 63, 73, 74, 155n3, 155n4; translation as *dérive*, 47; translation as drive, 43, 47, 48, 51, 52, 120; translation as instinct, 44–52, 120, 125–26; translation as *pulsion*, 43,
47, 50, 60, 118, 129. See also *Geschlechtstrieb*; instinct; *Instinkt*; perversion; sexuality; sexuality, infantile; *Sexualtrieb*; soldering; translation; *Trieblehre*
Trieblehre, 61–64, 66, 67, 74, 155n3, 155n4

unconscious, xiv, 60, 91, 105, 106, 117, 143n2, 151n20, 153–54n2, 161n11

Van Haute, Phillipe, 86–93, 98, 103–104, 116, 141n2, 141n3, 145n1, 146n8, 157n2, 157n4, 158n12
variability, 29, 31, 33, 35, 76, 77, 89
vital function/instinct, 16, 18, 80, 81, 89, 90, 109–12, 113–15, 128, 131–32, 138, 156n9. See also instinct; vital order
vital order, 112–13
voyeurism, 23, 76

Westerink, Herman, 86–93, 98, 103–104, 141n2, 141n3, 145n1, 146n8, 157n2, 157n4, 158n12
Winnicott, D. W., 79, 156n6
World War I, 54, 62, 152–53n27

Žižek, Slavoj, 5, 133, 166n2, 164n6
Zupančič, Alenka, 118, 133, 135, 144n7, 164n6